Battle Studies

MODERN WAR STUDIES

Theodore A. Wilson
General Editor

Raymond Callahan
Jacob W. Kipp
Allan R. Millett
Carol Reardon
Dennis Showalter
David R. Stone
James H. Willbanks
Series Editors

Battle Studies

Charles Jean Jacques Joseph Ardant du Picq

Translated, edited, and
with an Introduction by
Roger J. Spiller

 University Press of Kansas

Published by the University Press of Kansas (Lawrence, Kansas
66045), which was organized by the Kansas Board of Regents
and is operated and funded by Emporia State University,
Fort Hays State University, Kansas State University, Pittsburg
State University, the University of Kansas, and Wichita State
University.

Library of Congress Cataloging-in-Publication Data
Names: Ardant du Picq, Charles Jean Jacques Joseph, 1821–
    1870, author. | Spiller, Roger J., translator.
Title: Battle studies / Charles Jean Jacques Joseph Ardant du
    Picq ; translated, edited, and with an introduction by Roger
    J. Spiller.
Other titles: Etudes sur le combat. English
Description: Lawrence, Kansas : University Press of Kansas,
    [2017] | Series: Modern war studies | Includes index.
Identifiers: LCCN 2016051186| ISBN 9780700623914 (cloth :
    alk. paper) | ISBN 9780700623921 (pbk. : alk. paper) |
    ISBN 9780700623938 (ebook)
Subjects: LCSH: Military art and science. | Battles.
Classification: LCC U102 .A7 2017 | DDC 355.4/8–dc23
LC record available at https://lccn.loc.gov/2016051186.

British Library Cataloguing-in-Publication Data is available.

Printed in the United States of America
10 9 8 7 6 5 4 3 2 1

The paper used in this publication is recycled and contains 30
percent postconsumer waste. It is acid free and meets the minimum requirements of the American National Standard for Per-
manence of Paper for Printed Library Materials Z39.48-1992.

to
CRS
sans peur et sans reproche

Contents

Foreword

When Colonel Charles Jean Jacques Joseph Ardant du Picq fell on the field at Longeville-lés-Metz in August 1870 during the Franco-Prussian War, France lost her most astute military observer and commentator of the last half of the nineteenth century. Born in 1821, Ardant du Picq graduated from the Saint-Cyr military academy in 1844, served in the Crimean War during the siege of Sebastopol, where he was captured, and subsequently in Syria and Algeria. Promoted to colonel in 1869, he had been in command of the 10th Regiment of the Line for a little more than a year and a half.

At the time of his death, Colonel Ardant du Picq had published only fragments of his cogent studies on the behavior of men in battle and the dynamics of combat. Some of his observations were edited by a family friend and published in 1880 by Hachette et Dumaine, but it was not until 1903 that his published writing and unpublished notes were edited and presented in a complete edition by the well-known journalist Ernest Judet. The 1903 edition, published by Librairie Chapelot under the title *Études sur le combat: ancienne et moderne*, became popular in the French army during World War I, being used to support the disastrous doctrine of *offensive à outrance*, a doctrine that Ardant du Picq himself would probably have rejected.

Ardant du Picq's interests were not in strategy or tactics, but rather the behavior of men in combat and such related topics as courage, fear, and unit cohesion. His observations were based on a thorough reading of the literature on ancient battles as well as eighteenth-century and Napoleonic warfare. Of course, his own experiences in the Crimea, Syria, and Algeria were also considered. He was among the first military commentators to address war at its sharpest end in a comprehensive way.

Almost a century after the first and only English translation of Ardant du Picq's masterwork, Dr. Roger J. Spiller has brought forth a felicitous new English translation of Ardant du Picq's cogent observations on the behavior of men in combat. Dr. Spiller's work has two principal virtues. First, it is a fresh, readable English translation of Judet's 1903 edition. Second, the translation, as well as Dr. Spiller's commentary and notes, are infused with a thorough knowledge of almost 100 years of evidence and study accumulated since World War I on such subjects as the psychology of battle, shell shock, unit cohesion, and post-traumatic stress syndrome. He has thus aligned the classic work of Ardant du Picq with the scientific scholarship of the past century and produced what will no doubt become the standard English translation of Ardant du Picq's classic work for some time to come.

Charles R. Shrader
Carlisle, Pennsylvania

Introduction
Toujours la question essentielle

At about seven o'clock one morning in August 1870, the French army's *10e régiment d'infanterie de ligne* halted its march along a road just south of Longeville-lés-Metz. The regiment had been on the move since before dawn. The troops had just started their coffee when they came under shellfire from two guns of the Prussian 2nd Horse Artillery positioned across the Moselle on the heights of Montigny.[1] The troops scattered for the cover of an embankment, but one shell landed amid members of the 3rd Battalion, killing its commander and several other officers, and wounding ten more. One of the wounded was the commanding officer of the regiment. He had remained standing while his men ran for protection.

The shell had shredded the colonel's legs, "mutilated in a frightful manner," the regiment's history reads. His abdomen had also been severely contused by a shell fragment. The colonel's men pulled what was left of him to the lee of the embankment, and a surgeon rushed to his aid. The regimental history does not tell us whether the colonel's wounds were at all survivable, but they were serious enough for the colonel, no doubt suffering from shock by then, to suggest to the surgeon where his right leg should be amputated. The surgeon demurred. The colonel was evacuated to a military hospital across the river in Metz, where he died a few days later.[2]

---

1. F. C. H. Clarke, trans., *The Franco-Prussian War, 1870–1871, Volume 1: From the Outbreak of Hostilities to the Battle of Gravelotte* (orig. publ. London: HMSO, 1874; repr. Nashville, TN: Battery Press, 1995), 325. The two six-pound guns that took Ardant du Picq's regiment under fire accompanied Colonel Count von den Groben's 3rd Lancers and were commanded by a Captain Wittstock, 2nd Horse Artillery of the 3rd Field Artillery Regiment. Ibid., appendix 5, 135. This minor action is mentioned briefly in Field Marshal Helmuth von Moltke, *The Franco-German War of 1870–1871*, trans. Clara Bell and H. W. Fischer and rev. Archibald Forbes (London: James Osgood, McIlvaine, 1893), 33 (hereinafter cited as "von Moltke").
2. Appendix IV, 173–176.

The death of Colonel Charles Jean Jacques Joseph Ardant du Picq marked the end of a career that any French officer of his day might have admired. His comrades would not have valued his bookishness, on display since his cadet days at *École spéciale militaire de Saint-Cyr*. Such reputation as he had was not as an intellectual but as a seasoned soldier, as a decorated veteran of campaigns in the Crimea, Syria, and Algeria. Without the distinguished pedigree or powerful friends that aided so many careers, he had advanced steadily if not spectacularly through the officer ranks. At a time when the average age of a captain in the French army was forty-three, he became a colonel at the age of forty-seven.[3] When he died, he had commanded his regiment for nearly a year and a half.

Du Picq's death marked the beginning of another career, one in which his influence as the author of *Études sur le combat*, or *Battle Studies*, was far greater than when he lived. Yet as his posthumous reputation grew, the more du Picq himself gradually passed from historical view. That he left behind few traces of his life and career made his obscurity all the more complete. The Ardant du Picq who comes to us now is little more than a shadow behind his book.[4]

Battle Studies is now regarded as a minor classic of military literature, the first systematic exploration of human behavior in the extremities of combat. Du Picq was not interested in the grand problems of military theory or strategy that preoccupied other military thinkers. He spent his life in the tactical world, and this was the world that shaped his values and formed the boundaries of his studies. And it was in the tactical world that du Picq believed the source of victory could be found, not in elegant theories or inventive strategies. For him, the wellspring of victory was an army that succeeded where

---

3. Richard Holmes, *The Road to Sedan: The French Army, 1866–1870* (London: Royal Historical Society, 1984), 104 (hereinafter cited as "Holmes").

4. Three French scholars have attempted to rescue Ardant du Picq from obscurity. The first was the French army officer Lucien Nachin. As a captain in 1925, he wrote the first critical study of du Picq for the *Revue militaire française*, nos. 51 and 52 (September and October 1925) (hereinafter cited as "Nachin 1925"). This essay appears to have drawn on a more extensive record of his service, which has long since disappeared. Nachin published an edition of *Études* in 1942 and, in 1948, another edition with commentary for Berger-Levrault. Six years later, LTC Victor Petit, a friend of Nachin, produced a small study: *A la recherché d'Ardant du Picq* (Paris: Editions Berger-Levrault, 1954) (hereinafter cited as "Petit"). Much later, *Chef de bataillon* Frederic Guelton published "Qui est Ardant du Picq?" in *Revue historique des Armées*, no. 3 (1991): 3–14 (hereinafter cited as "Guelton"). Taken together, the work of these scholars has extended considerably our knowledge of du Picq's life and career.

it mattered most: in direct violent contact with the enemy. All else in war was subordinate to success here, and failure here meant failure everywhere.

In the last few years of his life, du Picq feared that war was outgrowing the capacities of armies to fight. How could his army's antiquated mass formations survive on the fire-swept battlescapes of modern industrial warfare? Conventional military wisdom held that a fighting unit's offensive power was best spent by its mass—the collective physical weight of its soldiers—densely organized in line or column, hurled like a rock against the enemy. Ideally, it was believed, a properly trained and commanded formation sustained its physical cohesion from the onset of its attack through the final assault when the enemy was overwhelmed, regardless of the punishment inflicted on the attackers by enemy fire.

Du Picq's experience taught him, as it no doubt taught others, that such an ideal bore little resemblance to reality. The offensive power of any massed formation, no matter how cohesive at the beginning of an attack, dissipated with each step toward the enemy. Commanders bent every effort to retain as much control over their troops for as long as possible, knowing that at some point the cohesion of their formation would dissolve into so many individual soldiers, struggling to live out the day.

Military leaders proposed various remedies. The most promising of these envisioned assigning skirmishers a more decisive role in battle. Some of France's colonial regiments such as the Zouaves had "opened" their formations, relying less on mass than on soldiers' initiative. These elite units were renowned for tactical speed and aggressiveness, but France's military leaders doubted such exotic formations, while successful against native peoples, were capable of withstanding sustained battle against orthodox European armies.

Anyway, who could imagine an army of Zouaves, who could conceive how to command tens of thousands, perhaps hundreds of thousands, of soldiers fighting in this way, deciding for themselves when to fire or not, when to advance or retreat? The very thought was anathema. Opening tactical formations meant that commanders would surrender control over their troops, with no assurance of achieving tactical objectives. Exchanging control for mere survival was no answer at all: that would accomplish what the enemy wanted to do in the first place, to destroy an opponent's physical cohesion—its unity of purpose and action. Soldiers fighting on their own or in small groups could never compensate for the loss of such an advantage. Du Picq believed that the answer to this puzzle could be found in those parts of the tactical world and human behavior that military thinkers had barely touched.

Du Picq was not especially well equipped for the task that lay before him, and his army was not then distinguished for its intellectual vitality. Most of his colleagues were content not to think about national policy, grand strategy, or the changes besetting the world of battle. France could look back with satisfaction on its army's victories in the Crimea, in the Italian War of 1859, and in Algeria, although none of these successes bore up under close inspection. Beneath appearances lay an institution that had steadily devolved since the Revolution. Instead of keeping abreast with the ever-changing strategic landscape of Europe and advancements of military technology, its leading operational principle was "*le système D: on se debrouilla toujours*—we'll muddle through somehow."[5] Little was demanded of du Picq's fellow officers, each of whom society regarded as "a great overgrown child, decent enough but still a little uncouth and backward."[6] Their social origins and professional upbringing seemed calculated to defeat any intellectual impulses, so much so that the career of any officer who dared to venture into the written world stood at some risk. The memoirist Théodore Fix recounts Napoleon III's minister of war, Marshal César-Alexandre Randon's reaction to discovering an officer, studying at late hours in the *Dépôt de la guerre*: "I didn't expect to find *you* in the archives; you loved to be on horseback in the old days!"[7] As Michael Howard has written, it was enough for the French army to assume an "inborn genius in its commanders and [in] its junior officers only obedience to orders, a good seat on a horse, and unflinching bravery under fire."[8]

The egalitarian composition of the officer corps, in which two-thirds once had been rankers, sustained this professional climate. On the eve of the Franco-Prussian War, 11,347 of the 18,643 officers had been promoted from the ranks. As an infantry officer, Ardant du Picq would have been in the minority; the 3,557 academy-trained infantry officers served alongside 6,633 rankers who had been commissioned.[9] Nor could Saint-Cyrians claim

---

5. Michael Howard, *The Franco-Prussian War* (London: Methuen, 1961), 15–17 (hereinafter cited as "Howard, *Franco-Prussian War*"). See also Holmes, 164–165.

6. David Ralston, *The Army of the Republic: The Place of the Military in the Political Evolution of France, 1871–1914* (Cambridge: MIT Press, 1967), 84.

7. Théodore Fix, *Souvenirs d'un officier d'état-major, 1846–1870* (Paris: Berger-Levrault, 1898), 227–228, quoted in Dallas Irvine, "The French Discovery of Napoleon and Clausewitz," *Journal of the American Military Institute*, vol. 4 (1942): 146.

8. Michael Howard, "The Influence of Clausewitz," in Carl von Clausewitz, *On War*, trans. and ed. Michael Howard and Peter Paret (Princeton: Princeton University Press, 1976), 36.

9. Holmes, 100. For a vivid portrait of the French army on the eve of the war, see Geoffrey Wawro, *The Franco-Prussian War* (Cambridge: Cambridge University Press, 2003), 41–57.

much social distinction over their fellow officers. Most cadets came either from military families, gendarmes, or the minor ranks of the civil service. In 1869, 54 percent could not pay for their schooling.[10] As the son of a minor civil servant, du Picq would at least have fit in socially with his classmates.[11]

Whether hostile or merely indifferent to intellectual pursuits, the outlook of the army produced officers who were not keeping pace with the professional demands that modern warfare was about to make of them. Indeed, they were not keeping pace with society at large; whereas public education had expanded in France during the first half of the century, the widespread illiteracy of French officers taken prisoner during the Franco-Prussian War astounded their German captors.[12] In the ranks, the picture was even gloomier: a survey in 1863 found that "a quarter of all army recruits were said to speak 'patois' and nothing else [and] some recruits never learned French at all."[13]

In this environment, the few officers who shared du Picq's intellectual traits stood out all the more. From his earliest days, he seemed to make no effort to conceal the reading habits he had acquired as a boy. Despite a certain intractability, he was apparently well liked and respected as a cadet at Saint-Cyr and later as a junior infantry officer, "gaining naturally and without effort the affection of his equals and the respect of his subordinates," according to his brother. His superiors spoke of his quirkiness, his "*excentricitie.*"[14]

He was no scholar. He was almost twenty-one when he finished public schooling at Perigueux. He had designs on joining the navy, but he was deficient in mathematics and turned to Saint-Cyr instead and here was required to take his entrance exam twice before being admitted at the rank of 218

(hereinafter cited as "Wawro"); as well as Douglas Porch, *The March to the Marne* (Cambridge, UK: Cambridge University Press, 1981), 17 (hereinafter cited as "Porch"). See also Dallas D. Irvine, "The French and Prussian Staff Systems before 1870," *Journal of the American Military Foundation*, vol. 2, no. 4 (Winter 1938): 261–263; and Terry Strieter, "An Army in Evolution: French Officers Commissioned from the Ranks, 1848–1895," *Military Affairs*, vol. 42, no. 4 (December 1978): 177–181.

10. Porch, 17.

11. Petit, 10.

12. Howard, *The Franco-Prussian War*, 16. See also Patrick Harrigan, "France: Education," in *The Encyclopedia of the 1848 Revolutions*, ed. James Chastain, accessed online at www.cats .ohiou.edu/chastain/dh/franedu.htm, October 29, 2012.

13. Graham Robb, *The Discovery of France* (New York: W. W. Norton, 2007), 65.

14. Appendix V, 178. See also Nachin 1925, 359–360; and Lucien Nachin, *Ardant du Picq, Présente et annote* (Paris: Berger-Levrault, 1948), xxii (hereafter cited as "Nachin, ADP 1948").

out of 316 in his class. But he was a voracious reader and, after graduating from Saint-Cyr in 1844, when he was assigned as a *sous-lieutenant* to the 67e *régiment d'infanterie de ligne* at Lyon, he spent all his spare time in garrison with books.[15]

More worrisome still, Ardant du Picq displayed an independence of mind that worked at odds with his lowly station as a junior garrison officer. On the anniversary of the battle of Austerlitz in 1851, Napoleon III staged a coup d'état, dismissed the *Corps législatif,* and called on the people of France to endorse him for a ten-year term as president. In the plebiscite that followed Ardant du Picq refused to support the coup, an act that earned him the disapproval of his colonel, who counseled him against jeopardizing his career. "Colonel," he said, "since my opinion was asked for, I must suppose it was wanted."[16]

Had he been an incompetent officer, inattentive to his duties, his intellectual bent and his forthright personality might have damaged his career, but his advancement seemed not to suffer. His performance was sufficient for promotion to lieutenant four years after leaving Saint-Cyr, and four years after that, in 1852, he was advanced to captain, all while serving with the 67th Regiment at Lyon.[17]

He was still with the 67th when the Crimean War began two years later. Public enthusiasm over the prospect of a glorious adventure with the new Army of the Orient filled the volunteer ranks. He was keen to go as well. When he learned that the 67th was not among the formations selected for the French expedition, he managed a transfer on January 24, 1854, to one that was: the 9th Battalion, *chasseurs à pied,* then posted at Fort de Nogent-sur-Marne.[18] The chasseurs were light infantry, already regarded as a cut above regular line infantry, as were the already famous Zouaves, all toughened by their service in Algeria.[19] The 9th was to be part of General Fran-

15. Guelton, 4.

16. Appendix V, 178–179.

17. Thus by the age of thirty-one, Ardant du Picq had already attained the rank at which most French officers expected to retire, regarding their career as having been successful. See Porch, 17.

18. Guelton, 6.

19. The chasseurs had only been organized in 1839 and made permanent formations a year later, when ten battalions were established and their name formally approved. The chasseurs prided themselves on superior marksmanship, tactical agility, and speed of maneuver. The regular infantry required ten commands to deploy from column to line, the chasseurs, one. Their distinctive marching speed was partly the result of training in gymnastics, and so their "double-quick step" of 160–180 paces per minute was known as *pas gymnasium.* For a

coise Canrobert's 1st Division, one of the three in the original expedition. In April, Ardant du Picq's battalion boarded the *Ville-de-Marseille* and *l'Alger* at Toulon, bound for Camp de Fontaines at Gallipoli.[20]

British and French Allied forces poured into the camp on the Dardanelles, but without any discernible strategy. How the armies might best be used to protect Turkish sovereignty against Russian claims on the Balkan principalities of Moldavia and Wallachia, no one seemed to know quite yet. But the increasing congestion in the camps and the inevitable appearance of disease prompted the Allies to decide on a relief expedition to the Danube Delta, ostensibly to encourage the Russians to withdraw farther than they had already. The withdrawal of the Russians from the provinces removed the declared casus belli and supposedly settled the long-standing "Eastern Question," but the Allies were ill disposed to call for a cease-fire. Nor were the Austrians being helpful, moving troops into the area as the Russians departed. The French and English worried that the Austrians' true aim was a more permanent occupation of the principalities. The result, in short order, was an Allied expedition aimed at "rescuing" the Danubian principalities.[21]

The seaport town of Varna was chosen as the Allies' first base of operations, and by mid-July a considerable force was ordered into the Dobruscha region of the Danube Delta. The enemy the Allies found in the Dobruscha was not the Russian army, but cholera, which struck Canrobert's 1st Division with particular force. After only two days, Canrobert's men were dying "like rotten sheep," and sick lists were growing so rapidly he was forced to retreat to Varna, carrying with him several hundred infected soldiers after having buried many more. By the end of July, sixty French soldiers were dying every day.[22] Between July 14 and August 5, the French admitted 1,287 soldiers to its hospital at Varna, of whom 705 died outright. Two days later, 257 more were admitted to the "rat infested barracks" used as a hospital. The situation grew so serious the French dispersed their hospital, establishing several smaller ones around the town for occupation by cholera victims alone.[23]

---

contemporary view of the chasseurs, see W. J. Rose, "The *Chasseurs à Pied*," *Atlantic Monthly*, vol. 11, no. 64 (February 1863): 250-259. See also Brent Nosworthy, *The Bloody Crucible of Battle* (London: Carroll and Graf, 2003), 397-398.

20. Guelton, 6.

21. Orlando Figes, *The Crimean War* (New York: Picador, 2010), 188-190 (hereinafter cited as "Figes").

22. Ibid., 192.

23. [Somerset John Gough Calthorp], *Letters from Head Quarters: or, the Realities of the War in the Crimea, by an officer of the Staff* (London: John Murray, 1856), 38-41.

If du Picq had been moved by the same romantic impulses that had driven so many volunteers into the army, he was quickly disabused of them on this expedition. As Canrobert retreated from the Dobruscha, du Picq was one of those detailed to dispose of the dead and escort the sick back to Varna. Soon enough, he contracted the disease himself yet managed to make his way back to Varna, where he was carted off to the hospital on August 10.[24] That was the night a suspicious fire destroyed much of Varna and the military stores the Allies had collected there, including his hospital. He escaped by dragging himself to a field, where, as his brother recalled, "the healthfulness of the air gave him unexpected relief."[25]

By then, the Allies had already decided their next port of call on the Black Sea would be Sebastopol. Collecting what was left of their stores, they hastily abandoned the pestilential region and sailed toward a fortress that had not figured in anyone's original campaign plans. Ardant du Picq was not among them, however; he was invalided back to France to recover and did not rejoin the 9th Battalion until December 1854, when it was well entrenched at Sebastopol.[26]

Spurred on as much by the mounting sick lists as by any strategic imperative, the Allies landed at Calamita Bay in early September and began fighting their way toward the objective. Success at the battle of Alma opened the way to Sebastopol, but not until the victories at Balaclava and Inkerman were the Allies' positions sufficiently secure to invest the town. By the time Ardant du Picq returned from his convalescence the Allies had settled in for the long siege and the miseries that beset the field.[27]

The siege was to last eleven months, the greater part of which was devoted to each sides' strengthening positions, building redoubts and intricate trench works to defend them, advancing and ranging hundreds of artillery pieces, and managing support arrangements for the several armies that eventually numbered more than 1.5 million men. The French alone dug sixty-six kilometers of trench lines to encircle the town, the British fifteen.

Du Picq's battalion, still part of Canrobert's 1st Division, was placed on the Allied left flank, opposite the Russians' Central Redoubt. As elsewhere along the lines, the terrain in the no-man's-land between the French and the

---

24. Appendix V, 178.
25. Ibid. Figes, 191–192. See also [Marie Octave Cullet], *Un Régiment de Ligne pendant la guerre d'Orient: Notes et souvenirs d'un officier d'infanterie* (Lyon: Librairie Générale Catholique et Classique, 1854), 61–62.
26. Appendix V, 178.
27. Ibid. Figes, 191–192. See also [Marie Octave Cullet], *supra*, 61–62.

Russians was a welter of ravines, most of which were exposed to direct fire from Russian batteries.

The British army occupied the center of the Allied position, while the strongest sector of the Russian defenses around the Malakoff Redoubt on the right flank was invested by the main French force. From the outset, the Malakoff Redoubt was the centerpiece of the Russians' defenses and attracted the greater part of the Allies' efforts. As the two sides perfected their positions, harassing artillery fire and trench raids, often at night and some involving thousands of men, became routine.[28]

As the siege ground on through the winter months, and as the generals bickered with one another and with their home governments, all sides looked ahead impatiently toward the grand assault that would decide the fate of the war. By April, the Allies had laid a track from the port of Balaklava to move up more heavy artillery and mortars, bringing the total number of their guns to 500. Finally, on April 9, the Allies began a ten-day bombardment, to be followed by a general attack all along the line. The Allies fired 2,000 rounds per day throughout the bombardment, killing or wounding nearly 5,000 Russian soldiers and civilians. The Russians replied with their own 409 guns and 57 mortars. Aside from one doomed sortie against the Russian lines, the British gave up the offensive for the time being.

Canrobert gave up his command to General Aimable Pélissier in May, however, and Pélissier was as avid for an attack as were the British. Another plan was laid on that focused the Allied attack more directly against the Malakoff by seizing the critical Mamelon and Quarry outworks guarding the great redoubt. Yet this attack, launched early in June, misfired as well. Despite the French having captured the outworks at the cost of 7,500 killed and wounded, the Russians broke the momentum of the assault. The Malakoff remained in Russian hands.[29]

But the Malakoff was now vulnerable, and another attack was set for June 18. To the soldiers who were to make the assault, however, vulnerability was only relative. Several hundred yards of open ground separated the lines between the outworks and the Malakoff. The assaulting troops would be exposed to frontal and flanking fire as they navigated the ditches and abbatis, only to be met by concentrated rifle fire as they used ladders to scale the walls of the great redoubt. Their commanders told them half of them would

---

28. Figes, 294–357.
29. Ibid., 359–361.

be killed before reaching that point.[30] Moreover, General Pélissier decided to cancel the three-hour preparatory bombardment planned before the assault, presumably to preserve some element of surprise. Pélissier could not have been more wrong: a deserter from the French general staff had already given the details of the attack to the Russians. Several of Pélissier's commanders protested his decision. One was relieved of command. Another, one General Mayran, having failed to dissuade Pélissier, returned to his place at the head of the assaulting regiment, saying "there's nothing left to do but get killed." He was killed, along with perhaps as many as 6,000 others in the French columns. No French soldier got as far as the Malakoff that day. Both sides agreed to a truce the following day to collect the dead and wounded, while Allied commanders spent their day apportioning blame—or defending themselves against it—for the misbegotten assault.[31]

So began the miserable summer of 1855 at Sebastopol. Whereas the French had suffered less illness than the British during the winter of 1854–1855, now the tables were turned. Cholera and typhus made their inevitable appearance in the French trench works. The work of the gunners on both sides was prodigious. During June and July, Allied artillery rained down on the Russian positions, killing 250 Russians for the 75,000 rounds fired each day. Allied losses were about the same.[32] The prospects of victory were as far away as they ever had been.

Du Picq and the 9th Battalion were posted on the left of the Allied lines, opposite the city of Sebastopol proper, and although the so-called Town Front was not the focal point of the Allied assaults, no part of the line was immune to Russian fire. In the intervals between the more dramatic attacks, life in the trenches was a dangerous monotony as ever, punctuated by harassing artillery fire, sharpshooting, night raids back and forth, and a constant struggle to improve fighting positions while exposed to the enemy.

The dominant Russian stronghold on the Town Front was the Central Bastion, built to bar the way into the town. The Russians protected the bastion with forty guns along with flanking bastions, the Bastion du mat to the south and the Bastion de la Quarantine to the north. On June 18, General de Salle, who had succeeded Canrobert to command the sector, ordered a general attack against all three bastions, aiming storming columns toward each. None succeeded. Two days later, French troops began to sap toward

---

30. Ibid., 364–365.
31. Ibid., 364–371.
32. Ibid., 376–377, 386.

the Central Bastion, a project expected to last three weeks. By mid-August, they were within just a few yards of the ditch protecting the bastion.[33]

But the French commander in chief, General Pélissier, had a grander project in mind. Even after the disasters and disappointments of that summer, Pélissier was convinced the Russians were now dangerously weak. He called for a new attack all along the line with massive artillery support, and for once the Allied commanders were in accord. Pélissier's new plan guaranteed that Ardant du Picq and his men would face the Russian guns yet again. The new attack on September 8 would be preceded by a three-day artillery preparation, along with a supporting attack against the Central Bastion. Du Picq makes no mention of having participated in this attack, which in any case gained no ground at all. If he did, he obviously survived with whole bones, because he was then assigned to lead the storming column of the 9th Battalion in the grand attack three days hence. His objective, once again, was the Central Bastion.

The preparatory bombardment that began on September 5 was of a scale unprecedented in the siege—and perhaps in military history up to that point. Fifty-thousand shells rained down on the Russian defenders every day. Whatever was left of the town was pulverized, leaving "essentially a phantom," according to a Russian officer who suffered through the bombardment.[34] At 5 A.M. on September 8, the bombardment became even more furious, and then, unaccountably, the firing stopped at 10 A.M. The Russians tensed, ready to meet the expected Allied assault. But nothing happened. The Russians relaxed. Then at noon, ten and a half French divisions emerged from their positions to storm the Russian lines. In du Picq's sector, at 2 P.M., five divisions rose to the assault against the Town Front and its three bastions. The official history of the 9th Battalion records the scene—and Captain du Picq's eventual capture:

> The demi-battalion on the left is encouraged with remarkable energy by Captain Ardant du Picq. A terrible fire of musketry, 20 guns, the shock from exploding fougasses every moment, all tell of the terrible obstacles before us. Nothing can arrest the *élan* of our brave chasseurs. Our ranks are decimated. . . . Captain Ardant du Picq and Lt. Becdelievre, carried forward by their courage, are made prisoners in the same trench where

---

33. Guy Arnold, *The Historical Dictionary of the Crimean War* (Lanham, MD: Scarecrow, 2002), 21.
34. Figes, 376–377, 387.

the flag of the 9th falls. Everyone in the trenches sees their glorious failure.[35]

Perhaps as many as 250 men attacked with du Picq that day.[36] Twelve actually got into the Russian trenches.[37] But the French assault on the Malakoff Redoubt finally succeeded; launched so unexpectedly and with such overwhelming force the defenders barely had time to reach their guns, it spelled the end of any effective defense of Sebastopol. The Russian commander, General Mikhail Gorchakov, immediately ordered the forts blown up, the ships scuttled, and the town evacuated.[38]

Du Picq made no reference in his later writing to his next few months in Russian hands. The scant record of his service has no entry as to where or in what conditions he was held, whether he was evacuated, or whether he had to live through another conflagration like the one he had survived at Varna. But when he was finally released on December 13, he had a promotion to major (chef de bataillon) waiting for him, a promotion by preferment for meritorious service rather than mere seniority. His brigade commander, Louis Trochu, who would later become president of France, had trooped the 9th Battalion's line that morning, trying to steel the men for what awaited them. He evidently had watched du Picq's column attack the bastion and was responsible for his commendation.[39] Years later, the trajectories of du Picq and Trochu would intersect again.

The Crimea had shown du Picq the worst that war could offer: a major conflict, ignited by the most dubious motives, in which nearly a million soldiers died, mostly from diseases spread by their own ignorance[40]; a war in which the combatants were comparable numerically, technically, and professionally; a war fought with tactics that had fallen dangerously behind the capacities of the weapons employed; indeed, a war in which the art of war itself had regressed. A decade later, when du Picq attempted to paint a picture of modern war, the Crimean War was his canvas.

---

35. *Historique du 9e bataillon de chasseurs à pied*, quoted in Guelton, 5-6.

36. The demi-battalion du Picq commanded that day consisted of the 5th, 6th, 7th, and 8th Companies. Nachin, ADP 1948, xxiv.

37. Appendix V, 178-179.

38. Figes, 392-394.

39. Appendix V, 179. Nachin, ADP 1948, xxv.

40. One of du Picq's few direct references to the Crimean War in *Études sur le combat* is a bitter outburst against his army's inadequate medical services. See 119-120. The French army lost 10,240 killed in action at Sebastopol, but a further 75,000 died from disease. The original French contingent at Sebastopol was 75,000. See Figes's accounting at page xix.

Du Picq emerged from the war unscathed, a decorated veteran. His experiences in the trenches were not appreciably different than those of other company grade infantry officers at Sebastopol. After the war, a general public that had been fed an almost daily diet of frontline journalism was treated to an outpouring of war memoirs.[41] He seemed in no hurry to write about his war, but when he did begin to write, his war experience invested his writing with a credibility that could not have been achieved in any other way.

Now a thirty-three-year-old major, du Picq was granted leave and made his way back to his father's house in Limoges. Temporarily assigned to the *100e régiment d'infanterie de ligne*, he would take up his permanent posting with the *16e Chasseurs à pied* in March 1857. During his leave, he married the nineteen-year-old daughter of a physician in nearby Saint-Leonard, Catherine Fraissex du Bost, and during the next year his son Georges was born.

Over the next two years, du Picq nearly disappears from historical view, caught up in the busy life of a field grade garrison officer, now the head of a growing family. Only once does he resurface, mentioned in an inspector general's 1858 report on his regiment, which pronounced the young officer as difficult and withdrawn ("*peu convenable avec ses superieurs et manqué de tact avec ses inferieurs*") a verdict that echoed his reputation at Saint-Cyr, but that was apparently at odds with his domestic behavior as a devoted husband and doting father.[42]

His family life was about to be disrupted, however. In May 1859, Napoleon III intervened in the Italian struggle to overthrow Austrian rule in the Piedmont. His regiment was not among those ordered to the front, and he did not petition to join the intervention as he had before the Crimean War, perhaps content to attend to his new family in Toulouse. He watched the great battles at Magenta and Solferino from afar, and not without interest.[43] But he was not to remain in Toulouse much longer. The French army did not lack for work in 1860. Napoleon III already had designs on Mexico that would lead to the French expedition of 1863, and France and Great Britain were already engaged in the Opium War in China. And in the summer of 1860, du Picq found himself once again at sea with his troops, this time bound for Beirut.

In the region of Greater Syria known as Mount Lebanon, then under Ottoman rule, long-standing sectarian hatreds between the Maronite Christians

---

41. See Figes, 304–315.
42. Nachin, ADP 1948, xxiv–xxv. Guelton, 6. Petit, 16.
43. Appendix II.

and the Druze erupted in a violent uprising in early 1859, when Maronite peasants revolted against their feudal overlords. The so-called Keserwan Uprising spread throughout Mount Lebanon, where more than sixty villages near Beirut had been put to the torch. The Druze, traditionally favored over the Maronites by the Ottoman Porte, soon retaliated. By the spring of 1860, sixty Maronite villages had been burned, their inhabitants either killed or made refugees, all with the connivance of Ottoman troops. In early June, the Druze successfully laid siege to the Maronite town of Deir al Qamar and massacred more than 1,500 Maronites. The violence spread as far as Damascus, where in mid-June, Druze and Sunnis killed between 7,000 and 20,000 Maronites. The Ottoman governor of the Damascus *vilayet* refused to intervene, and indeed some Turkish troops participated in the massacre. Among the dead were the American and Dutch consuls.[44]

European embassies in Istanbul were already appealing to the Ottoman Porte to quell the violence. The Porte did send a frigate and two battalions to Beirut, which had not yet been touched by the uprisings, and an Ottoman emissary arranged for a temporary cease-fire. None of this satisfied the European powers, however. Napoleon III, evoking an ancient commitment to defend Christianity in the Holy Lands, led an international chorus of outrage, enlisting Great Britain, Prussia, Austria, and Russia to join France in demanding that the Ottoman Porte intervene to put an end to the bloodshed. On August 3, the five powers agreed to mount a relief expedition. France was to provide the bulk of the force, some 7,000 troops. The French general Beaufort d'Hautpoul was named commander in chief of the expedition. Addressing his troops before departure, the general said their mission was to help the Sultan's troops "avenge humanity shamefully outraged."[45]

Du Picq and his battalion received orders to deploy immediately. The *16e* left Toulouse for Marseilles, where they boarded the steamer *La Borysthene* on August 6, to sail for Beirut via Malta and Alexandria. A week later, he

---

44. Inevitably, the exact number of those killed in these massacres varies considerably between different sources. See Ernest Louet, *Expédition de Syrie: Beyrouth-le Liban-Jérusalem, 1860-1861* (Paris: Amyot, 1862) (hereinafter cited as "Louet"); P. Camille de Rochemonteix de la Campagnie de Jesus, *La Liban et l'expédition française en Syrie, 1860-1861: Documents inédité du general Ducrot* (Paris: Librarie August Picard, 1921) (hereinafter cited as "Rochemonteix"); and Kamal Suleiman Salibi, *The Modern History of Lebanon* (New York: Frederick A. Praeger, 1965), esp. 80-104 (hereinafter cited as "Salibi"), which sets the French intervention in its larger imperial context.

45. Leila Fawaz, *An Occasion for War: Civil Conflict in Lebanon and Damascus in 1860* (Berkeley: University of California Press, 1994), esp. 147-116 (hereinafter cited as "Fawaz"). See also Sabili, 107; Louet, 15 and 17.

wrote to his wife, describing a pleasant, uneventful voyage, a picture at some variance with the account of another passenger.[46] The French expedition to Greater Syria is now cited as the only instance of humanitarian intervention in the nineteenth century.[47] News of the massacres quickly reached the European public through a press invigorated by improvements in communications since the Crimean War. Moved in part by public interest, the Great Powers' convention authorizing the expedition declared their intention only to quell the violence in Lebanon, especially toward the Maronites, and made no claims to territory or other concessions. The Ottoman Porte consented to the expedition, although by the time du Picq arrived Ottoman troops had suppressed most of the violence.[48] Only the thousands of refugees choking Beirut and the smoldering ruins of villages along the road to Damascus were left to greet him and his men.

Toward the end of September, du Picq marched a day and a half with his battalion up the Damascus road, into the Bekka Valley as far as Kab Elias, now "devastated, burned, or abandoned." Ottoman troops had already been in the vicinity and were nowhere to be found. Twelve companies of infantry were left to defend what was left of Kab Elias, and two more on the road toward Beirut, at Baada. These postings would be augmented by cavalry, artillery, and engineers over the coming months. Du Picq thought the march was to "no military purpose," and by October he was back in camp "without incident in the Druze mountains." He did not go into detail about the human devastation he would have seen along the road, telling his wife instead to read accounts then being reported in *Le Press* by a journalist who was traveling with him.[49]

---

46. Charles Ardant du Picq to Catherine Ardant du Picq, August 12, 1860, in Petit, 19. Baptistin Poujoulat, who was returning to Syria after a twenty-five-year absence, complained of the "unbearable heat" both on deck where the soldiers berthed and the cabins, which were "sweating rooms where one cannot breathe." He evidently suffered from seasickness for much of the voyage. Poujoulat is quoted in Fawaz, 115.

47. Ian Brownlee, *International Law and the Use of Force by States* (Oxford: Clarenden Press, 1963), 34; and Simon Chesterman, *Just War or Just Peace? Humanitarian Intervention and International Law* (Oxford: Oxford University Press 2001).

48. In contrast to the many demands made of China by France and Great Britain at the onset of the Opium War, by this time only a few months old. Louet, 15. Napoleon III's address to the troops of the French expedition before embarkation is quoted in Fawaz, 115.

49. Ardant du Picq to Catherine Ardant du Picq, October 1 and October 4, 1860, in Petit, 25-26. G. deLaux, "Nouvelles d'Orient," *Le Press* (October 18, 1860), n.p. See also Fawaz, 125.

From the beginning of the expedition, du Picq seems to have been under no illusions about the state of affairs in Lebanon. He was in accord with the mission of his expedition, but he believed his government was altogether too conciliatory toward the Ottomans. He thought that behind the Ottomans' concessions to the Great Powers lay a desire to rid the region of Maronites altogether. Du Picq thought that, of all the sects in Lebanon, the Maronites alone were "active, industrious, intelligent," and with a "sense of law." Meanwhile, "these brave Turks . . . put all possible obstacles in our way," refusing the French permission to march on to Damascus. "Damascus is quiet, we do not need you," they were told.[50]

The tenuous peace, still complicated by the growing number of refugees, nevertheless held over the succeeding months. Ardant du Picq's chasseurs and a battalion of Zouaves watched over the peace, resettled several destroyed villages, helped Maronites rebuild houses, and shared their rations with "the unfortunate victims of Turkish fanaticism and cruelty of the Druze."[51] The expedition had been intended originally to last only six months, but the Great Powers agreed on a second convention, extending the mission six months more. Not surprisingly, during the spring du Picq's letters reveal an increasing frustration and impatience over official inaction, as well as skepticism that the realities of life in Lebanon will have changed by the time he left. Du Picq's brigade commander, August Ducrot, was equally frustrated. "We are still in the same uncertain future," Ducrot wrote in January, "the country's situation changes little, lot of miseries, of worries among Christians, a great insolence and continuing threats from Turks. Absolute inaction by our army."[52] When the date for the expedition's withdrawal was set for the end of May, few protests were likely to have been heard from the French camp.

On the eve of his return to France, du Picq considered his future in the army. He warned his wife of future separations. As *chef de bataillon*, he would be obliged as usual to spend summer training away from garrison, "not to mention still very likely chances of war with anyone." Although he had been made chevalier of the *Légion d'honneur* in December, he thought he would be lucky to be promoted to lieutenant colonel, but of course that meant even

---

50. Ardant du Picq to Catherine Ardant du Picq, November 22, 1860, in Petit, 30. In this letter, Ardant du Picq accurately describes in some detail relations between the various sects in the region.

51. These "hearts and minds" operations are described by August Ducrot to Madame Ducrot, October 17, 1861, in Rochemonteix, 126.

52. August Ducrot to Madame Ducrot, October 18 and 27, 1861, in ibid., 132.

greater responsibilities and "following the cycle of the military machine and all its movements." He seemed content; higher rank did not interest him. "You know my indifference to rank," he wrote. "The rank of Marshal of France is therefore not for me."[53]

Du Picq and his chasseurs returned to Toulouse in the summer of 1861, but in the following year they were to move again, this time to the garrison of Paris. The garrison was composed of the Imperial Guard and three line infantry divisions and meant to enforce public order, but they also served as show troops for ceremonial duty. This meant constant drills and inspections for the troops, in which "not a gaiter button" could be left undone, and schooling for officers on the niceties of comportment and regulation. But du Picq was no ceremonial soldier, nor were his troops, and his personality almost guaranteed he would run afoul of his superiors eventually. In January 1863, the *16e* failed an inspection by their brigade commander, General Julius de Marguenat, who in du Picq's presence declared the chasseurs the worst troops he had seen in thirty years of soldiering.[54]

Du Picq reacted furiously, four days later writing a letter directly to Field Marshal Bernard Magnan, the commander of the Paris garrison. His dignity had been insulted, he protested, and his capacity to serve as the chasseurs' *chef de bataillon* had been questioned in front of his troops. Honor, as well as the wounded reputation of his troops, required him to relinquish his post and be assigned elsewhere. Magnan agreed to his demands, and less than two weeks later du Picq was reassigned to the *37e régiment d'infanterie de ligne* in Lyon. Not long after his transfer, he drew a quite different appraisal from another inspector, who praised his dignity and character, although the general noted he was rather "inflexible" in the performance of his duties, which, the general also noted, du Picq freely acknowledged. Nevertheless, the inspector believed he was a "*tres bon officier de guerre.*"[55]

Du Picq may have already been on the list for promotion to lieutenant colonel when he challenged the commander of the Paris garrison. If this episode was not enough to cement his reputation as a "difficult" and "eccentric" officer, an encounter with the minister of war, Marshal Randon, may

---

53. T. Lamathier, ed., *Pantheon de la Légion d'honneur* (Paris: Depot de Guerre, 1903), 282. Ardant du Picq to Catherine Ardant du Picq, May 29, 1861, in Petit, 61.

54. Nachin, ADP 1948, xxx.

55. Ibid., xxxii. Since the chasseur battalions were "tainted" by having originated in Algeria, some part of this contretemps may have been due to the well-known mutual disdain of the metropolitan army and the *Armee d'Afrique*, which Trochu called the "African Mutual Admiration Society." Trochu is quoted in Holmes, 32.

have been reason to delay his promotion. According to du Picq's brother, Randon had asked du Picq for his opinion on the quality of the chasseurs' shoes, to which he bluntly replied they were very bad.[56] Perhaps it was just as well du Picq was shipped off to Lyons and the 37e, far from the capital and the chance of further insubordination. A year later, his sins forgiven or forgotten, he was promoted to lieutenant colonel of the 55e *régiment d'infanterie de ligne* on the eve of its deployment to Tlemcin, Algeria.[57]

Save for a brief mention in his brother's reminiscence of du Picq's having taken part in two campaigns, no record of his service in Algeria has survived. Effectively second in the regiment's chain of command, du Picq's life in garrison would have been much the same as in his earlier assignments, but with even more responsibility for the maintenance, training, and discipline of the command. For the moment, the western reaches of the colony were quiescent, but the scars of France's 1830 invasion and Marshal Thomas Robert Bugeaud's brutal pacification campaigns would never really heal.[58]

What is more likely is that du Picq not only kept to his reading habits after the day's duties had ended but also began writing, for it was in the garrison at Tlemcin that in 1865 he took his first steps toward the essays that eventually became *Études sur le combat*. He composed two short pieces, "The Employment of the Rifle and the Chasseurs," and "The Companies of the Center."[59] None of his surviving work tells us whether these pieces were simply aides-memoir to share with a small circle of colleagues, or whether he was planning a larger work, but both of these pieces contributed to a longer "Memorandum on Infantry Fire" that served as one of the appendices to the 1903 edition of *Études*.[60]

Scholars have speculated that the catalyst for du Picq's study was the Prussians' defeat of the Austrians, contrary to French expectations, at the battle of Sadowa in 1866. A leading historian of the war a generation later was not wrong in writing that the "thunderbolt of Sadowa fell on Paris . . . pro-

---

56. Appendix V, 179.

57. Appendix III.

58. Bugeaud's subsequent influence over French colonial campaigning as well as tactical thinking in both the Algerian and in the metropolitan army are detailed in Bruce Vandevort, *Wars of Imperial Conquest in Africa, 1830–1914* (Bloomington: Indiana University Press, 1998), esp. 56–67.

59. "The Center," that is, the main body of the battalion formation for combat, exclusive of skirmishers, or *voltigeurs*.

60. See Appendix I. See also Nachin 1925, 368.

ducing as much effect as if it concerned a French Army."[61] Sadowa ignited furious debates throughout the government of Napoleon III, the *Corps législatif*, the army, the leading journals of opinion, and the greater public. As Richard Holmes has written, the leading military question before France from 1866 until the outbreak of the Franco-Prussian War was "not whether reform should take place, but the form it would take."[62] Sadowa was not the catalyst of du Picq's work, but the news of the battle no doubt contributed to the sense of urgency that flows through his essays. Although he would have been loath to admit it, his references to Sadowa in *Études* suggest that he thought the Prussians' performance in the battle was the highest expression of the military art as it then existed.

Du Picq was certainly not the only French officer driven to the pen by the news of Sadowa. Louis Trochu, his old brigade commander from the Crimean War who had watched him lead the demi-battalion against the Central Redoubt and who had recommended his promotion, had himself advanced in rank. When France entered the Italian War, he had command of a division. In a war noted for the incompetence of commanders high and low, Trochu stood out at Magenta and Solferino for his composure under fire and for maneuvering his troops "with an almost peacetime precision." He finished the war with his reputation not only intact but much enhanced by a Grand Cross added to his *Légion d'honneur*.

Yet Trochu's personality and opinions often counterbalanced his successes. By the 1860s he had assumed the pose of a uniformed aesthete. Worse yet, he was an unregenerate Orleanist, a stance guaranteed to excite the deepest suspicions of Napoleon III and especially Empress Eugenie, who came to hate him enthusiastically.[63]

Even before the shock of Sadowa interrupted French complacency, Trochu was expounding on the inherent superiority of the Prussian army, declaring before an audience at the Artillery School at Metz in 1864 that the Prussian army had the best morale in Europe.[64] Despite his transgressions, he was assigned to study problems of mobilization in the Ministry of War in 1866, and he participated in what was supposed to have been a secret

---

61. Pierre Lehautcourt (pseudo. Palat, General B. E.), *Guerre de 1870–1871, Aperçu et Commentaires* (Paris: Berger-Lavrault, 1871), 10, quoted in Holmes, 91.

62. Holmes, 93. Holmes (at 91–97) has expertly summarized the labyrinthine interplay of official policymaking and public opinion during the prewar period.

63. See the sketches of Trochu in Alistair Horne, *The Fall of Paris* (New York: Penguin, 1985), 72–73, and 98; Howard, *The Franco-Prussian War*, 37; and Wawro, 42–43.

64. Wawro, 43.

commission that was to report to Napoleon III on the state of the French army. Trochu made the results of the report public in *L'armée française en 1867*, published anonymously, that leveled a searing indictment of the nation's preparedness and the army's decrepitude.[65]

L'armée française en 1867 aroused not only official but public interest, going through sixteen editions in three weeks.[66] For Napoleon's opponents in the *Corps législatif*, the book became a manifesto for deputies set against the emperor's military plans. And yet, the citizens of France did not share their government's sense of urgency. For good and sufficient reasons, among them the draft lottery for active service and the widely abused system permitting paid replacements for unlucky recruits, the public "loathed soldiering, and Sadowa did not make it more palatable for them."[67] Inside the army, Sadowa stimulated articles in both military and public journals as well as "a rash of projects . . . by soldiers and civilians alike, ranging from the rational to the widely impracticable."[68] This was the national atmosphere in which du Picq began to write his own book.

In April 1866, three months before Sadowa, du Picq and his regiment traded their colonial garrison in Tlemcin for a new posting in metropolitan France, at Besançon. This was where he began his work in earnest. Now within the reach of libraries, he could draw on the works that would form the foundation for the essays that he published privately and anonymously as a pamphlet in 1868 as *Études du combat d'apres l'antique*.[69]

Even as he published and distributed copies of his pamphlet in 1868, du Picq was expanding the scope of his research, this time addressing contemporary warfare. He was clearly not interested in the grand questions of

65. [Louis Trochu], *L'armée française en 1867* (Paris: Amyot, 1867).

66. Howard, *The Franco-Prussian War*, 37.

67. Arpad F. Kovacs, "French Military Institutions before the Franco-Prussian War," *American Historical Review*, vol. 51, no. 2 (January 1946): 224 and 231. See also Lynn M. Case, "French Opinion and Napoleon III's Decision after Sadowa," *Public Opinion Quarterly*, vol. 13, no. 3 (Autumn 1949): 441–461.

68. Holmes, 94. See, for one example, the lead essay of the managing director, M. Noirot, "Projet d'organisation militaire," in *Spectateur militaire*, vol. 7 (January–May 1867): 1–30.

69. [Ardant du Picq], *Études du combat d'apres l'antique* (Besançon: Veuve Valluet et fils, 1868). One of the recipients of his pamphlet, Andre Alfred Poilecot, a fellow officer of chasseurs who had fought at Sebastopol with the 9th Battalion, replied with a fulsome thank-you, expressing his regret that du Picq was not advertising his work more broadly, and assuring him that he would place it in the local library at Limoges for the edification of all, especially fellow officers. Poilecot reprinted his letter to du Picq in his *Histoire du siège de Sébastopol suivie du siège de Saragosse* (Limoges: Editions Ardant et C. Thibaut, 1872), 123.

statecraft and national defense policy that so animated Trochu. He was not interested in pronouncements on the higher art of war or the military theories that purported to explain them. He believed this approach, often based on vacuous assumptions, and uninformed by the realities of the battlefield, led inevitably to dogma whose only merit was that it did not demand much thinking.

The references du Picq cited both in his pamphlet and in his later notes reflected a lifetime of reading in the history of the military art, yet by 1868 he had concluded that his arguments could not rest solely on a foundation of history, however illuminating.[70] Instead, he believed the evidence for his arguments lay beyond the reach of history as it was then written. "The smallest detail," he wrote, "taken from an actual incident in war, is more instructive for me, a soldier, than all the Thiers and Jominis in the world. They speak, no doubt, for the heads of states and armies but they never show me what I wish to know—a battalion, a company, a squad, in action."[71]

But how to get at those "smallest details"? The solution he reached was by no means obvious. He would call on his fellow officers to recount their own experiences in order to unearth the sine qua non of war, the human nature of combat itself.

Du Picq's solution was not original, however. In 1830, the British army commissioned Captain William Siborne to construct a precise model of the battle of Waterloo at its most critical moment. As part of his research, Siborne sent out a circular letter to all the officer veterans of the battle, asking them to recount their actions. Siborne also wrote to the Ministry of War in Paris, which responded with an understandable silence.[72]

Du Picq gives no sign of knowing about Siborne's labors, but the practice of collecting primary data, especially statistical data, by means of surveys was well understood and practiced in France, where professional organizations had existed since the beginning of the century. There is no reason to think du Picq was ever involved with these societies. His decision to employ

---

70. Among the better-known authors cited by du Picq in *Études sur le combat* were Marshal de Saxe, Polybius, Caesar, Xenophon, Thucydides, Marshal Bugeaud, Froissart, Frederick the Great, Turenne, Cromwell, Napoleon I, Prince de Ligne, General Ambert, Marshal Blücher, General Gouvion Saint-Cyr, Epaminondas, Jomini, Folard, Prud'homme, Cuizot, Machiavelli, Gustavus Adolphus, Montecuccoli, Marquis de Cambray, and Plutarch.

71. See Appendix VI.

72. Siborne's work eventually led to a two-volume history of the battle and, as John Keegan notes, the "largest single collection of primary sources material on Waterloo ever assembled." Keegan drew extensively on this collection for his own analysis of Waterloo in *The Face of Battle* (New York and London: Viking, 1976).

questionnaires—as well as Siborne's, whose purpose was descriptive, not ana-
lytical—was innovative, but not the stroke of genius as it has been portrayed.
The quest for social data of all sorts was well under way by du Picq's day.[73]

Early in 1868, du Picq sent out his circular letter, and by the summer
some were replying.[74] He told his correspondents that his objective was to
collect data "to serve as a base for what might be a rational method of fighting." The questions he posed, the implications behind them, and what he
expected to learn would combine to set his course as he composed what
eventually became *La guerre moderne*, the second part of *Études*.[75]

Given the attitudes then prevailing among his professional colleagues, one
wonders how du Picq's questions were received. "At what point," he asks,
"has this control [in the attack] escaped from the battalion commander?
When from the captain, the section leader, the squad leader?" Such a question must have seemed presumptuous or impertinent, and most of his colleagues were satisfied not to think about its implications.[76]

In April 1869, du Picq was promoted to colonel and command of the
10e régiment d'infanterie de ligne, then garrisoned at Limoges. Two regimental
inspections dating from this time conform to the now-accepted view of a
competent but unusual officer: "Mind a bit weird," wrote one inspector,
while another suggested du Picq could do "with a little less eccentricity,"
even thought he was "a very distinguished senior officer."[77]

As he worked on his essay on modern battle, and even as he refined his
ideas, du Picq attempted to make his views on "the defective state of the
army and the perils of the situation" known to his superiors in Paris. His
reception in Paris was disappointing: "they take all that philosophically," he
told his brother.[78] He was right. Beyond the heated debates over military

---

73. John T. Howard's *The State of Prisons in England and Wales* (London: Warrington, 1777)
is usually credited as the first true social survey, and one whose purpose was not merely the
collection of data but that of reform. The first Statistical Society of Paris was established in
1802, was defunct by 1848, and rejuvenated in 1860. See Carl C. Taylor, "The Social Survey,
Its History, and Methods," Social Science Series 3, *University of Missouri Bulletin*, vol. 20, no.
28 (October 1919): 22–23. I have greatly benefitted from Azar Gat's perceptive analysis of du
Picq's scientism in his *History of Military Thought: From the Enlightenment to the Cold War* (New
York: Oxford University Press, 2003), 296–310 (hereinafter cited as "Gat").

74. One of the earliest replies, dated August 23, 1868, recollecting a company-grade officer's experiences at the battle of Magenta, is reproduced in Appendix II.

75. Appendix VI.

76. Howard, *The Franco-Prussian War*, 7.

77. Nachin, ADP 1948, xlii.

78. Appendix V, 179.

policy, little had changed in the French army, Sadowa or not. Marshal Edmond Leboeuf, who had succeeded Marshal Adolphe Niel as minister of war, was confident his army was ready to meet the Prussians. "From Paris to Berlin," he said, "it will be a mere stroll, walking stick in hand."[79]

The stroll would begin in earnest when the French army was ordered to mobilize after war was declared on Prussia on July 19, 1870. Napoleon III had found a pretext for the war he had dreamed of since Sadowa.[80]

The French mobilization was something of a comic opera. Some postwar critics claimed France had no war plan, but as Douglas Porch and Richard Holmes have written, the problem was there were altogether too many, none of them definitive. By the end of the month, Napoleon III and his marshals had reached a consensus of sorts to concentrate two armies, one at Metz, and the other at Strasbourg. Once the movement to the frontier was complete, the two armies would join near Strasbourg and advance across the Rhine, then northeast to meet the main body of the Prussian army. A third army, held momentarily in reserve at Châlons, would then advance to cover the rear at Metz.[81]

The regiment was the largest standing formation in the French army. Mobilization required swiftly organizing higher echelons of control and the staffs that went with them; brigades, divisions, corps, and armies alike had to be brought to life, commanders and their staffs assigned, then moved to assembly points to oversee the concentration of troops and materiel.[82] "The confusion," Trochu would write later, "was indescribable."[83]

Ardant du Picq assembled his *10e régiment* from its posts at Limoges and Angouleme to join the VI Corps, then concentrating at Châlons under the command of General Canrobert, his old division commander from Crimea days. The *10e* was assigned to Julien-Charles Pechot's brigade of the 1st Division, commanded by General Michel Tixier. The regiment stood in corps

---

79. David Baduley, *Napoleon III and His Regime* (Baton Rouge: Louisiana State University Press, 2000), 373.

80. The onset of the war can be briefly explained by a paraphrase of Thucydides: the war began because of the growth of power in Prussia and the fear this inspired in France. The chain of events leading to the war is concisely detailed in Wawro, 16–40. Wawro's description compares favorably with Émile Zola's in *Le Debacle*, trans. Leonard Tancock (New York: Penguin, 1972), 34–35.

81. Holmes, 165–171, esp. 170; and Porch, 45.

82. William Seman, "French Mobilization in 1870," in *On the Road to Total War: The American Civil War and the German Wars of Unification, 1861–1871* (Cambridge: Cambridge University Press, 1997), 283–294.

83. Trochu is quoted in Porch, 46.

review on July 31 and, six days later, was ordered to Nancy with the rest of the division. There they remained until the French defeats at Forbach and Reichshofen, when forward elements of the VI Corps were ordered to return to Châlons. By August 10, the regiment received new orders, this time to move forward with VI Corps to reinforce the defense of Metz. By this point, the two French armies had been reorganized, and Canrobert's VI Corps now formed part of the Army of Metz. The 10e took up defensive positions at Metz in front of the Montigny repair shops of the eastern railroad lines just south of the fortress on August 12.[84] By the morning of August 15, Prussian cavalry had reached the outskirts of Metz, unsure whether the French meant to defend the city or retreat. In fact, by that time, elements of VI Corps, including Ardant du Picq's regiment, had already withdrawn across the Moselle and were at Rezonville. The Prussian high command, riding up to the heights of Montigny and seeing "immense clouds of dust," soon concluded the French were evacuating and ordered their II Army to pursue the retreating forces.[85] That was the point at which the Prussian 3rd Lancers and the horse artillery battery accompanying them reached the heights of Montigny, unlimbered their guns, and fired on the mass of troops collecting on the road across the river. Not long after, Ardant du Picq was carried back to the military hospital in the city. He died of his wounds on August 19.[86] His regiment had yet to fire a shot in the war.

Ardant du Picq left behind a mass of notes, far from a finished manuscript, in the care of his still-young family at Limoges. Six years after his death, some of these notes were published in the Revue de la Reunion des officiers, but with changes to the manuscript Lucien Nachin describes as un-

---

84. Appendix IV.

85. Von Moltke, 26–33.

86. La guerre de 1870–1871, Volume 1: Les opérations autour de Metz, Journées de 15 et 16 août (Paris: Chapelot, 1901), 11, n. 2. Judging from the brief description of Ardant du Picq's wounds, his chances of survival were virtually nil. Seventy percent of all deaths from wounds in the French army were caused by sepsis, which would have set in whether or not du Picq's legs were amputated. French medical services during the war, plagued by a shortage of physicians, were portrayed as "the most complete triumph of anarchy," staffed by medical officers whose low status in the army was underscored by their subordination to administrative officers. At Metz, where Ardant du Picq was treated, the medical officers could not keep pace with casualties, even when they were assisted by local physicians. One source calculates that each medical officer at Metz attended 400–500 casualties. Alexander Lambert, "Medicine, a Determining Factor in War," Presidential Address to the American Medical Association, Journal of the American Medical Association, vol. 72, no. 24 (June 14, 1919): 1717–1721. See also Holmes, 78–79.

accountable.[87] Three years later, with the help of an officer in the territorial army, du Picq's family arranged for Hachette's publication of his essays free of creative editing, in the first edition of *Études sur le combat*.[88]

Beyond receiving perfunctory notices in *Le Figaro* and in the *Revue critique d'histoire et de litterateur*, as well as the scholarly *Journal des Economistes*, *Études* was not reviewed in either public or military circles.[89] Yet there is reason to believe that within the cloisters of the newly reorganized *École superieur de guerre* of the 1880s Ardant du Picq was not entirely forgotten. As the early notices showed, it was all too easy to reduce Ardant du Picq's work to little more than a cheer for the much-cherished traditions of *élan*, however disappointingly it had served the army against the Prussians. By fits and starts, the French army was already attempting to reconstruct itself in order to prepare for the *revanche* that most officers believed was inevitable.[90] Ardant du Picq's book began to appear in the syllabi of the *École* in the 1890s. One of his leading promoters, not surprisingly, was an officer who came to the faculty from command of chasseurs, Louis de Maud'huy, who was assigned to instruct the course in infantry. Maud'huy introduced the latest works in psychology and physiology to his students, and du Picq's work was among those.[91] Just how widely Ardant du Picq's ideas were broadcast through the rest of the faculty is difficult to judge; the capacity of faculty to ignore each other's work should never be underestimated. Yet, by 1896, the reach of Ardant du Picq's book already extended to Great Britain. That year, Douglas Haig was recording notes from *Études* cited during lectures at the British Staff College.[92] Claims made for Ardant du Picq's influence during the

---

87. Nachin 1925, 64.

88. Ardant du Picq, *Études sur le combat* (Paris: Librairie Hachette, 1880), n.p., n. 1.

89. *Le Figaro*, April 28, 1880, 5; *Revue critique d'histoire et de littérateur* (Paris: Librairie de Societé Asiatique 1880), 113–114; *Journal des Economistes*, vol. 11 (1880): 451–453.

90. French military expenditures reflected the urgency felt in military circles in the 1890s. Although overall French military spending from 1870 to the beginning of the Great War ran to 3.7 percent of gross national product, from 1894 to 1913 spending increased by 91.5 percent. Holmes, 159; Niall Ferguson, *The Pity of War* (New York: Basic Books, 2000), 106; and Jari Eloranta and Mark Harrison, "War and Disintegration, 1914–1950," in *The Cambridge Economic History of Modern Europe*, ed. Stephen Broadberry and Kevin H. O'Rourke (Cambridge: Cambridge University Press, 2010), 138.

91. Nachin 1925, 67. General John M. Rene Cugnac, "*Le Général de Maud'huy (1857–1921)*," *Mémoires de l'Académie nationale de Metz* (Metz: Académie nationale de Metz, 1924), 60.

92. Tim Travers, *The Killing Ground: The British Army, the Western Front, and the Emergence of Modern Warfare, 1900–1918* (London: Allen & Unwin, 1987), 90. By 1910, at least one young American officer had acquired an interest in Ardant du Picq as well. See Steve Dietrich, "The

closing decade of the century could easily be overstated, but he clearly had not been forgotten by some of the professionals.[93]

Études rose to military and public prominence with the publication of a new edition in 1903. What, exactly, drove Ernest Judet, the right-wing editor of *Le Petit Journal*, controversialist, and anti-Dreyfusard, to bring out this new edition is unknown. Judet's edition coincided with a constellation of social anxieties in the leading industrial nations that had been in the making for more than a generation. The intersection of democratic, social, and technological change in the nineteenth century and the urban congestions it produced gave rise to widespread hand-wringing over the battleworthiness of modern man. Within military circles, this anxiety translated into questions about whether the new democratic, urban man was equal to the mental and physical demands of war, and if not, how to compensate for his assumed weaknesses. One of the more elaborate expressions of this anxiety was Ivan Bloch's pioneering multivolume study, *The Future of War*, published in 1898. But Bloch's massive work, its argument against the utility of modern battle, and its statistical reasoning offered no relief. Although professional soldiers seemed happy to ignore Bloch's findings or deride them, echoes of his concerns were increasingly voiced in Western military circles.[94] For the professionals, Ardant du Picq was approachable in a way Ivan Bloch was not, and his prescriptions for the creation, management, and sustainment of soldierly morale in the extremities of offensive combat—even short-term soldiers—seemed to offer a counterweight to their concerns.

But whether du Picq's work was one of the foundation stones of the French School of modern warfare is more problematic. What is more certain is that Judet's edition appeared at a propitious time, when the army was being battered by the effects of the Dreyfus controversy and the new republican government.[95] Judet's anti-Dreyfusard sentiments coincided nicely with those of the younger generation of officers who believed their *armée de métier* was being sacrificed at the altar of republicanism. *Études* came to serve a talismanic function in *fin de siècle* French military thought. Robert Doughty has written

---

Professional Reading of General George S. Patton, Jr.," *Journal of Military History*, vol. 53, no. 4 (October 1989): 396.

93. See Gat's reservations about Ardant du Picq's influence in his *History of Military Thought*, 308.

94. See Gat, 377–380.

95. The environment that greeted Judet's new edition is described in Jack Snyder, *The Ideology of the Offensive: Military Decision Making and the Disasters of 1914* (Ithaca: Cornell University Press, 1984), 73–74 and 90–96.

that Ardant du Picq's ideas "permeated the entire French army and provided the inspiration for the *offensive a outrance.*" His emphasis on moral supremacy in battle flowered most luxuriantly in Loyzeau de Grandmaison's 1906 influential study on infantry training, promoting superior morale as the ultimate weapon, one that drove attacking troops the last few yards against fire into the enemy's line.[96] No one cited Ardant du Picq's few excursions into tactical design; as doctrines and weapons advanced, those were soon out of date. His pronouncements on human psychology, poorly schooled to begin with, were seized upon by writers who were little more conversant with the subject than he was. Military writers found him useful chiefly to shore up their own arguments, ignoring Ardant du Picq's often qualified and conditional judgments. Their technical arguments were founded more on the results from recent wars in the Balkans, Manchuria, and South Africa.[97]

From the appearance of the second edition of *Études*, one could hardly find an issue of a military journal in France that did not pay homage to Ardant du Picq's work. The well-known historian of the Franco-Prussian War, Pierre Lehoutcourt, published an extensive essay on Ardant du Picq and his influence, significantly titled "Un Précurseur," in *Le Revue de Paris* in 1904, further promoting his work in the public eye.[98]

Du Picq's public reputation grew steadily and went through eight editions in the years before the Great War. When France went to war once again, his book went into the trenches with the *poilus*. In what is perhaps the most widely cited scholarly essay on Ardant du Picq in English, Stefan Possony and Étienne Mantoux wrote that "with the exception of [Leo Tolstoy's] *War and Peace*," *Études* was "the most widely read book in the French trenches during the First World War." Possony and Mantoux offered no evidence in support of this claim, however.[99] This claim had been made before, and

---

96. While it is true that de Grandmaison overemphasized the value of morale, even he argued that on the modern battlefield a frontal assault over open ground was impossible. See Hew Strachan, *The First World War, Volume I: Call to Arms* (Oxford: Oxford University Press, 2001), 188.

97. Robert Doughty, *Pyrrhic Victory: French Strategy and Operations in the Great War* (Cambridge: Harvard University Press, 2005), 25. See also Leonard V. Smith and Stephane Audoin-Rouzeau, *France and the Great War* (Cambridge: Cambridge University Press, 2003), 21–22; and Gat, 408–411.

98. Pierre Lehautcourt, "Un Précurseur," *Le Revue de Paris* (May–June 1904): 347–366.

99. Stefan T. Possony and Étienne Mantoux, "Du Picq and Foch: The French School," in *The Makers of Modern Strategy: Military Thought from Machiavelli to Hitler*, ed. Edward Mead Earle (Princeton: Princeton University Press, 1943), 207. Possony later claimed sole authorship of the du Picq segment of this joint essay. If so, the speculation that Trochu's work

more authoritatively, by Jean Norton Cru, in his remarkable and controversial study of French combatant literature of the Great War. The same claim, based on Cru's earlier judgment, was made in L. M. Chassin's anthology of French military literature published only a few years before Possony and Mantoux wrote.[100] Either of these works could have been the missing source in Possony and Mantoux's important essay.

In the many appraisals of *Études*, it is forgotten that it is above all an unfinished work. The book is commonly treated as a fully realized study, but du Picq only left behind a statement of his ambitions, and those were never fulfilled. He was still unable to see his intellectual horizon when he took his regiment off to meet the Prussians. He left behind a body of manuscripts, only part of which—his essays on ancient combat—he was able to publish. Those could be regarded as finished to his satisfaction, but it would be optimistic to think that the larger portion of what became *Études sur le combat*, Part II, "Modern Battle," was a finished work. Moreover, readers cannot be confidant that the order in which those later essays were placed was what Ardant du Picq himself would have decided. The two final chapters—on "Command, General Staff, and Administration," and "Social and Military Institutions; National Characteristics"—seem better suited to introduce Part II. Given their imperfect state, he might well have decided not to include those at all.[101]

Seeing his work as it stands now, outside the context in which it was written, readers are free to see connections where none exist, and to read into his text messages Ardant du Picq never intended. Such dangers lurk for any book once freed of their authors, but not many books have been so popular with military writers, their authority invoked in selective or tendentious quotes.

"suggested to Ardant du Picq the composition of his own" was Possony's. Mantoux was on active service with the FFI by then. He did not survive the war. Michael P. M. Finch, "Edward Mead Earle and the Unfinished Makers of Modern Strategy," *Journal of Military History*, vol. 80, no. 3 (July 2016): 798.

100. Teaching in America when the war began, Cru immediately returned home to enlist in the army and served in the trenches until 1917; if anyone had known what his comrades were reading, Cru would have. Jean Norton Cru, *Témoins: Essay d'analyse et de critique des souvenirs de combattants édités en française de 1915 à 1928* (Nancy: Presses Universitaires de Nancy, 1993; orig. publ. Paris: Les Etincelle, 1929), 75, n. 2; and L. M. Chassin, *Anthologie des classiques militaires française* (Paris: Charles-Lavauzelle, 1938), 200, n. 1. The leading American authority on Cru's work is Leonard Smith; see his "Jean Norton Cru and Combatants' Literature of the First World War," *Modern and Contemporary France*, vol. 9, no. 2 (2001): 161-169.

101. The sequencing of a manuscript is no small matter in textual reconstruction. An author's ideas may evolve as the writing advances, and misplacing the order in which its parts are conceived may have the effect of rendering the author's ideas contradictory or illogical.

Not until the publication of S. L. A. Marshall's *Men Against Fire* in 1948 did any writer make a name for himself exploring the parts of war that interested Ardant du Picq, and not until the appearance a generation later of John Keegan's seminal work, *The Face of Battle*, did any scholar improve on what this obscure French officer had written in his spare time. Moreover, the intellectual resources available to any writer in nineteenth-century France who wished to address the questions that interested Ardant du Picq were very limited. Even had he spent his career in Paris, the tools he could draw upon would have been of little help to him. The state of knowledge about human psychology in France at midcentury was on the verge of a sea-change, in which scientific medicine was about to shoulder aside older schools that opposed psychology as a natural science. Just as he was writing, Jean-Martin Charcot was beginning his experiments on hysteria at the *Salpêtrière* in Paris, but the work of Charcot and others belonged to the realm of elite medicine, well beyond the garrison gates at Limoges.[102] Ardant du Picq was left to his own devices, in far-flung garrisons and encampments, to deduce from his readings a set of ideas that passed his own test of experience and that of his comrades.

How, then, is the modern reader to regard the manuscripts that Ardant du Picq left behind? Surely not as history. Although history plays a critical role in his work, his reconstructions of ancient battles and later references to modern battles are employed not as proofs, but as illustrations.[103] Then as now, historical knowledge alone, however much it might illuminate a contemporary question, was insufficient to carry a point of argument. But it was important to him to show how historical knowledge could prompt new insights on modern questions; "nothing, especially in the trade of war, is sooner forgotten than experience. . . . Nevertheless, let us try to hold to facts," he wrote in 1869.[104]

---

102. Serge Nicholas, "'A Big Piece of News': Theodule and the Founding of *Revue philosophique de la France et de lEtranger,*" *Journal of the History of the Behavioral Sciences*, vol. 49, no. 1 (Winter 2013): 1–17. Edward Shorter, *A History of Psychiatry* (New York: John Wiley & Sons, 1997), 82–85.

103. Ardant du Picq has been criticized because the statistics from ancient battles concerning the balance of forces engaged and the number of casualties have been revised by modern scholars. I am not convinced that, had he more modern findings available, he would have drawn different conclusions. His arguments did not rest on these case studies alone.

104. Appendix I.

Which of Ardant du Picq's "facts" attracted so much attention from admirers and critics alike? Of all the military writers in nineteenth-century France, he alone attempted to escape the prison of orthodoxy, demonstrating that new, alternative paths to understanding war were still open, investigating parts of war where even Clausewitz had not ventured. It was in those parts, Clausewitz wrote, that "the light of reason is refracted in a manner quite different from that which is normal in academic speculation."[105] Orthodox military thought, long the handmaiden of statesmen and high commands, was organized to elucidate grand principles aimed at controlling the entirety of war with little thought for the parts of war that interested Ardant du Picq most. In the rare instances where they were considered at all, they were treated as derivatives of larger truths, which if correctly understood, will naturally act in accord with them. Ideally, national policies and their strategies will determine the shape of the army built to serve them. That army will prepare accordingly, raising its recruits, training its soldiers and commanders, devising its operational and tactical doctrines, and acquiring the materiel necessary to accomplish its mission. And yet, Ardant du Picq insisted, reality always intervenes; "the difference between theory and practice is incredible," he wrote.[106]

His approach was the polar opposite of orthodox theory, which he denounced as "mechanistic." His theoretical world was composed almost exclusively of the infantry battalion at the moment of contact with the enemy. Although innovations in small arms contributed substantially to the violence of modern battle, he had little to say about their proper distribution and employment. His treatment of other arms, the cavalry and artillery, was perfunctory, and his few mentions of logistics amounted to little more than complaints about its inadequacy. He declared he would waste no time on the proper design of battle formations, examining the merits of attacking in column or line, a subject he dismissed as "pedantry."[107] His only real interest, "*toujours la question essentielle*," around which all his thinking turned, was the soldier, "the fundamental instrument of battle," within the world of combat.[108] This perspective was at once his study's greatest strength, and, so easily misread, its greatest weakness.

---

105. Carl von Clausewitz, *On War*, trans. by Michael Howard and Peter Paret (Princeton: Princeton University Press, 1976), 113.

106. See below, 69. See also John Keegan's indictment of orthodox military thought and, not incidentally, orthodox military history's treatment of battle, at 39, 65.

107. See below, 69.

108. Ibid., 51.

Du Picq's insistence that war is best understood from the perspective of the soldier was by no means original. He paid due homage to the observations of Marshals Maurice de Saxe and Auguste Marmont, among others. Much of his study of ancient combat was meant to show how the ancients, chief among them the Romans, intuitively anticipated his own thinking on how to shape and use armies in accord with human rather than material capacities. But his predecessors had not elaborated on their insights to the degree that satisfied him. Too, the lessons that could be drawn from them belonged to earlier times and places, and du Picq was interested most of all in the army that stood before him.

Equipped with what he could glean from his readings in history, responses to his questionnaire, and not least his own experience, he painted a picture of the soldier in extremis, stripped of the patriotic devotion, romantic image, or heroic poses so beloved in popular literature. Nor was this soldier's behavior constant, as it is so often assumed, neither consistently brave, cowardly, or stoic.[109] He admitted that some soldiers seemed capable of banishing their fears to act heroically, but such acts were extremely rare and momentary. Ardant du Picq's soldier was psychologically fragile. His performance in battle was the product of his fears, which, if he were left to his own devices, drove him from one act to another in the service of *l'instinct de conservation*, the instinct of self-preservation.[110]

He had little patience for time-worn notions of *élan* and *l'esprit militaire*, usually promoted as near-magical qualities supposedly unique to the French, by which most military writers convinced themselves their nation would prevail in any war.[111] When he used these terms he was more precise, trying to explain exactly what produced such qualities. He took it as a given that men were more alike than not and that "centuries have not changed human nature." In a passage often overlooked, he could not give up the

---

109. Ibid., 46. "We assume that all the personnel present with an army, with a division, with a regiment on the day of battle, fights. Right there is the error," he wrote. Professional soldiers needed no convincing; few would have contested Marshal de Saxe's well-known dictum that "the courage of men must be reborn daily, that nothing is so variable." Marshal de Saxe, *Mes reveries*, in *The Roots of Strategy*, vol. 1, trans. Thomas R. Phillips (Harrisburg: Stackpole Books, 1940), 190.

110. Ibid. The concept of an instinct of self-preservation was well established by the time Ardant du Picq wrote. See, e.g., Jean-Louis Alibert, *Psychologie des passions, ou Nouvelle doctrine des sentiment moraux* (Brussels: Chez August Wahlen, Tarlier, C-J Dematfile, et al., 1825), 11, in which the author declares this instinct innate in all animals.

111. Holmes, 161. These qualities, when combined with *le systéme D*, supposedly protected the nation from its enemies, especially the stolid Prussians.

commonly held notion that every nation possessed certain attributes. He conceded that human nature "may be manifested in various ways according to the time, place, the character and temperament of the race."[112] Even so, national characteristics alone were never of sufficient power to overcome the soldier's first instinct.

The instinct of self-preservation as Ardant du Picq understood it posed important questions.[113] If this instinct were so all-powerful, how could soldiers function at all in combat? Soldiers obviously did fight. What enabled them to overcome their instinct? Ardant du Picq's answer was discipline, created and sustained by the commander, the one who would lead them into combat. Yet, no matter how adept the commander, his efforts would inevitably fall short. He argued that in any battle there came a point at which the commander could no longer attenuate fear.[114] That was the moment in which the commander would lose control of his troops. "The animal instinct of self-preservation always gains the upper hand," he wrote.[115]

The mere suggestion that commanders were not all-powerful, not all-seeing, not at every moment in contact with the enemy presiding over an orderly unfolding of his intentions, must have struck many of Ardant du Picq's colleagues and superiors as anathema. His battle was not under control from beginning to end but inevitably degenerated into one of chaos and uncertainty, filled with men fighting, whether on the attack or in defense, not for glory or victory but to preserve themselves.

Ardant du Picq believed the violence of modern warfare induced fear that was more intense than ever. Because of modern weaponry, battles were more terrifying even though they were less deadly, even though man's capacity to withstand fear was as fixed as it had been when Caesar met the Gauls. "Man is capable of standing before only a certain amount of terror," he wrote. "Today there must be swallowed in five minutes what took an hour under Turenne."[116] Behind this passage, one can hear the incessant barrages at Sebastopol.

---

112. Indeed, his case studies of ancient combat depend heavily on national characterizations: "The Gaul," he wrote, was "a fool in war," while the Roman was a "politician above all," and "not essentially brave." See below, 8–10.

113. I am indebted to Richard McNally, professor and director of clinical psychology at Harvard University, for his tutelage on the current scientific literature concerning the instinct of self-preservation.

114. Ibid., 7–10.

115. Ibid.

116. Ibid., 47.

Yet, du Picq did not argue that battle depended on an individual's performance alone, nor were formations merely collections of individuals. Then as now, battle is a test not only of individual strengths and weaknesses but also of the collective power of a military formation contending against its enemy. Yet, military units are never as robust and unchanging as theorists and military writers imagine them to be. He would have understood John Keegan's dictum that "inside every army is a crowd struggling to get out," that the moment a formation begins to take action it begins to disorganize itself.[117]

He believed that discipline was essential even though it was insufficient to resist the formation's tendency to disintegrate under the stresses of battle. The discipline he imagined could not be achieved by a commander without first binding his unit together socially. A cohesive unit could accomplish feats of arms beyond that which could be accomplished by soldiers who had not been socially integrated. This social integration, he believed, was the engine of morale itself. And, "in the last analysis," he wrote, "success in battle is a matter of morale."[118] Without morale, armies were doomed to defeat.

Of all Ardant du Picq's assertions, his claims for the power of morale in battle may have excited the most admiration and criticism.[119] Morale meant for him the sum of a military unit's collective psychology, which expressed itself in the unit's performance in battle. A talented commander might inspire morale in his unit, but the real source of morale lay in the comradeship among the troops themselves, and he thought it was stronger in troops who had soldiered together for a long time. The relationships created by long-standing association, he believed, encouraged the troops to support one another in combat with no prompting from their chain of command. Given proper arms and realistic training, soldiers thus carried with them into battle another advantage. As attacking formations tended to disperse

---

117. Keegan, 175.

118. Ibid., 109.

119. Much of the modern criticism may have begun with the essay by Possony and Mantoux, "Du Picq and Foch: The French School," 206–233, which scholars have argued overstated the debt Foch owed to du Picq's thinking. Ardant du Picq does not figure in Douglas Porch's formidable *The March to the Marne*, while Jack Snyder, in his *The Ideology of the Offensive: Military Decision Making and the Disasters of 1914* (Ithaca: Cornell University Press, 1984), 57–106, accords his work a more influential role in French military thought. A more recent assessment of Ardant du Picq's influence can be found in Gat, 408–411; and in Wawro, 174, 307, for whom Ardant du Picq's theory was "nonsense on stilts," but lived on despite its obvious contradiction by the course of the Franco-Prussian War.

as they closed with the enemy, comradeship acted as a counterweight, delaying the point at which the unit lost its cohesiveness and the tactical control of the commander. The value to the commander of this "mutual surveillance" among the troops was therefore more important than ever: even if the course of battle separated him from most of his troops, the troops themselves could rely on one another to fight their way through the danger. "Let us ensure cohesion by the mutual acquaintanceship of men and officers; let us call French sociability to our aid," he wrote.[120] With indifferent leadership, without comradeship, a mass of troops approaching one's defenses might be intimidating, he thought, but there were "only fifty or twenty-five percent who really fight."[121]

Though powerfully expressed and argued in greater detail, du Picq's assertions were not appreciably different than those of the most tub-thumping proponents of *l'esprit militaire* and *élan* of his day. The degree of power he assigned to morale was another matter, however. Ardant du Picq believed superior morale could achieve victory even in the face of superior numbers and arms. "He will win who has the resolution to advance," he wrote.[122] In his discussions of both ancient and modern battle, he derided the assumption that battles were decided when forces collided in a frenzied melee. For that reason he had little faith in massed assaults, which he found "incomprehensible" and wasteful. Instead, he thought, a force armed with greater morale would inevitably find that its enemy would rather retreat, often in disorder, than engage in sustained physical contact. He was sure this explained why casualties were so high in ancient warfare: soldiers in disordered retreat were easy prey, exposing themselves to slaughter. In modern warfare, he argued, "there is no shock of infantry on infantry. There is no physical impulse, no force of mass. There is but moral impulse."[123] Such dicta as these overshadowed more reserved, if not outright contradictory, assertions elsewhere in his text. Even while extolling the virtues of superior morale, he cautioned

---

120. See 130.

121. Ibid., 66. This passage may have been the inspiration for the American military writer S. L. A. Marshall's often cited "ratio of fire," in which he made the same assertion as Ardant du Picq, also without convincing evidence. Marshall claimed he had not read Ardant du Picq before he wrote *Men Against Fire*, forgetting that he had quoted Ardant du Picq's dictum that "the heart of man does not change" in his text. S. L. A. Marshall, *Men Against Fire: The Problem of Battle Command in Future War* (Gloucester, MA: Peter Smith, 1978; orig. publ. New York: William Morrow, 1947), 154. See also Roger J. Spiller, "S. L. A. Marshall and the Ratio of Fire," *Journal of the Royal United Services Institute*, vol. 133, no. 4 (December 1988): 63–71.

122. See 61.

123. Ibid., 63–64.

his readers to remember that during the attack one should "cover infantry troops before their entry into action; cover them as much as possible and by any means; take advantage of terrain, make them lie down." Throughout his text, he revealed a preference for skirmishers, whose dispersion and tactical flexibility seemed to better suit the modern battlefield, but he believed an army could rely on skirmishers too much; "this talk of skirmishers in large bodies is nothing else but an euphemism for absolute disorder," he wrote. Unified formations must be employed, not for the shock of their mass, but for their moral effect, and for that, formations must remain under the control of the commander until the crucial moment. In one of the few passages in which he discussed tactics in a conventional way, the mass of the battalion serves mainly as the means by which the commander can move his troops up to the assault itself, at which point unity of action and tactical control devolves to small groups or individual soldiers. For the commander, "determining the moment when man abandons reason and becomes instinctive is the essence of the science of combat."[124]

Contrary to prevailing opinion that the French citizen could only learn soldiering in nine years, Ardant du Picq believed that troops properly recruited, trained, formed, and led could be made into the kind of army he imagined within three years.[125] The raw human material from which armies at the time were raised was the subject of no small amount of hand-wringing by government officials and social commentators alike from the middle of the nineteenth century to the Great War. Ardant du Picq was not immune to these concerns. Resigned to the need for a mass army rather than a long-standing corps of professionals, he believed that the progress of democracy in France made raising such an army all the more difficult. "A democratic society is antagonistic to the military spirit," he wrote, and for that reason "the military spirit is dead in France." And although there was an inherent "lack of power in mob armies," France had set its course, and there was little to do but accept the military liabilities that came with it. Resigned as he was to the realities of the day, he nevertheless saw qualities in his fellow citizens that might be drawn upon: "The French are indeed worthy sons of their fathers, the Gauls. . . . The good Frenchman lets himself be carried away, inflamed by the most ridiculous feats of arms into the wildest enthusiasm. . . . French sociability creates cohesion in French troops more

---

124. Ibid., 71–73.
125. Ibid., 45.

quickly than could be secured in troops in other nations. . . . How much better modern tactics fit the impatient French character?"[126]

Ardant du Picq's optimism was at odds with that of his old brigade commander, Louis Trochu, who lacerated French soldiery every bit as much as French policymakers in his denunciations of the army in 1867, reserving his most biting comments for long-service soldiers, the "old grumblers," *grognards*. They were "Whoremongers," wastrels of the worst kind, drunkards who habitually evaded their duties by any means at hand, insular, taking refuge in grimy garrisons in out-of-the-way provinces. What could be made of such men without stern discipline?[127]

Even with his more forgiving view of the potential of his soldiers, Ardant du Picq was careful to emphasize the role of discipline throughout his manuscript. If indeed France was to have a mass army made of such imperfect material, her only salvation lay in the quality of her professional officers and noncommissioned officers, and among these, he emphasized, officers of the line, not the staff, mattered more than anyone. If the military spirit had indeed vanished from French society at large, the professionals were its last remaining repository.[128] Inasmuch as modern democracy prized wealth above all, he thought officers should be paid more and allowed more leisure in order to elevate their prestige and attract candidates. "There is little taste for the military life in France; such a procedure would lessen it. The leisure of army life attracts three out of four officers, laziness, if you like. But such is the fact," he wrote.[129] The officer corps could take up the place of the aristocracy of old, but it would be an aristocracy of valor. And in return, France would have its mass army, commanded by officers lacking "in firmness" but with no little pride; "in the face of danger they lack composure, they are disconcerted, breathless, hesitant, forgetful, unable to think of a way out. They call 'Forward! Forward!' at the head of their formations."[130]

There was no such drama in Ardant du Picq's last moments commanding his regiment. No painter would bother to stretch his canvas to depict Ardant du Picq's wounding, and no one would record his death a few days later, one of the tens of thousands of French soldiers to follow. He left behind a collection of manuscripts, some nearer final draft than others, whose se-

---

126. Ibid., 126.
127. See Wawro, 43–44, for an especially pungent description of the army on the eve of the war.
128. See below, 123.
129. Ibid.
130. Ibid., 127.

quence could only be assumed, and whose line of argument was marred by inconsistencies, contradictions, and digressions. Once collected in a single volume, Ardant du Picq's work could be seen as an attempt to think about war differently, one that turned conventional military thought on its head. Although unschooled in psychology, even the crude schools that then prevailed, he reached into parts of war that until then had been addressed, if at all, in hoary aphorisms and clichés. His hopes to substantiate his insights with more precise, systematically researched evidence had not been satisfied when he died. In spite of its shortcomings, *Études sur le combat* had opened the door to the heart of the soldier's war like no other work before its time and few works after.

About This Translation

The original edition of Ardant du Picq's *Études sur le combat* was published in Paris in 1880 by Hachette. This edition consisted of a compilation of du Picq's unpublished essays. A family friend, one Captain Letellier, about whom little is known, undertook the compilation at the family's request. Captain Letellier did not explain the condition of the manuscripts he worked with, and internal evidence suggests he did little if anything to edit them. Both the content and the organization of the book reflect its unfinished state. For all its deficiencies, this was the only edition readers knew for nearly a generation, and today it can be freely accessed online.

In 1903, Ernest Judet, a well-known and controversial journalist, published a much improved edition. Judet enlisted the support of du Picq's family, and one of the more valuable features of Judet's edition was the addition of a biographical sketch of du Picq by his brother. For the main body of the text, Judet used a light editorial hand, but he did make one significant change: the introduction in the old edition became Part One's chapter VII in Judet's edition, a change that made good editorial sense.

Judet's 1903 edition drew a great deal more notice than the original, running through eight printings before the Great War. And one authority has claimed that with the exception of *War and Peace*, *Études sur le combat* was the most popular book in the French trenches during the war. There is good argument, then, for regarding Judet's edition as the "definitive" edition in French.

In 1921, two American army officers, Colonel John N. Greely and Major Robert Cotton, translated the Judet edition into English. Their work has served as the "standard" English edition since then. They modestly described their translation as "unpretentious," but Anglophone readers have depended on it for nearly a century, and it has served them well. I suspect Greely and Cotton were working under something of a deadline, as I was

li

not. Too, the emergence of considerably more biographical information about du Picq's life and career over the years since has permitted me to see his work in a better perspective than was available to them, and to introduce his work in a way that I hope will assist the reader in understanding just how remarkable du Picq's work was. Inevitably, this better perspective has influenced my translation.

This translation is also based on Judet's 1903 edition. Any disquisition on the trials and tribulations of translation is of little use to readers who find their way to this book. There are almost as many schools of the art of translation as there are translators. One practical principle has guided me in this work, and it takes the form of a question: Were Ardant du Picq as fluent in English as he was in French, what would his text have looked like when he wrote it in the late 1860s? In part, that will explain both the Gallic flavor of his diction, and also what some may regard as rather old-fashioned—that is, mid-nineteenth-century—English.

My own editorial interventions have been conservative, consisting mostly of footnotes as a means to identify or explain references and military terms whose meaning have faded into obscurity. I have taken care not to disturb the paragraphing in du Picq's text, and my intention here was to retain the epigrammatic qualities in a text that in many instances will strike the reader as du Picq's thinking with his pen. This book, after all, was a work very much in progress.

BATTLE STUDIES

*Ancient and
Modern Battle*

PART ONE

Ancient Battle: Introduction

Battle is the ultimate purpose of armies, and man is the ultimate instrument of combat. Nothing can be prescribed wisely in an army; its makeup, its organization, its discipline, its tactics—all of which are like the fingers of a hand—without an exact understanding of its ultimate instrument, man, and his morale at the defining instant of combat.

It often happens that those who discuss matters of war, taking the weapon as the starting point, assume without hesitation that the man called upon to serve it will always use it as expected and directed by rules and regulations.

But the soldier is a reasoning being; without his excitable, changeable nature, he becomes a mere pawn, an abstract unit in battle plans, born of speculation in the ministry [of war], and not a real man. He is flesh and blood; he is body and soul. And strong as the soul often is, it cannot master the body so that its flesh does not revolt or its spirit is not weakened in the face of destruction.

The human heart, in the words of Marshal de Saxe, is the starting point for all matters of war; to understand this, it must be studied.

Let us study, not modern combat at first—too complex to be easily understood—but ancient combat, which is simpler, clearer, although nowhere explained in detail.

The centuries have not changed the human heart; the passions, the instincts, above all the instinct of survival, all of which have been manifested according to the time, place, and character of the races. Thus, today we can admire—even under the pressure of the same danger—the composure of the English, the *élan* of the French, and the stolidity of the Russians that is called tenacity. But, basically, we always find the same man; and it is this man, always the same, whom we see in the organization and discipline of

3

the soldiers when the masters prepare them for action. The greatest of the masters knew man best, modern man as well as historical man. This is clear from a close analysis of the formations and great events of ancient warfare.

This analysis has led us to the study of man in combat.

We will even go beyond ancient battle, to primitive combat. By progressing from the savages to our own time, we shall have a clearer view of the man. Then, shall we know as much as the masters? No more than a painter who knows only the methods of painting; but we will better understand these able men and the great examples they left behind.

From them, we will learn to suspect mathematics and materiel calculations when they are applied to matters of combat; we shall be skeptical of illusions drawn from the firing range and training ground, where the soldier is calm, sedate, rested, well fed, attentive, obedient, intelligent, and tractable—and not with the nervous, impressionable, agitated, troubled, distraught, excitable creature incapable of self-control who is every fighting man from commander to private (except for the strong, and they are very rare).

However, illusions, persistent and tenacious, always recover the day after experience inflicts the greatest damage on them. At the very least, illusions lead to ordering the impractical, as if it were not really an attack on discipline, and would not lead to commanders and soldiers being baffled by the unexpected and by being surprised by the difference between battle and peacetime training.

Certainly, battle always surprises. But it surprises less if understanding and realism have influenced the fighting man's training and are widespread throughout the ranks. Let us therefore study man in combat, for it is he who actually fights.

I

Man in Primitive and Ancient Combat

Man does not enter combat to fight, but for victory. He does everything he can to avoid the first and guarantee the second.

War between savage peoples, between Arabs, even in our own day,[1]* is a war of ambush by small groups of men, each of whom at the moment of surprise chooses not his adversary but his victim, and is an assassin.[2] Because the weapons on both sides are the same, the only way to find an advantage is by surprise; the man who is surprised needs a moment to think and defend himself. In this moment, he is killed if he does not flee.

The surprised enemy does not defend himself, he tries to escape; and face to face or body to body combat with primitive arms, ax or knife, so terrible among combatants without defensive arms, is exceedingly rare. It can only take place between enemies who are mutually surprised and without a chance of safety for anyone except in victory.

And yet . . . in such a case there is another chance for safety, that of one side or the other falling back, and that chance is often taken. An example—and if it does not concern savages but soldiers of our own time, it is none-

---

1. *Général Dumas, *Meurs et coutumes d l'Algérie, surprise nocturne et extermination d'un compement.* [Editor's note: Asterisks indicate original notes written by Ardant du Picq.]

2. Melchior Joseph Eugène Daumas (1803–1871), the French general whose work du Picq notes above, was an early Arabist and ethnologist as well as a professional soldier. First posted to Algeria in 1835, he took part in several early campaigns under Marshal Clausel, and became a close student of Algerian life and culture, and was the author of several well-known works in the field. He put this knowledge to work in early Arab affairs departments under Marshal Bugeaud in Algeria and in 1850 was appointed director of Algerian Affairs in the Ministry of War in Paris. He was elevated to the Senate in 1857.

theless significant—is a man of warlike temperament who has related what he was forced to witness with his own eyes while disabled by his wound.

During the Crimean War, on a day of heavy fighting, among numerous movements over broken ground, two groups of soldiers, A and B, come unexpectedly face to face, at ten paces, and freeze. Then, forgetting their rifles, they threw stones and withdrew. Neither group had a leader to urge them forward, and neither dared to shoot first for fear the others would also bring their rifles to bear. They were too close to escape, or so they thought—although in reality opposing fire at such close range is almost always too high. The man who would fire sees himself already killed by return fire. So he throws stones instead, not very hard, to distract himself from his rifle, to distract his enemy, to win a little time, until he sees some chance of escaping point-blank fire.

This agreeable situation does not last long, a minute perhaps. The appearance of a troop B on the flank sees the flight of group A and opens fire.

Certainly, the encounter is farcical and laughable.

Let us see, however. In a dense forest a lion and a tiger meet face to face on a trail. They stop, rearing backward, their knees bent, ready to lunge, their eyes measuring the other, their throats rumbling. Their claws flex, their hair stands up. Their tails batting the ground, necks extended, ears back, lips curled, they display their formidable fangs in that terrible menacing gesture common to felines.

An unseen observer, I shudder.

For the lion as well as the tiger, the situation is frightful. One movement means the death of a beast. Which? Perhaps both.

Slowly, very slowly, one of the legs flexed to jump, still bent, moves back. Slowly, very slowly, the foreleg follows, then the other legs. Little by little, still face to face, they retreat farther than a single leap could carry them. Lion and tiger turn away slowly and, still watching the other, calmly walk away with the sovereign dignity of the great lords. I no longer shudder, but neither do I laugh.

There is no laughing at man, because he has in his hands a more terrible weapon than the teeth and nails of a lion or tiger, the rifle, which without cover can send you instantaneously from life to death. It is understandable, therefore, that no one is in a hurry to shoot, to put into action a force that may kill him. He is not anxious to set fire to the wick that may blow up the enemy and himself at the same time.

Who has not seen similar examples between dogs, between dogs and cats, cats and cats?

In the Polish War of 1831, two Russian regiments and two Polish regiments of cavalry charged each other. With equal *élan*, both went forward with the same dash to meet each other; then, when they drew close enough to see each other's faces, they both withdrew. The Russians and the Poles, at this terrible moment, saw each other as brothers, and rather than spill fraternal blood, they withdrew from combat as if it were a crime. That is the testimony of a witness, a Polish officer.

Cavalry troops who see each other as brothers?

But to resume:

When a society becomes more populous, and when surprising an entire people occupying a vast territory is no longer possible, when a sort of public knowledge has risen within society, one is forewarned before war is formally declared. Surprise is not the entirety of war, but it is still one of the means, one of the best means, even today.

Man can no longer slay his defenseless enemy without warning. He must expect to find the enemy waiting in force. He must fight, taking as little risk as possible to win, using the mace against the staff, arrows against the mace, shield against arrows, shield and cuirass against the shield alone, the long lance against the short lance, the armed chariot against the infantry, and so forth.

Man strains his ingenuity to kill without the risk of being killed. His bravery rests on his feeling of strength and it is not absolute; in the face of greater strength, he flees shamelessly. The natural survival instinct is so powerful he feels no reluctance to obey it. However, with the defensive power of arms and armor he can fight at close quarters, who could expect otherwise? He must test himself before knowing who is stronger, and once the strength is known, no one can face it.

The strength and valor of individuals played a dominant role in ancient combat, and when the hero was killed, the nation was vanquished. By mutual, tacit agreement, combatants stopped fighting to watch in wonder and anguish as two heroes struggled. Whole peoples placed their fate in the hands of these heroes, who stood to fight in single combat. Everyone agreed since no one could stand against heroes.

But intelligence defies force. No one can stand against an Achilles, but no Achilles can stand against ten opponents who, uniting their efforts, act in concert. Tactics are born, in which organized means and action are decided first to ensure concerted efforts and the discipline that counteracts the individual fighter's weaknesses.

So far we have seen man against man on his own, in the manner of wild beasts, hunting to kill, fleeing that which can kill him. From now on, discipline and clear tactics unite the commander and the soldier, and the soldiers with each other. In addition to intellectual progress, there is moral progress. To ensure solidarity in combat, and to make tactical decisions that make it practical, we must see that everyone is dedicated to one another. This raises all fighters to the same heights as the champions of primitive combat. Pride is born. Flight is disgraceful because the soldier is no longer alone in battle but part of a legion, and he who runs away abandons his commander and his comrades. In all respects, the soldier is now more valuable.

Thus reason makes clear the strength of wisely concerted effort; discipline makes it possible.

Will we see terrible struggles, battles of extermination? No. Men assembled in a disciplined formation in tactical battle order are invincible against undisciplined troops. But against similarly disciplined troops, men revert to the primitive, fleeing before stronger forces of destruction that are real or imagined. Nothing changes in the heart of man. Discipline keeps him face to face with his enemy a little longer, but the instinct of survival reigns supreme, and the sense of fear with it.

Fear!

There are commanders, there are soldiers, who do not know it, but they are men of rare character. The mass trembles because one cannot suppress the flesh, and the trembling born of apprehension must be an essential calculation in all matters of organization, discipline, dispositions, movements, maneuvers, and plan of action—all of which is exactly why the soldier's human weakness that causes him to exaggerate his enemy's strength must be taken into account.

If we study this weakness in ancient battle, we see that of the nations best at war, the strongest have been those who best understood war in general, and who acknowledged human weakness and took measures to overcome it. It is remarkable that the most warlike people are not always those in which military institutions and methods of combat are the best or most rational. And indeed, among warlike nations there is a good dose of vanity. They only demand courage in their tactics; one might think they refuse to admit their weakness.

The Gaul, a fool in war, used barbarian tactics, and after the first surprise, he was always beaten by the Greeks, by the Romans.

The Greek, a warrior and also a politician, had tactics far superior to those of the Gauls and the Asiatics.

The Roman, a politician above all, for whom war was only a means to an end, demanded perfect means. He had no illusions; he acknowledged human weakness and found the legion.

But this is merely affirming what should be demonstrated.

II

Knowledge of Man Made Roman Tactics, the Successes of Hannibal, and Those of Caesar

The tactics of the Greeks are embodied in the phalanx, Roman tactics in the legion; the tactics of the barbarians in the square phalanx, the wedge, or the diamond.

The mechanics of these different formations are explained in all the elementary texts; Polybius discusses their mechanical value when he contrasts the phalanx and the legion (Book XVIII).

The Greeks were intellectually superior to the Romans and so their tactics should have been far more rational. But it was not so. Greek tactics were founded on mathematical reasoning; Roman tactics from a profound understanding of the human heart,[3]* but they were preoccupied by more diverse interests.

What formation obtained the maximum effort from the Greeks?

By what means did the Roman army ensure that all their soldiers fought effectively?

The first question requires discussion. The Romans found a solution to the second.

---

3. *In both cases, mechanics and morale are so closely related that one comes to the aid of the other and neither is ever weakened.

The Roman was not essentially brave; he did not produce any warrior the caliber of Alexander. The impetuous bravery of the barbarians, Gauls, Cimbres, Teutons—it is commonly said—always frightened him. But the glorious bravery of the Greeks, the brave temperament of the Gauls, the Romans opposed with a far stronger sense of duty, led by patriotic commanders who enforced a terrible discipline upon the soldiers.

The discipline of the Greeks was secured by punishment and reward; the discipline of the Romans too, and also by death: they were beaten to death; they were decimated.

A Roman general considers how to defeat these enemies who terrify his men. He raises their spirits not by enthusiasm but by hatred. He makes his soldiers' lives miserable with hard labor and privation. He imposes discipline to the point where at a certain moment it will break or spend itself on the enemy.

A Greek general has Tyrtee[4] sing.

It would have been curious to see the two armies face to face.[5*]

But discipline alone does not make for superior tactics. The man in combat, we repeat, is a being in whom the survival instinct dominates all other feelings at a certain moment. Discipline aims to dominate that instinct by means of a greater fear, but it cannot dominate it completely; there comes a point where fear will not be denied. Certainly, I do not deny there are glorious instances of discipline and devotion in which man transcends himself; but if these instances are acclaimed, it is because they are so rare; it is because they are exceptions, and exceptions confirm the rule.

Determining this moment when man abandons reason and becomes instinctive is the essence of the science of combat, and which in its general application was the strength of Roman tactics; it is in such moments that we see the superiority of Hannibal and that of Caesar.

At this time, combat was fought between groups in more or less deep formation, commanded and overseen by leaders with a fixed role. Massed combat was a series of individual fights, juxtaposed, in which the man in the front rank fought alone. If he fell, if he was wounded or exhausted, the man in the second rank who had watched and guarded his flanks took his

---

4. Tyrtaeus, a Spartan poet of the seventh century B.C. who was renowned for his military elegies.

5. *The Romans did not disparage Tyrtaeus. They did not disparage any means. But they knew the value of each.

place, and so on to the last rank. Man spends all his energy in hand-to-hand fighting and is physically and mentally exhausted.

These fights usually did not last long. With equal morale, those least fatigued always won.

While the first rank fights—the second rank closely watching the other—the men posted behind, watching the two, are inactive, waiting their turn only if their predecessors are killed, wounded, or exhausted. They are shocked by the violent fluctuations in the first ranks, they hear the clash of arms and perhaps those that bite into the flesh. They see the wounded, the exhausted, crawl between the intervals to the rear; passive spectators in the face of danger, they calculate its approach. They see their chances turn against them at each moment. All these men experience the poignant emotions of combat, unable to relieve them in the struggle, and thus are burdened by the pressures of intense anxiety. Often they cannot hold on there, and they take flight.

The best tactics, the best dispositions, were those that created a succession of efforts, by assuring relief of the ranks in action, and in actually employing only those necessary and keeping the rest in reserve, beyond the range of immediate moral tension. The superiority of the Romans lay in such tactics and in the dreadful discipline that shaped and gave life to their execution.[6]*

Their tenacity under fatigue, their hard and continuous drill, and their continuous renewal of fighters enabled them to fight longer.

Without thinking, the Gauls saw only the inflexible rank, and *they bound them together*, making relief impractical. They believed, as did the Greeks, in the power of mass and the momentum of deep ranks, and they did not see that massed ranks are powerless to push the front ranks forward when they recoil in the face of death. Strange mistake to think that the last ranks will rush to meet what has already repelled the first, while the contagion of retreat is so strong that halting the front means the rear must first retire!

Certainly the Greeks also had reserves and supports in the rear of their dense ranks, but the idea of the mass predominated. They placed their supports and reserves too close to the front, forgetting man.

The Romans believed in the power of mass, but only from the perspective of morale. They did not multiply the files in order to add to the mass, but to give the soldiers the confidence they would be supported and relieved;

---

6. *Their common sense also enabled them to adopt arms that were better than their own.

and the number was determined by the degree of moral pressure that the last ranks could sustain.

There is a time beyond which man can no longer bear the anxiety of combat without being directly engaged. The Romans did not increase their ranks and avoided this problem. The Greeks did not see or calculate so well and sometimes formed as many as thirty-two files, and their last files—which in their minds were doubtless the reserves—found themselves forcibly dragged into the material disorder of the first.

In the Roman legion's formation by maniples the best soldiers, those who had proved their courage in battle, waited stoically in the second or third lines. They were far enough back to avoid being wounded, *to see clearly*, and not to become entangled as the anterior lines withdrew in the intervals. They were close enough for support when necessary or to finish the fight by moving forward.

When the three separate and successive maniples of the first cohort were united in order to form the united battle cohort of Marius and of Caesar, the same thinking placed the most reliable men—that is, the oldest—in the last lines; the youngest, the most impetuous, in the front ranks. And the legion was not composed simply for numbers or mass. Each had his turn in action, and when the unit made up a maniple, each cohort had its place in the order of battle.

What we see is the Roman concept that dictated a depth of ranks that provided for a succession of soldiers. The general adjusted the disposition of these formations. If the soldiers were battle-hardened, well trained, reliable, tenacious, quick to relieve the leaders of their file, full of confidence in their leaders and their own comrades, the general reduced the depth of the ranks, even the lines, in order to strengthen the number of combatants on the front line. His men possessing moral, and sometimes physical, capacity greater than the enemy, the general knew that the last ranks of the enemy would not stand long enough to relieve his first lines or prevent the relief of his own. Hannibal had part of his infantry, the Africans, armed and drilled in the Roman way; his Spanish infantry had the endurance of the Spaniards of today; his Gallic soldiers, tested by their trials, were also fit for long campaigns. Hannibal, empowered by the confidence with which he inspired his people, formed a line half as deep as the Romans and at Cannae surrounded an army twice his size and exterminated it. Caesar, at Pharsalus, for similar reasons did not hesitate to reduce his depth while facing double his strength in Pompey's army, a Roman army like his, and crushed it.

As we have mentioned Cannae and Pharsalus, we shall study the mechanics and the morale in ancient combat, two matters that cannot be separated. We cannot find better examples of battle more clearly or impartially explained, due in one case to the clear account of Polybius, who spoke with survivors of Cannae, and possibly even some of the victors; and in the other case, it is due to the impassive clarity of Caesar in teaching the art of war.

III

Analysis of the Battle of Cannae

The account of Polybius:

Varro placed the cavalry on the right wing, and rested it on the river; the infantry was deployed near it and on the same line, the maniples drawn close to each other, with smaller intervals than usual, and the maniples presenting more depth than front.

The cavalry of the allies, on the left wing, completed the line, in front of which were posted the light troops. There were in that army, including the allies, 80,000 foot and a little more than 6,000 horse.

Meanwhile Hannibal had his slingers and light troops cross the Aufidus and posted them in front of his army. The rest crossed the river at two places. He placed the Iberian and Gallic cavalry on the left wing, next [to] the river and facing the Roman cavalry. He placed on the same line, one half of the African infantry heavily armed, the Iberian and Gallic infantry, the other half of the African infantry, and finally the Numidian cavalry that formed the right wing.

After he had thus arrayed all his troops upon a single line, he marched to meet the enemy with the Iberian and Gallic infantry moving independently of the main body. As it was joined in a straight line with the rest, on separating, it was formed like the convex face of a crescent. This formation reduced its depth in the center. The intention of the general was to commence the battle with the Iberians and Gauls, and have them supported by the Africans.

The latter infantry was armed like the Roman infantry, having been equipped by Hannibal with arms that had been taken from the Romans in preceding battles. Both Iberians and Gauls had shields; but their swords were quite different. The sword of the former was as fit for thrusting as for cutting while that of the Gauls only cut with the edge, and at a limited distance. These troops were drawn up as follows: the Iberians were in two bodies of troops on the wings, near the Africans; the Gauls in the center. The Gauls were naked, the Iberians in linen shirts of purple color, which to the Romans was an extraordinary and frightening spectacle. The Carthaginian army consisted of 10,000 horse and a little more than 40,000 foot.

Aemilus commanded the right of the Romans, Varro the left; the two consuls of the past year, Servilius and Attilius, were in the center. On the Carthaginian side, Hasdrubal had the left under his orders, Hanno the right, and Hannibal, who had his brother Mago with him, reserved for himself the command of the center. The two armies did not suffer from the glare of the sun when it rose, the one being faced to the south, as I remarked, and the other to the north.

Action commenced with the light troops, which were in front of both armies. The first engagement gave advantage to neither the one nor the other. Just as soon as the Iberian and Gallic cavalry on the left approached, the conflict became hot. The Romans fought with fury and rather more like barbarians than Romans. This falling back and then returning to the charge was not according to their tactics. Scarcely did they become engaged when they leaped from their horses and each seized his adversary. In the meanwhile the Carthaginians gained the upper hand. The greater number of the Romans remained on the ground after having fought with the greatest valor. The others were pursued along the river and cut to pieces without being able to obtain quarter.

The heavily armed infantry immediately took the place of the light troops and became engaged. The Iberians and Gauls held firm at first and sustained the shock with vigor; but they soon gave way to the weight of the legions, and, opening the crescent, turned their backs and retreated. The Romans followed them with impetuosity, and broke the Gallic line much more easily because the wings crowded toward the center where the thick of fighting was. The whole line did not fight at the same time. The action commenced in the center because the Gauls, being drawn up in the form of a crescent, left the wings far behind them, and presented the convex face of the crescent to the Romans. The latter then followed the Gauls and the Iberians closely, and crowded toward the center, to the place where the enemy gave way, pushing ahead so forcibly that on both flanks they engaged the heavily armed Africans. The Africans on the right, in swinging about from right to left, found themselves all along the enemy's flank, as well as those on the left that made the swing from left to right. The very circumstances of the action showed them what they had to do. This was what Hannibal had foreseen, that the Romans pursuing the Gauls must be enveloped by the Africans. The Romans then, no longer able to keep their formation[7*] were forced to defend themselves man to man and in small groups against those who attacked them on front and flank.[8*]

Aemilius had escaped the carnage on the right wing at the commencement of the battle. Wishing, according to the orders he had given, to be everywhere, and seeing that it was the legionary infantry that would decide the fate of the battle, he pushed his horse through the fray, warded off or killed everyone who opposed him, and sought at the same time to reanimate the ardor of the Roman soldiers. Hannibal, who during the entire battle remained in the conflict, did the same in the center.

The Numidian cavalry on the right wing, without doing or suffering much, was useful on that occasion by its manner of fighting; for, pouncing upon the enemy on all sides, they gave him enough to do so that he might not have time to think of helping his own people. Indeed, when the left wing, where Hasdrubal commanded, had routed almost all the cavalry of the Roman right wing, and a junction had been effected with the Numidians, the auxiliary cavalry did not wait to be attacked but gave way.

Hasdrubal is said to have done something that proved his prudence and his ability [and] contributed to the success of the battle. As the Numidians were in great number, and as these troops were never more useful than when one was in flight before them, he gave them the fugitives to pursue, and led the Iberian and Gallic cavalry in a charge to aid the African infantry. He pounced on the Romans from the rear, and having bodies of cavalry charge into the melee at several places, he gave new strength to the Africans and made the arms drop from the hands of the adversaries. It was then that L. Aemilius, a citizen who during his

---

7. *This is an excuse. The maniple was perfectly mobile and without the least difficulty could face in any direction.

8. *This was an enveloping attack of an army and not of men and groups. The Roman army formed a wedge and was attacked at its point and side; there was not a separate flank attack. That day the maniple presented more depth than front.

whole life, as in this last conflict, had nobly fulfilled his duties to his country, finally succumbed, covered with mortal wounds.

The Romans continued fighting, giving battle to those who were surrounding them. They resisted to the last. But as their numbers diminished more and more, they were finally forced into a smaller circle, and all were put to the sword. Attilius and Servilius, two persons of great probity, who had distinguished themselves in the fighting as true Romans, were also killed on that occasion.

While this carnage was taking place in the center, the Numidians pursued the fugitives of the left wing. Most of them were cut down, others were thrown under their horses; some of them escaped to Venusia. Among these was Varro, the Roman general, that abominable man whose administration cost his country so dearly. Thus ended the battle of Cannae, a battle where prodigies of valor were seen on both sides.

Of the 6,000 horse of which the Roman cavalry was composed, only seventy Romans reached Venusia with Varro, and, of the auxiliary cavalry, only 300 men found shelter in various towns. Ten thousand foot were taken prisoner, but they were not in the battle.[9]* Of troops in battle only about 3,000 saved themselves in the nearby town; the balance, numbering about 20,000, died on the field of honor.[10]*

Hannibal lost in this action about 4,000 Gauls, 1,500 Iberians and Africans, and 200 horses.

Let us analyze:

The light infantry scattered in front of the armies and skirmished without result. The real fighting began with an attack on the legionnaire cavalry of the Roman left wing by Hannibal's cavalry.

There, says Polybius, the fight became thickest, and the Romans fought with a fury more like barbarians than like Romans because this falling back then returning to the charge did not accord with their tactics. Hardly did

---

9. *They had been sent to attack Hannibal's camp. They were repulsed and taken prisoner in their own camp after the battle.

10. *This extract is taken from the translation of Dom Thuillier. [Dom Vincent Thuillier, *Historie de Polybe: Nouvelle traduits du Grec par Dom Vincent Thuillier, avec un commentaire du corps de science militaire; avec un commentaire par Chevalier Folard.* 6 volumes. Paris: Grandouin, 1720–1730.] Livy does not state the exact number of Roman combatants. He says nothing had been neglected in order to make the Roman army the strongest possible, and from what he was told by some it numbered 87,200 men. That is the figure given by Polybius. His account has killed, 45,000; taken or escaped after the action, 19,000. Total 64,000. What can have become of the other 23,000?

they come to blows when they dismounted and each seized his adversary, and so on.

That is, the Roman cavalry usually did not fight hand to hand like the infantry. It hurled itself at a gallop toward the enemy cavalry and, if the enemy's cavalry had not retreated, wisely slowed its pace, threw some javelins, and turned about, then rode to the rear to prepare another charge. The opposing cavalry did the same, and this might be repeated several times, until one or the other, persuaded that his enemy was going to attack him in earnest, retreated, and was pursued to the death.

That day the battle intensified, actually coming to blows; that is to say, the two cavalries attacked for real and one man fought another. The engagement was being forced; there was no retreating by one side or the other. It was necessary to attack. There was no room for skirmishing. Confined between Aufide and the legions, the Roman cavalry could not maneuver (Livy). The Iberian and Gallic cavalry, confined as well and twice the strength of the Roman cavalry, was forced into two lines; it could maneuver even less. This limited front served the Romans, inferior in numbers, well; they could only be attacked in front, that is, by an equal number. As we have said, it made contact inevitable.

These two bodies of cavalry engaged chest to chest had to fight close, man to man, and for riders mounted on simple saddle blankets and without stirrups, burdened with a shield, a lance, a saber or sword, to grapple man to man is to grapple together, fall together, and then fight dismounted. That is what happened as Titus Livius explains it in elaborating on Polybius, and the same thing happened every time two ancient cavalries really had to fight, as the battle of the Ticinus showed.[11]

This mode of action was all to the advantage of the Romans, who were well armed and well trained. Consider the battle of Ticinus, in which the Roman light infantry were cut to pieces, while the elite of the Roman cavalry, although surprised and surrounded, fought dismounted and on horseback, inflicted more casualties on Hannibal than they suffered, and returned to their camp with their wounded general. The Romans, moreover, were well commanded by a man of head and heart, the Consul Aemilius, who, instead of escaping when his cavalry was defeated, went to his death in the ranks of the infantry.

---

11. The battle of Ticinus (218 B.C.), a cavalry battle in the Second Punic War in which the legions of Hannibal defeated those of Publius Cornelius Scipio, the father of Scipio Africanus, who was said to have rescued his father from the disastrous engagement.

And yet [at Cannae] we see 3,000 to 3,400 Roman cavalrymen almost exterminated by about 6,000 or 7,000 Gauls and Iberians who lost less than 200 men. Hannibal's entire cavalry only lost 200 men that day.

How to explain this?

Because most of them died without any thought of giving up their lives; because they ran away while their first line fought and were struck down from behind with impunity. The words of Polybius, "Most of them remained on the spot after having defended themselves with utmost valor," were consecrated long before Polybius. The vanquished always console themselves with their bravery, and their conquerors never object.

Unfortunately, the numbers are there. No matter how we try to consider this engagement, we are obliged to see it as a short one. Both the Gallic and Roman cavalry had already made brave attacks on each other's front. These attacks were followed by the terrible anxiety of close combat. Roman cavalrymen, who were behind those fighting dismounted and could see the Gallic second line mounted, fell back. Fear very quickly drove the disengaged ranks to their horses, where they wheeled about like a flock of stampeding sheep and abandoned their comrades and themselves to the mercy of their conquerors.

Yet these cavalrymen were brave men, the elite of the army, noble, guards of the Consuls, volunteers from noble families.

With the Roman cavalry defeated, Hasdrubal led his Gallic and Iberian horsemen behind Hannibal's army to attack the allied cavalry still engaged by the Numidians.[12]* The allied cavalry did not wait for their enemy. They retreated immediately, pursued to the utmost by the Numidians, who were numerous (3,000) and excellent in the pursuit. The allied cavalry was exterminated, reduced to about 300 men, without fighting.

After the light infantry skirmished the foot soldiers of the line met. Polybius has explained how the Roman infantry allowed itself to be enclosed by the two wings of the Carthaginian army and to be attacked in the rear by

---

12. *The Numidian horsemen were irregular light cavalry, excellent for skirmishing, harassing, terrifying with their extraordinary shouts, and unbridled gallop. They could not stand against a regular, disciplined cavalry equipped with bits and substantial weapons. They were like a swarm of flies that always harasses and kills at the least mistake; elusive and perfect for long pursuit and massacre of the defeated whom the Numidians never permitted rest or quarter. They were like Arab cavalry, poorly armed for combat, but sufficiently for butchering, as results show. The Arab knife, the Kabyle knife, or the Indian knife of our day, favored by the barbarian or the savage (the Indians scalp, the Arabs bleed or mutilate), will play its role.

Hasdrubal. It is also probable that the Gauls and the Iberians, repulsed in their first attack and forced to retire, returned, and, supported by part of the light infantry, charged the head of the angle formed by the Romans and filled in their encirclement.

But we know, as will be seen further on in examples taken from Caesar, that the ancient cavalryman was powerless against infantry in formation, even against the isolated infantryman with *sangfroid*. The Iberian and Gallic could have found behind the Roman army the reliable Triarians[13]* hemmed in, armed with pikes and steady soldiers. They might have held them in check, forced them to face them, but done them little or no harm as long as the ranks were preserved.

We know that those of Hannibal's infantry who carried Roman arms amounted to only 12,000 men. We know that his Gallic and Iberian infantry, protected by simple shields, had to retire, turn back, and probably lost in this part of the action nearly all of the 4,000 men that the battle cost them.

Deduct the 10,000 men who had attacked Hannibal's camp and the 5,000 that Hannibal must have left there. There remains: a mass of 70,000 men, surrounded and slaughtered by 28,000 foot soldiers, or, including Hasdrubal's cavalry, by 36,000 men, or half their number.

One may ask how 70,000 men could have allowed themselves be slaughtered; in fact by 36,000 fewer weapons as each fighter had one man opposing him, because in close combat, especially in an engagement this big, the number of fighters directly engaged are the same on both sides. Then there were neither guns nor rifles to penetrate the mass by a converging fire and destroy it by the superiority of this fire over diverging fire. Arrows were all spent in the first phase of the engagement. It seems that, by virtue of their mass, the Romans must have posed an insurmountable resistance, and that by allowing the enemy to exhaust itself against it, that mass merely had to defend itself in order to repel its assailants.

But they were exterminated.

When, in pursuit of the Gauls and the Spaniards, who even with comparable morale could not stand against the superior arms of the legionnaires, the [Roman] center pushed ahead vigorously, the wings followed in support by oblique movement so as to preserve the intervals and form the sides of the salient. The entire Roman army, in wedge formation, marched to victory. All of a sudden, the wings were attacked by the African battalions; the

---

13. *They formed the third line in the order of battle of the legion. The contraction of the first line into a point would naturally confine them.

Gauls and the Iberians who had been in retreat returned to the fighting.[14*] Hasdrubal's cavalry, in the rear, attacked the reserves.[15*] Everywhere, without warning, unforeseen, there was fighting, and just when they thought they were victorious, in front, on the left, and in the rear, the Roman soldiers heard the furious clamor of fighting.[16*]

The physical pressure was of little moment; the ranks that they were fighting were not half their own depth. The moral pressure was enormous. Apprehension, then panic, took hold. The first ranks, fatigued or wounded, wanted to retreat, but the rear ranks, frightened, recoiled and swirled into the middle of the wedge. Demoralized and despairing of support, the engaged ranks followed them and the whole disordered mass let itself be slaughtered. The weapons fell from their hands, alleges Polybius.

The analysis of Cannae is finished. Before passing on to the account of Pharsalus, we cannot resist the temptation, though a little beyond the subject, to say a few words about the battles of Hannibal.

These engagements have a particular character of relentlessness, reflecting the necessity of dominating Roman tenacity. It seems that victory is not enough for Hannibal: he wants destruction, and he always aims to cut off all retreat for the enemy. He knows well that, with Rome, destruction was the only way to finish.

He does not believe in the desperate courage of the masses; he believes in terror, and he knows the value of improvisation to inspire it.

But it was not the losses of the Romans that were most surprising in these engagements; it was Hannibal's. Who before Hannibal or after had lost as many as the Romans and was still victorious? To keep troops fighting on until victory ensues, with so many casualties, requires a very powerful hand.

He inspired his subjects with absolute confidence. Almost always his center, where he placed the Gauls, his cannon fodder, was broken. But that did not seem to disturb or trouble either him or his soldiers.

We can say that his center was penetrated by the Romans who were fleeing the pressure of the two Carthaginian wings, that they were disorganized because they had engaged and pushed back the Gauls, whom Hannibal knew how to make fight with singular tenacity. They probably felt as though they had been passed through a press, and, glad to be free, they thought only

---

14. *Recalled by Hannibal, who had retained command of the center.

15. *The Triarians, the third Roman line.

16. *We know how, in the battle of Alisia, even when Caesar's men were forewarned, they were unsettled by the war cries behind them. The noise of battle in the rear has always demoralized troops.

of getting farther from the battle—and by no means returning to the flanks or rear of the enemy. Without a doubt, although he said nothing about it, Hannibal had taken measures against any thought of their ever returning to the battle.

All that is probably true. The confidence of troops so completely broken is nonetheless astonishing.

To inspire his followers with such confidence, Hannibal had to explain his plan of action before the engagement in such a way that treachery could not harm him. He must have warned them that the center could be penetrated, but that he was not worried about it because it was an expected and prepared action. And his troops, in fact, did not worry about it.

Leaving aside his conception of campaigns, his greatest glory in the eyes of all, Hannibal was certainly the greatest general of antiquity because of his admirable understanding of the morale of combat, of the morale of the soldier, his own or the enemy's. He displays his greatness in this respect in all the different circumstances of war, of campaign, of action. His soldiers were not better than the Roman soldiers; they were not as well armed, and half their number, and yet they were always victorious because their strength lay in their morale. And always, he had the absolute confidence of his people and the art, in commanding them, of always drawing on their superior morale.

If Hannibal was defeated at Zuma, it was because genius cannot do the impossible. Zuma proved again Hannibal's perfect knowledge of man and his influence over his troops. His third line, the only one in which his soldiers were reliable, was the only one that was engaged. Before they were vanquished, attacked from all sides, they killed 2,000 Romans.

We shall see what high morale and what desperate fighting entails.

IV

Analysis of the Battle of Pharsalus and Some Characteristic Examples

Here is Caesar's description of the battle of Pharsalus:

As Caesar approached Pompey's camp, he noted that Pompey's army was placed in the following order:

On the left wing were the II and III Legions that Caesar had sent to Pompey at the commencement of the operation, pursuant to a decree of the Senate, and that Pompey had kept. Scipio occupied the center with the legions from Syria. The legion from Cilicia was placed on the right wing together with the Spanish cohorts of Afranius. Pompey regarded the troops already mentioned as the most reliable of his army. Between them, that is, between the center and the wings, he had distributed the remainder, consisting of 110 complete cohorts in line. These were made up of 45,000 men, 2,000 of whom were veterans, previously rewarded for their services, who had come to join him. He had scattered them throughout the whole line of battle. Seven cohorts had been left to guard his camp and the neighboring forts. His right wing rested on a stream with inaccessible banks; and, for that reason, he had placed all his 7,000 cavalry,[17]* his archers and his slingers (4,200 men) on the left wing.

---

17. *His cavalry consisted of 7,000 horses, of which 500 were Gauls or Germans, the best horsemen of that time, 900 Galicians, 500 Thracians, and Thessalians, Macedonians, and Italians in various numbers.

Caesar, keeping his battle order,[18]* had placed the X Legion on the right wing, and on the left, the IX, which was much weakened by the combat of Dyrrachium. To the latter he added the VIII Legion in order to form something like a full legion from the two, and ordered them to support one another. He had eighty very completely organized cohorts in line, approximately 22,000 men. Two cohorts had been left to guard the camp. Caesar had entrusted the command of the left wing to Anthony, that of the right to P. Sylla, and of the center to C. Domitius. He placed himself in front of Pompey. But when he saw the disposition of the opposing army, he feared that his right wing was going to be enveloped by Pompey's numerous cavalry. He therefore withdrew immediately from his third line a cohort from each legion (six cohorts), in order to form a fourth line, placed it to receive Pompey's cavalry, and showed it what it had to do. Then he explained fully to these cohorts that the success of the day depended on their valor. At the same time he ordered the entire army, and in particular the third line, not to move without his command, reserving to himself authority to give the signal by means of the standard when he thought it opportune.

Caesar then went through his lines to exhort his men to do well, and seeing them full of ardor, had the signal given.

Between the two armies there was only enough space to give each the necessary distance for the charge. But Pompey had given his men orders to await the charge without stirring, and to let Caesar's army break its ranks upon them. He did this, they say, on the advice of C. Triarius, as a method of meeting the force of the first dash of Caesar's men. He hoped that their battle order would be broken up and his own soldiers, well disposed in ranks, would have to fight with sword in hand only men in disorder. He thought that this formation would best protect his troops from the force of the fall of heavy javelins. At the same time he hoped that Caesar's soldiers charging at the run would be out of breath and overcome with fatigue at the moment of contact. Pompey's immobility was an error because there is in every one an animation, a natural ardor that is instilled by the onset of combat. Generals ought not to check but to encourage this ardor. It was for this reason that, in

---

18. *The legions of Caesar in battle order formed three lines: four cohorts in the front line, two in the second, and three in the third. Thus, the cohorts of a legion in battle were always supported by cohorts from the same legion.

olden times, troops charged with loud shouts, all trumpets sounding, in order to frighten the enemy and encourage themselves.

In the meanwhile, our soldiers at the given signal advanced with javelins in hand; but having noticed that Pompey's soldiers were not running toward them, and taught by experience and trained by previous battles, they slowed down and stopped in the midst of their run, in order not to arrive out of breath and worn out. Some moments after, having taken up their run again, they launched their javelins and, immediately afterward, according to Caesar's order drew their swords. The Pompeians conducted themselves perfectly. They received the darts courageously; they did not stir before the dash of the legions; they preserved their lines, and, having dispatched their javelins, drew their swords.

At the same time Pompey's entire cavalry dashed from the left wing, as had been ordered, and the mass of his archers ran from all parts of the line. Our cavalry did not await the charge, but fell back a little. Pompey's cavalry became more pressing, and commenced to reform its squadrons and turn our exposed flank. As soon as Caesar saw this intention, he gave the signal to the fourth line of six cohorts. This line started directly and, standards low, they charged the Pompeian cavalry with such vigor and resolution that not a single man stood his ground. All wheeled about and not only withdrew in full flight, but gained the highest mountains as fast as they could. They left the archers and slingers without their defense and protection. These were all killed. At the same time the cohorts moved to the rear of Pompey's left wing, which was still fighting and resisting, and attacked it in the rear.

Meanwhile, Caesar had advanced his third line, which up to this moment had been kept quietly at its post. These fresh troops relieved those that were fatigued. Pompey's men, taken in rear, could no longer hold out and all took to flight.

Caesar was not in error when he put these cohorts in a fourth line, particularly charged with meeting the cavalry, and urged them to do well, since their effort would bring victory. They repulsed the cavalry. They cut to pieces the slingers and archers. They turned Pompey's left wing, and this decided the day.

When Pompey saw his cavalry repulsed and that portion of the army upon which he had counted the most seized with terror, he had little confidence in the rest. He quit the battle and galloped to his camp, where, addressing his centurions who were guarding the praetorian gate, he told them in a loud voice heard by the soldiers: "Guard well the camp and defend it vigorously in case of attack; as for myself, I am going to make the tour of the other gates and assure their defense."

That said, he retired to the praetorium, despairing of success and awaiting events.

After having forced the enemy to flee to his entrenchments, Caesar, persuaded that he ought not to give the slightest respite to a terrorized enemy, incited his soldiers to profit by their advantage and attack the camp. Although overcome by the heat, for the struggle was prolonged into the middle of the day, they did not object to greater fatigue and obeyed. The camp was at first well defended by the cohorts on watch and especially by the Thracians and barbarians. The men who had fled from battle, full of fright and overcome with fatigue, had nearly all thrown their arms and colors away and thought rather more of saving themselves than of defending the camp. Even those who defended the entrenchments were unable long to resist the shower of arrows. Covered with wounds, they abandoned the place, and, led by their centurions and tribunes, they took refuge as quickly as they could in the high mountains near the camp.

Caesar lost in the battle but 200 soldiers, but nearly thirty of the bravest centurions were killed therein. Of Pompey's army 15,000 perished, and more than 24,000 took refuge in the mountains. As Caesar had invested the mountains with entrenchments, they surrendered the following day.

Such is the narrative of Caesar, so clearly written it hardly needs comment.

At first Caesar's order of battle formed three lines as customary in Roman armies, but not absolute since Marius fought with two only. But as we have said, depending on the circumstances, the genius of the leader dictated the battle formation. There is no reason to think that Pompey's army was organized differently.

To face this army, twice the size of his own, Caesar—if he had been forced to keep to ten ranks in each cohort—would have been able to form only one complete line, the first, while the second, half as strong, acted as reserve. But he knew the bravery of his troops, and he also knew, as we have said, the illusory force of deep ranks. He did not hesitate to reduce his depth to preserve the order and the morale of three-fifths of his troops until the instant of their engagement. And to be certain of his third line of his reserves, to be sure it would not be carried away by its impatience for action, he gave them explicit orders. Perhaps—because the text is open to interpretation—he kept it twice the usual distance behind the fighting lines.

Then, to protect against a turning movement by the 7,000 cavalry and 4,300 slingers and archers of Pompey, a maneuver on which he pinned his hopes, Caesar positioned six cohorts of nearly 2,000 men. He was perfectly confident that these 2,000 men would force this cavalry to turn about, and that his 1,000 horsemen would then press their counterattack so forcefully that Pompey's cavalry would not even think of rallying. And so it was: the 4,200 archers and slingers were slaughtered like sheep by these cohorts, doubtless aided by 400 foot, young and agile,[19]* whom Caesar had integrated with his horsemen and who kept at this task, freeing the horsemen whom they had relieved to pursue the terrified fugitives.

Thus were 7,000 cavalry swept away and 4,200 foot slaughtered without a fight, all demoralized simply by a vigorous demonstration.

Pompey's order to his infantry to await the charge was judged too severely by Caesar. He certainly was right as a general rule; the élan of the troops must not be denied, and the initiative of the attack indeed invests the assailant with moral courage. But with steady soldiers one can try a ruse, and Pompey's men had proven their steadiness by waiting in place, without moving, a vigorous enemy attacking in good order, when they expected to meet him disordered and out of breath.

Though it may not have produced success, the advice of Triarius was not bad; even the conduct of Caesar's soldiers proves this; and it demonstrates the soldier's confidence in the heavy ranks of ancient combat in assuring his mutual support and confidence.

Even though Caesar's soldiers had initiated the attack, the first shock decided nothing. It was fighting in place, fighting for several hours; and 45,000 good troops lost barely 200 men in this engagement. With similar arms, courage, and ability, Pompey's infantry should not have lost more than Caesar in hand-to-hand fighting. These 45,000 men broke, and between the battlefield and their camp, 12,000 were slaughtered.

---

19. *Caesar said that to compensate for his numerical inferiority, he had chosen 400 of the most alert young men (adolescentes) from among those marching with the standards (ex antesignatis), and by daily drills they had learned to fight between horsemen (inter equites praeliari). He had thus obtained such results that his 1,000 riders did not hesitate to encounter Pompey's 7,000 cavalry without being frightened by their number (neque magnopere eorum multitudine terrerentur).

Pompey's soldiers had twice the depth of Caesar's ranks, whose attack did not force them to fall back a step. On the other hand, their mass was not enough to repel them, and they fought in place. Pompey had told them, Caesar says, that the enemy's army would be turned by his cavalry, and all of a sudden, when they were fighting bravely, step by step, they heard the clamor of the attack by Caesar's six cohorts (2,000 men).

It would seem that for a similar mass to parry this danger would be easy. No. The wing taken from behind in this way loses ground, step by step, and the contagion of fear spreads to the rest. And the terror is so great, they give no thought of reforming in their camp, which at the moment is defended only by the cohorts on guard. As at Cannae, their arms dropped from their hands. Without the steady demeanor of the camp guards that permitted the fugitives to reach the mountains, the 24,000 prisoners taken the next day would have been corpses that very day.

The examples of Cannae and Pharsalus are enough to understand ancient combat. However, we shall add some other brief representative examples, presented in chronological order. Then our inquiry will be complete.[20*]

Livy recounts how in an action against some of the people near Rome, I do not remember where now, the Romans did not dare pursue for fear of breaking their ranks.

In fighting against the Hernici, he observes the Roman cavalry, who had not been able to do anything while mounted to break up the enemy, asking the Consul permission to dismount and fight on foot. And this was not only the Roman cavalry. Later on, we see the best horsemen, the Gauls, the Germans, the Parthanians even, dismounting to fight in earnest.

The Volsci, the Latini, the Hernici, and others joined forces to fight the Romans, and as the action drew toward its end, Livy writes: "Finally, the first ranks having fallen, and carnage being all about them, they threw away their arms and started to scatter. The cavalry then dashed forward, with orders not to kill the isolated ones, but to harass the mass with their arrows, annoy it, to delay it, to prevent dispersion in order to permit the infantry to come up and kill."

---

20. *For those who wish to read *in extenso*: in Xenophon, the combat of the 10,000 against Pharnabase in Bithynia, par. 334, page 569, Lisken & Sauvan edition. In Polybius, the battle of Tecinus, chapter XIII of Book III. In Caesar or those who followed him in the battles against Scipio, Labiennus, and Afranius, the Getae, and the Numidians, par. 61, page 282, and par. 69, 70, 71, 72, pages 283, 285, and 286, in *The African War*, Lisken & Sauvan edition.

In Hamilcar's fight against the mercenaries in revolt, who before had always beaten the Carthaginians, the mercenaries believed they could envelop him. Hamilcar surprised them with a new maneuver and defeated them. He marched in three lines: elephants, cavalry and light infantry, followed by heavily armed phalanxes. As the mercenaries attacked vigorously toward him the first two lines, formed by the elephants and the cavalry and light infantry, pivoted and quickly drew alongside the flanks of the third line. The third line now in view met an enemy who had thought only of pursuit, and whose surprise now moved them to escape. Now it was at the mercy of the elephants, horses, and the light infantry, who massacred the fugitives.

Hamilcar killed 6,000 men, took 2,000 men prisoner, and perhaps lost no one. There was a question whether he lost anyone at all, because there had been no real fighting.

At Trasimenus, the Carthaginians lost 1,500 men, nearly all Gauls; the Romans lost 15,000 killed and 15,000 prisoners. The desperate fighting had raged for three hours.

At Zama, Hannibal lost 20,000 killed and 20,000 taken prisoner; the Romans lost 2,000 killed. This was a momentous struggle in which Hannibal's third line fought alone and broke only when its rear and flank were assailed by the cavalry.

In the battle of Cynocephalae between Philip and Flaminius, Philip pressed Flaminius with his phalanx, thirty-two ranks deep. Twenty maniples took the phalanx from behind. The battle was lost by Philip. The Romans lost 700 dead; the Macedonians lost 80,000 dead and 5,000 prisoners.

At Pydna, Aemilius Paulus against Perseus, the phalanx was not checked as it advanced, but disorder naturally resulted from the resistance it met. Hundreds penetrated gaps in the phalanx and killed soldiers encumbered by their long pikes who were only effective when unified, abreast, and at pike's length. Frightful confusion and butchery: 20,000 killed, 5,000 captured from 44,000 engaged? The historian does not deign to speak of the Roman losses.

After the battle of Aix against the Teutons, Marius surprised the Teutons from the rear. Frightful carnage: 100,000 Teutons and 3,000 Romans killed.[21]*

Sulla's battle of Chaeronea against Archelaus, a general of Mithridates: Sulla had 30,000 men, Archelaus, 110,000. Archelaus was defeated by a sur-

---

21. *In ancient warfare, there was almost only the dead or lightly wounded. In action, a severe wound or one that incapacitated a man was immediately followed by a coup de grâce.

prise from the rear. The Romans lost fourteen men and killed their enemies until they were exhausted by the pursuit.[22]

[Here the author recounts the battle of Orchomenus against Archelaus—a repetition of Chaeronea.]

Caesar recounts that his cavalry could not fight the Britons without exposing itself too much, because they pretended flight to separate the cavalry from the infantry and then, leaping from their chariots, *fought dismounted with advantage.*

Less than 200 veterans embarked on a boat that they ran aground at night to escape being taken prisoner by superior naval forces. They found an advantageous position and spent the night. At dawn, Otacilius sent some 400 horsemen and some infantry from the Alesio garrison to attack them. They defended themselves bravely, and after killing several, they rejoined Caesar's troops without the loss of a single man.

In Macedonia Caesar's rear guard was caught by Pompey's cavalry while crossing the Genusus River, the banks of which were very steep. With his cavalry of 600 to 1,000 men, among whom he had carefully placed 400 elite infantrymen, Caesar opposed Pompey's 5,000 to 7,000 cavalry. Caesar's men performed so well in the fighting that followed they repulsed the enemy, killed many, and fell back on their own army without having lost a single man.

In the battle of Thapsus in Africa against Scipio, Caesar killed 10,000, lost fifty, and had some wounded.

In the battle under the walls of Munda in Spain, against one of Pompey's sons, Caesar commanded eighty cohorts and 8,000 horsemen, about 48,000 men.

Pompey commanded thirteen legions with 60,000 troops of the line, 6,000 cavalry, 6,000 light infantry, 6,000 auxiliaries—in all about 80,000 men. The fighting, the narrator writes, carried on valiantly, step by step, sword to sword.[23*] In this exceptionally violent battle, which held in the balance for a long time, Caesar had 1,000 dead, 500 wounded. Pompey lost

---

22. Two of the fourteen Romans unaccounted for after the battle were said to have returned to the ranks later. Ardant du Picq's uncritical acceptance of Plutarch's account of the battle suggests he was unaware that Plutarch's account was based on Sulla's own memoirs, which none other than Hans Delbrück described as "a fantasy." See Hans Delbrück, *History of the Art of War, Volume I: Warfare in Antiquity*, trans. Walter J. Renfroe Jr. (Lincoln: University of Nebraska Press, 1975), 438.

23. *Face to face, sword to sword, intense close combat was rare then, just as in the duels of our own day swords are rarely crossed in actual fighting.

33,000 dead, and if Munda had not been so close by, barely two miles away, his losses would have been twice that. The defensive works of Munda were built from corpses and discarded weapons.

In studying ancient battle, one can see that almost always a surprise attack on the flank or rear won battles, especially against the Romans. This was why their excellent tactics might be misunderstood; Roman tactics were so good that a Roman general only half as skilled as his adversary was certain to win. Only by surprise could they be beaten. Consider Xanthippe, Hannibal, the improvisational fighting methods of the Gauls, and so on.

To paraphrase Xenophon, "Anything at all, pleasant or terrible, the less expected, the more does it excite pleasure or terror."

Fighters armed with cuirasses and shields were not often killed in the front lines. In his victories, Hannibal lost very few save the Gauls, his cannon fodder, who fought with poor shields and no armor. Nearly always driven in, they still fought with a tenacity that they never displayed under any commander before or after him.

Thucydides characterizes the fighting of light infantry, remarking "as a rule, the lightly armed on both sides fled."[24*] In combat between close ranks there was mutual pressure but little loss because the men could not strike at liberty and with all their power.

Against the Nervii, Caesar saw his men, who in the press of action instinctively concentrated to oppose the mass of barbarians, giving way under their pressure. He *made them open their ranks and files* so that his legionnaires, concentrated and paralyzed and forced to give way, might be able to kill and unnerve the enemy. And so, as soon as one in the front rank of the Nervii fell under the blows of the legionnaires, they were stopped and fell back. Then, after an attack on their rear and a melee, the Nervii were defeated.[25*]

---

24. *Today, the riflemen do nearly all the work of destruction.

25. *In light of Caesar's narrative, what of the mathematical theory of masses that is still discussed? If that theory was at all viable, how could Marius have stood against the rising tide of the armies of the Cimbri and Teutons? In the battle of Pharsalus, the advice Triarius gave to Pompey's army, advice that was followed and was from a man of experience who had seen much at close hand, shows that the shock, the physical impulsion of the mass, was only a word. They knew what to think.

V

The Dynamics
of Morale in
Ancient Combat

Now we have explained the dynamics of morale in ancient combat. The word "melee" used by the ancients was many times more powerful than the idea expressed; "melee" meant the crossing of weapons, not of men.

The results of battle, such as casualties, sufficiently demonstrate this, and a moment of reflection allows us to see the misunderstanding of the word. If, in pursuit one plunged into the middle of the sheep, in an engagement in which everyone relied too much on the next man, on his neighbor, who was protecting his flanks and back, he allowed himself to be killed because of feckless enthusiasm.[26*]

But in a melee, where are the victors?

In a melee, Caesar at Pharsalus, Hannibal at Cannae, would have been defeated; their shallow ranks, penetrated by the enemy, outnumbered two-

---

26. *The lone advance in modern combat, among blind projectiles that are not aimed, is much less dangerous than in ancient times, because it seldom gets as far forward as the enemy.

At Pharsalus, the volunteer Crastinius, an old centurion, advanced with about 100 men, saying to Caesar, "I am going to act, general, so that living or dead, today you may have cause to be proud of me."

Caesar, to whom these examples of blind devotion were not displeasing, and whose troops were too seasoned, too experienced, to fear the contagion of this example, consented and allowed Crastinius and his companions to go out and be killed.

Such blind courage influences the mass that follows, and probably for that reason Caesar permitted it. But against steady troops, as the example of Crastinius proves, to advance against the enemy in this way is to go to certain death.

to-one, would have been broken through and through by being taken from behind.

Have we not seen, between troops equally steady and desperate, mutual fatigue that leads, with tacit accord, to a rest on both sides only to resume the fighting after?

How could this be possible with a melee?

And so we repeat, in a melee, with intermingled combatants, there would be mutual extermination but no victors. How would they recognize each other?

Imagine two confused masses of men or groups, where everyone engaged face to face can be struck with impunity from the side or the back? That is mutual extermination, in which victory belongs only to the survivors, because in the confusion, in the melee, no one knows where to escape.

Are not mutual casualties a sufficient demonstration that there was no real melee?

The word is therefore misplaced; the imagination of painters and poets created the melee.

Here is how it happened:

At attack range the troops advanced on the enemy at the proper pace for fighting with swords and for mutual support. Quite often, the *momentum of morale*, that resolution to advance come what may, manifests itself in their order and easy gait. That momentum alone forces the retreat of a less resolute enemy.

Among good troops a clash was customary, but not the blind, headlong collision of the mass; the focus of the ranks was intense,[27]* as the conduct of Caesar's troops at Pharsalus revealed in their deliberate cadence, kept by the flutes of the Lacedaemonian battalions.

At the moment of closing with the enemy the pace slows of its own accord, because the man in the first rank, necessarily and instinctively, marks the positions of his support, his neighbors in the first line, their comrades in the second, and composes himself to strike and parry. Man fought man. Each aimed for the enemy in front of him and attacked, because by penetrating the ranks without having brought him down, he risked being wounded from the side by losing his flank supports. Each therefore hit his man with his shield, expecting to make him lose his balance, and when his enemy tried to recover, he struck his blow. The men in the second rank, allowing

---

27. *The comrades of the maniple, of the Roman company, pledged never to leave ranks except to retrieve an arrow, to save a comrade (a Roman citizen), or to kill an enemy.

space for the swordplay in the first, were ready to protect their sides against anyone who came between them and were prepared to relieve those in front who were exhausted. The third rank did the same, and so on.

As everyone was prepared for the first shock, it was rarely decisive, and the fencing, the real fighting at close quarters, commenced.

If the men in the first line were wounded quickly, if the other ranks did not quickly replace them, or if there was hesitation, defeat followed. This happened to the Romans in their first encounter with the Gauls. The Gaul parried the first blow with his shield, then furiously brought his great iron sword down on edge of the Roman shield, split it in two, and went after his man. The Romans, already wavering before the moral impulsion of the Gauls, their ferocious shouts, their nakedness—a sign of their contempt for wounds—at that moment fell in greater number than their enemies, and demoralization ensued. Before long they habituated themselves to the not so tenacious valor of their enemies, and after they protected the top of their shields with an iron band, they no longer fell, and their roles were reversed.

The Gauls, indeed, could not stand their ground against the better weapons and the sword thrusts of the Romans or against their individual superior tenacity, made ten times greater by the potential relay of eight ranks in their maniple. The maniples were self-renewing, while among the Gauls the duration of combat was limited to the strength of a single man because of the impediments of the crowded, tumultuous ranks and the impossibility of replacing losses as they fought.

If the weapons were roughly equal, maintaining ranks and thus breaking down, driving back, and confusing the ranks of the enemy was to be victorious. The man in disordered, broken ranks no longer felt sustained, but everywhere vulnerable, and he fled. It is true that it is almost impossible to break an enemy line without breaking one's own, but the one who breaks through first could only do so by forcing the enemy back with his blows, by killing or wounding. His courage has increased and so too that of his neighbor. *He knows, he sees* where he is marching, while the enemy who is overtaken because of the retreat or the collapse of the troops that were flanking him is surprised. He retreats to a line with the rear ranks in order to find support. But the lines in the rear are broken by the retreat of the first lines. If the retreat lasts a certain time, the result of the blows that struck down the first line, driving them back, is terror. And if, to make room for those pushed back upon them, the last lines turn their backs, there is little chance they will turn about again. Space has tempted them. They will not return.

So by that natural instinct of the soldier to worry, to assure himself of support, the contagion of flight spreads from the rear ranks to the first, closely engaged, which has been trapped in the fighting by the prospect of immediate death. One need not explain what happens next; it is butchery (Caedes).

But to return to combat:

It is evident that the order of the troops in a straight line, so close together, existed hardly an instant.

But each group ready for action was linked with the next group, and groups just as individuals were always worried about their support. The fight was all along the line of contact of the first ranks of the army, straight, broken, curved, bent in different directions, depending on the various chances of action at one point or another, but always limiting, separating the combatants of both sides. On this line, one engaged wholeheartedly or not, facing to the front, on pain of immediate death, and each one in these first ranks spent all his energy defending his life.

At no point did the line become entangled while there was fighting, for—whether general or soldier—everyone tried to preserve the continuity of support all along the line and to break or sever that of the enemy, because victory then ensued.

We see then that between men armed with swords it was possible to have penetration—and there was, if the fighting was serious—of one mass into the other, but never confusion, coalescence, melee[28*] of the ranks of men forming these masses.

Fighting sword to sword was the deadliest, because it was the sort in which the combatant's individual valor and dexterity had the greatest and most immediate influence on the action. Beyond this, other kinds of fighting were simpler.

Let us compare pikes and swords.

The advance of pikemen was irresistible; a forest of pikes kept you at a distance (the pikes were fifteen to eighteen feet long).[29*] Although it was easy to kill off cavalry and light infantry around the phalanx, it was a lumbering mass, marching in step, that mobile troops could always avoid. The phalanx might open as it marched because of the terrain, because of the thousand accidents of the struggle, because of the individual assault of brave men,

---

28. *A small group of men falling into a trap might make a sort of melee for a second, just enough time for a slaughter. In a rout it might be possible at some point in the butchery for fighting, resistance by some men of courage who mean to sell their lives dearly. But this is not a real melee. Men are trapped, overwhelmed, but not thrown into disorder.

29. *The Greek phalanx.

because of the wounded on the ground creeping under the pikes carried chest-high—who are barely noticed because those in the first two ranks could hardly see and had no freedom to strike. The slightest opening rendered these pikemen almost useless, good only for fighting at the length of their pikes (Polybius). They were struck with impunity by those who threw themselves into the intervals.[30]* And then, with the enemy inside the phalanx, it buckled as its morale wavered and it became a disordered mass, a flock of panic-stricken sheep falling over each other.

In a mob, in fact, men prod with their knives those who crowd them too much. The contagion of fear changes the direction of the flow of humans, first bending back on itself, then breaking apart to escape danger. If the enemy retreated before the phalanx there was no melee. If he tactically withdraws and avails himself of gaps penetrated by groups, still there was no melee or confusion of ranks. The wedge entering the mass does not become intermingled with it.

Between a phalanx armed with long pikes against a similar one, there was still less confusion. They were able to stand for a long time if one did not take them in the flank or in the rear with a detached body of troops. In ancient combat, even in victories won by methods that affected the morale, such methods are always effective, for man does not change.

It is unnecessary to explain again why, in every battle, demoralization and flight began in the rear ranks.

We have attempted to analyze the combat of the line infantry because in ancient warfare its action alone was decisive. The line infantry of both sides took flight, as Thucydides noted. Then they came back to pursue and massacre the defeated.[31]*

For the cavalry, the cavalry against cavalry, the momentum of morale, represented by the speed of the mass in good order, was most important. We rarely see two cavalry formations meeting in reciprocal action against each other. We saw this at Tecinus and at Cannae, engagements recounted precisely because they were so very rare. And even here there was no shock at top speed, but a halt to face off and then an engagement.

In fact, the hurricanes of cavalry who collide—that is poetry, never reality. The shock of collision at top speed would crush men and horses, and nei-

---

30. *The Romans lost no one as their companies penetrated the openings in the phalanx.

31. *The Roman velites of the early legion before Marius were given the mission of standing for a moment in the intervals of the maniples while awaiting the princes. They kept, if only for an instant, the continuity of support.

ther men nor horses wanted such an encounter. The hands of the cavalry-men reined back, their instinct and that of their horses to slow, to halt if the enemy did not, and to turn about if he kept coming. And if they ever met, the shock at this point was so absorbed by the men's hands, the rearing of the horses, the tossing of heads, that they halted face to face. Several blows were traded with sword or lance, but the equilibrium was too unstable, the fulcrum too weak for real swordplay and mutual support. Man felt too iso-lated, the moral pressure was too great, and though not deadly, the fighting lasted only a second precisely because man felt himself, saw himself, alone and surrounded. The leading men, who felt themselves unsupported, could no longer stand the anxiety, turned the bridle and the rest followed—unless the enemy had also turned. Then he could pursue until he encountered fresh cavalry, who pursued him in turn.

Between cavalry and infantry there was never a shock. The cavalry ha-rassed with its arrows, perhaps with the lance while passing quickly, but it never attacked.

Truth to tell, close combat on horseback did not exist. And in effect, the horse, by adding so much mobility to the man, enabled him to escape with equal swiftness when his menace did not shake the enemy. And man, ac-cording to his nature and his reason, could do as much damage as possible while risking the least possible. In brief, for riders without stirrups or sad-dle, for whom launching a javelin was a difficult matter (Xenophon), fight-ing was only a series of reciprocal harassments, demonstrations, menaces, and skirmishes with arrow. Each side looked for the chance to surprise, to intimidate, to exploit disorder, and to chase either the cavalry or the infan-try. Then, *vae victis*, the sword goes to work.

Man always has had the greatest fear of being trampled by horses, and surely, this fear has routed 100,000 times more men than real collision. This was always more or less because of the horse, and no one was run over. When two ancient cavalries really wanted to fight, were forced into it, they fought on foot—see the battles of Tecinus, Cannae, and the exam-ples of Livy. I find no real fighting on horse in all antiquity such as that of Alexander the Great at the passage of the Granicus. Even that? His cavalry traversed a river with steep banks defended by the enemy. He lost eighty-five men, the Persian cavalry 1,000, and both were equally well armed.

Combat in the Middle Ages revived the ancient battles, except in science. Perhaps the cavalry attacked each other more than the ancient cavalry did because they were invulnerable. It was not enough to dismount them; it was necessary to kill them when they were on the ground. They knew that fighting on horseback was not important as far as results went, because when they really wished to fight, they fought on foot (note the battle of the Thirty,[32] Bayard,[33] etc.).

The victors, clad in iron from head to foot, lost no one. The peasants did not count. And if the vanquished was taken, he was not massacred because chivalry had established a brotherhood of arms between noblemen, the mounted warriors of different nations, and ransom replaced death.

If we have spoken most of infantry combat, that is because it was the most serious. On foot, on horse, on the bridge of a ship, at the moment of danger, the same man is always found. Anyone who knows him well may deduce from his actions in the past what his actions will be in future.

---

32. See page 54, n. 2.

33. Pierre Terrail, seigneur of Bayard (1475–1524). Acclaimed as the model of the French knight, "*le chevalier sans peur et sans reproche*," Bayard was a military leader in France's First and Second Italian Wars, a much-praised veteran of the battles of Fornovo, Garigliana, and Ravenna, among others. He was killed by a harquebus ball while commanding the rear guard defending the crossing at the River Sesia as his army retreated from defeat at Robecco.

VI

Under What Conditions Real Combatants Are Made and How the Fighting of Our Own Days, in Order to Be Done Well, Requires Them to Be More Resolute than in Ancient Combat

Allow us to repeat now what we said at the beginning of this study. Man does not enter battle to fight, but for victory. He does all he can to avoid the first and secure the second. The continued perfection of all the instruments of war has no other purpose than the annihilation of the enemy. Absolute bravery, which does not refuse combat even on unequal terms, trusting only in God or destiny, is not natural in man. It is the result of moral culture, and it is infinitely rare because in the face of danger the animal instinct of self-preservation always gains the upper hand. Man calculates his chances, and with what errors, we are about to see.

Man has a horror of death. Among the elite souls, a great sense of duty that only they can understand and can obey, is supreme. But the mass always recoils at the sight of the phantom. Discipline aims at dominating that horror by a still greater one, that of punishment or disgrace. But always there comes an instant when natural horror overwhelms discipline and the fighter takes flight. "Stop, stop, only a few minutes, an instant more, and you are the victor—you are not even wounded—if you turn back you are dead!" He does not hear, he can no longer hear. He is gorged with fear. How many armies have sworn to conquer or perish? How many have kept their oaths? Oaths of sheep to stand against wolves. History records, not armies, but resolute souls who have fought to the death. The devotion of Thermopylae is therefore justly immortal.

In real combat, the serious, rough combat that we know now, to have any chance of success, it is not sufficient to have an army composed of valiant men like the Gauls or the Germans.

The army needs, and we provide, leaders with the firmness and decision of command that arises from habit and complete faith in their unquestioned right of command by tradition, law, and society.

We add good weapons, methods of fighting in concert with these weapons and those of the enemy and that do not overwhelm the physical and morale capacities of man. We add further a rational division that permits the direction and employment of every effort down to the last man.

We animate with passion, a violent desire for independence, a religious fanaticism, national pride, a love of glory, a madness to possess. We add a severe discipline that permits no one to escape fighting, that commands solidarity from top to bottom, among all the parts, among the commanders, between the commanders and the soldiers, among the soldiers.

Do we then have a steady army? Not yet. Solidarity, that first and supreme power of armies, is ordained, it is true, by severe laws of discipline and powerful passion. But an order is not enough. A surveillance from which no one can escape enforces discipline; it guarantees solidarity against failure in the face of dangers, those that we know and can feel, which is the point at which to exert the greatest moral pressure to persist and to advance above all. This watchful eye exists in all groups of men who know each other well and who understand their duty to one another.

It is necessary then that a wise organization requires at the outset that the same leaders and the same soldiers form combat groups so that the leaders and comrades in peace are the leaders and comrades in war. The habit of living together, obeying the same leaders commanding the same men, sharing hardships and amusements, cooperating in the execution of movements and warlike maneuvers, forge a unity, a sense of craft, a feeling, and, in a word, the intelligence of solidarity: the duty to submit, to impose discipline, and the impossibility to escape from it.

And now confidence appears.

It is not that the enthusiastic and mindless confidence of tumultuous armies that races up to the danger point and evaporates quickly, giving way to a contrary sentiment, which sees treason everywhere. Instead, it is that intimate confidence, firm and conscious, that does not lose itself in the moment of action and that alone makes true combatants.

Now we have an army. It is no longer difficult to explain how men are swept away by passions, even men who know how to die without flinching, without blanching, resolute in the face of death; but without discipline or organizational unity, they are beaten by others individually less brave but firmly, solidly formed.

One loves to imagine an armed mob, overcoming all obstacles, carried away by an explosion of passion.

There is more of the picturesque than truth in this imagination. If the fighting depended only on individuals, then passionate men, courageous, making up this mob, have the greater chance of victory. But in any body of troops facing the enemy everyone knows that the task is not the work of a single man but of everyone at the same time. And when this company in danger is hastily reformed by unknown commanders, each man instinctively wonders if he can depend on them. One moment of distrust leads to hesitation. The first serious threat will in a moment interrupt the passion of *élan*.

Solidarity, confidence cannot be improvised. But, as in everything, there are always degrees. Let us see if modern combat is less demanding than ancient combat.

In ancient combat there was danger only at close quarters. If a unit had enough morale (and Asiatic hordes seldom had enough) to meet the enemy at the length of a broadsword, there was fighting. Anyone at this distance knew that if he turned his back he would be killed, because as we have seen, the victors lost few and the vanquished were exterminated. This simple reason held men and made them fight, if only for an instant.

Today, aside from a few exceptional and very rare circumstances that may bring two forces nose to nose, combat is joined from afar. The danger begins at a longer distance; one must march for a long time under fire as each step grows heavier. The defeated lose prisoners, but often he does not lose more dead and wounded than the victor.

In ancient combat, groups fought close together in a confined space, in open terrain, in full view of everyone, without the deafening noise of modern weapons. Men marched in formation into action on a particular spot that was not thousands of feet away from their starting point. The commanders observed calmly, and individual weakness was immediately reprimanded. Only general confusion led to retreat.

Today, fighting is done over immense spaces by thinly drawn lines broken every instant by accidents and obstacles of terrain. From when action begins, as soon as there is rifle fire, the men disperse as skirmishers or, lost in the inevitable disorder of a quick march,[34]* escape the observation of their commanders. A considerable number hide themselves[35]*; they escape the engagement and reduce by just that much the material and moral effect and confidence of the brave ones who remain. This can lead to defeat.

But let us look at man himself in both ancient and modern combat. I am strong, adroit, vigorous, trained, full of sangfroid and presence of mind. I have good offensive and defensive weapons and solid comrades of long standing who will not allow me to be overwhelmed without coming to my aid. I am with them, they are with me, we are invincible, invulnerable. We have fought twenty battles and not one of us has been left on the field. We support each other just in time, and *we clearly see.* We quickly relieve each other to place a fresh fighter in front of a fatigued adversary. We are the legions of Marius, 50,000 who stood against the furious avalanches of the Cimbri, killed 140,000 and took 60,000 prisoners while losing only 200 or 300 maladroits.

Today, strong, firm, trained, courageous as I am, I can never say I shall return. I am no longer dealing with men, whom I do not fear. I deal with fate in the form of iron and lead. Death is in the air, invisible and blind, with blasts of breath that bend the head. As brave, as solid, as devoted as my companions are, they cannot protect me. Only—and this is abstract and less immediately obvious to all than the material support of ancient combat—only I calculate that the more numerous who run a dangerous risk, the greater is the chance to escape. I also know that if we have confidence that

---

34. *The result of the perfection of machines.
35. *In troops without cohesion, this movement begins fifty leagues from the enemy. Numbers enter the hospitals without any complaint other than the lack of morale, which very quickly becomes a real disease. Draconian discipline no longer exists; cohesion alone can replace it.

none of us should lack in action, we feel, and are, stronger; and the more resolutely we begin and sustain the struggle, the sooner we finish.

We finish! But, to finish it is necessary to advance; you have to get at the enemy.[36]* Infantryman, horseman, we are naked against the iron, naked against the lead, vulnerable at close range. All the same, let us advance resolutely. Our adversary will not stand against our rifles at close range, because we are certain there will be no collision. We have been told a thousand times; we have seen it. But what if it should change now? What if the enemy also stands?

How distant this is from Roman confidence!

We have shown elsewhere how in ancient times retiring from action was difficult and perilous for the soldier. A final remark on the difficulty will illustrate the matter.

Since the invention of firearms, muskets, rifles, and cannons, the ranges and mutual support between weapons will increase. In addition, the improvement of all kinds of communications permits the concentration of numerous forces. For this reason, we have said the battlefields will be immense.[37]*

Command becomes more and more difficult. Direction, being farther removed, tends more often to escape the commander and his subordinate leaders. In the certain, inevitable disorder that always besets a unit in action, the shock from the moral effect of modern devices accentuates the uproar and fluctuations in the battle lines so that the soldiers lose their commanders and the commanders lose their soldiers.

This should not be true! Perhaps, but all the same it is.

Not all troops in battle are immediately or directly engaged. Commanders always try to control as long as possible some troops who can march at any moment in any direction. Today, as in the past, as in tomorrow, the decisive action is fought by troops in formation at the right point. Therefore, success belongs to the commander who has kept them in good order, holds and directs them.

This is incontestable.

---

36. *It is a hard business, attacking men who fire six to eight shots a minute, no matter how badly aimed. Will he who has the last round have the last word, the one who knows how to make the enemy fire his last round without using his own? The same old idea. With arrows: let us use up their arrows. With the club: let us break their clubs. But how? That is always the question. In war, above all, *the principles are easy, but,* etc., etc.

37. *The more one imagines he is alone, the greater he has need of morale.

But it is also true that commanders can keep decisive reserves only if the enemy has committed his.

In troops that are fighting, *for factual reasons*, the soldiers and their commanders, from corporal to battalion commander, action is more independent than ever. And because it is only the vigor of that action, *more independent* of the higher commanders than ever, which can be directed at a decisive moment, that action becomes more *preponderant* than ever. Those actions always have been, because in the final analysis execution belongs to the man in the ranks. But his influence is greater than ever. From this comes a precept of the day: the battles of soldiers.

Beyond the regulations on tactics and discipline, common sense is necessary. It is necessary to counteract the hazardous predominance of action of the soldier over the commander. He must delay to the extreme limits of the possible that moment which modern conditions tend to accelerate powerfully, when the soldier escapes the control of his commander.

This fact, and the concerns it raises, underscores the truth already stated: combat today, in order to obtain the best results, requires a moral cohesion, a unity more binding than at any other time.[38*] The simple truth is that if one does not wish bonds to break, one must make them flexible in order to make them stronger.

---

38. *Are not naval battles chiefly the battles of captains, and do not all captains try to promote a feeling of solidarity that will enable all to fight together on the day of battle? See the battles of Trafalgar, Lissa.

In 1588, the Duke of Medina Sidonia, preparing for a naval engagement, sent three commanders on light vessels for the advance guard and three for the rear guard, accompanied by executioners who were to hang every captain who abandoned his post during battle.

In 1702, the English Admiral Benbow, a heroic man, was almost abandoned by his captains during three days of battle. Before dying from an amputated leg and arm, he brought four of them to trial. One was acquitted and three were hanged, and from that moment begins the inflexible English severity toward commanders of fleets and vessels, a severe necessity in order to force them to fight effectively.

Our commanders of battalions, our captains, our men, once under fire, are more at sea than the commanders of these vessels.

VII

The Purpose of This Study and What Would Be Necessary to Complete It

Other thoughts on this study must come from the meditations of the reader. To be of value in actual application these should be founded on a study of modern combat, and that study cannot be made from the accounts of historians alone.

Historians describe in a general way the actions of the troop formations, but in their narratives the detailed descriptions, as well as those of the individual soldier in action, as in reality, remain wrapped in a cloud of mist. And yet we must comprehend both because they form the rationale and the starting point for all methods of combat, past, present, and future. Where can these details be found?

We have very few narratives showing the action as closely as Colonel Bugeaud's account of the fighting at l'Hopital.[39] These narratives are more

---

39. Thomas Robert Bugeaud de la Piconnerie (1784–1849), marshal of France, governor-general of Algeria. Bugeaud rose from the enlisted ranks of Napoleon's *Garde Imperiale* to become one of France's most revered—and reviled—soldiers. A veteran of Austerlitz, Jena, Eylau, and the Spanish campaigns, after France's defeat in 1814, he was pardoned by the Restoration and reinstated to his rank of colonel. He defected to Napoleon during the Hundred Days Campaign to fight under Marshal Suchet. After Waterloo, he was forbidden to hold military rank and retreated to his home province of Périgord to farm. The July Revolution of 1830 restored Bugeaud to the army and in the following year he was appointed *marechal de camp* and was elected to the Chamber of Deputies, where he proved himself a relentless enemy of democracy. By 1836, he held the rank of lieutenant general, and although he disagreed with Louis Phillipe's Algerian policy, he was persuaded to take command of field

detailed, because the slightest detail is important, as are actors or witnesses who were able to see and remember, which is required to study combat today. The number and kind of troops killed, where they are injured, sometimes reveal more than longer narratives that do not analyze action.[40]

We must learn how man, and in particular the French, fought yesterday; how and to what extent, under the pressure of danger and the survival instinct, necessarily, inevitably, he followed, ignored, or forgot rules or recommended methods, or to say how he fought by his instinct or by his warlike intelligence.

Once we truly know this, without illusion, we will be closer to understanding how he will behave tomorrow, with and against today's faster and more destructive weapons. We can see, knowing that man is capable of only a given amount of terror, knowing the moral force of its destructive power, the speed of it; that tomorrow, more than ever, formal methods that give only the illusion of the battlefield, and contempt for our own experience, hold us back. Tomorrow, the value of the individual soldier will be greater than ever, and so too as a consequence the value of group solidarity.[41*]

Only the study of the past can give us a sense of what is practical, inevitable, for the fighting soldier tomorrow.

So informed, prepared, we will not be surprised because we can arrange our fighting doctrine, our organization, the best formation appropriately. This will have the effect of regularizing it to the extent possible and therefore leave the least to chance, extending the commander's control over the soldier when the soldier's instinct becomes absolutely incompatible with prescribed tactics. This is the only way to preserve discipline, which is broken at precisely the instant of the greatest need. And take care that above all this is before actual combat and not in maneuver.

Maneuvers are the march and movements of troops in the field in the largest formations with all possible order and speed; they are not the same as action itself. Action follows.

---

forces there. His campaigns against the Algerians were notable for their "flying columns," entailing the rapid, relentless pursuits of the enemy by his light forces. Louis Phillipe appointed Bugeaud governor-general of Algeria in 1840, a post he held until 1846. Bugeaud was a great favorite of his troops, who admired his pragmatic, if costly, style of desert warfare. He was in Paris during the Revolution of 1848 but chose not to participate. He was a prolific writer not only on military subjects but also political science, economics, agriculture, and farming.

40. For a concise, detailed account of Bugeaud's action at l'Hopital, see George B. McClellan, "A Marshal of France," *The Galaxy*, vol. 9 (January–July 1870): 674–675.

41. *Do we have a method of war?

It is the confusion [between] maneuver and action that leads many to doubt and oppose our maneuver regulations, which are good, very good, however. As a whole, they provide the means to execute all movements, to take all possible dispositions with all the rapidity and all practical, possible order.

Change them, discuss them, the matter does not advance a step. There is still the problem of definitive action. The solution is in the frank study of what happened yesterday, from which one can deduce what will happen tomorrow, and then all the rest follows.

This study is intended for all those leaders whose experience of war has endowed them with value and moral authority in the army, those of whom they say: he knows the soldier and he knows how to use him.

He knows the soldier, he knows how to use him. Who knew more than the Romans discovering the legion? But they knew, these masters of combat! Their *incessant* experience and reflection made for a complete science.

Today, experience is intermittent. It must therefore be carefully collected and studied; it will be a stimulus to reflection even among those who know, especially among those. And since so many things meet in extremes, who knows—if ancients with pick and sword were seen to defeat other armies twice as strong—who knows if the advancement of long-range weapons could improve these heroic victories in greater proportion by combining common sense or moral genius or machine?[42]*

Despite what Napoleon I says, it costs, always, to assume that victory is on the side of the larger battalions.

---

42. *Surprise today certainly doesn't last long. But wars are fast.

PART TWO
Modern Battle

I

General
Considerations

1. Ancient and Modern Combat

I have heard philosophers reproached for studying too exclusively man in
general and leaving aside the race, country, or era, so that their studies
of him permit little real application, social or political. The opposite criticism can be made of military men, whatever the country. They are quick to
expound traditional tactics and national organization appropriate to their
own race, always brave, the bravest of the brave. They neglect to consider
the study of man in the face of danger. They cannot imagine how practice
differs from their superb theories, all the theories. Perhaps in this time of
military reform, it is not out of place to think some of the man in combat,
and combat itself.

The art of war is subjected to numerous modifications to accord with
scientific and industrial and other progress. But one thing does not change:
the heart of man. In the final analysis, combat is a moral affair; in all the
improvements concerning an army, its organization, its discipline, and its
tactics, all must concede that the human heart in the supreme moment of
battle is always the essential question.

It is rarely contemplated, and it has led to some strange errors. Witness
armies with long-range and accurate weapons (the carbines), which have
never served as intended, because they were used mechanically, without
considering the human heart. Study it!

With the perfection of weapons, the power of destruction grows, the
moral effect of destruction increases, and the courage to face them grows
ever more difficult, and *man does not change*; he cannot change. What needs
to grow with the power of machines is the power of the organization, the

solidarity of the combatants; that is to say, all the means by which we can improve this cohesion that we so neglect. A million men in training exercises and maneuvers (which should be simpler as the power of weapons improves) are of little use if a sane, rational organization does not assure their discipline, and by their discipline their cohesion, that is to say, their courage in action.

Four brave men who do not know each other would not dare attack a lion. Four less brave, but who know each other well, with solidarity and with mutual support, resolutely attack. There is all the science of the organization of armies in brief.

At any moment a new invention may assure victory. Granted. But realistic weapons are not invented every day, and other nations very quickly keep pace with their own. The ultimate question always comes back (leaving aside generals of genius and luck, which can never be counted on) to the quality of the troops; that is to say, to the organization that best assures their spirit, their steadiness, their confidence, in a word their solidarity. Troops here mean soldiers. The soldiers, no matter how well drilled, who are assigned randomly to companies, battalions, etc., will never have, and have never had, that unity which can only be born of mutual understanding.

We have seen in our study of ancient battle what a terrible thing battle is, how man will not fight except under the pressure of discipline. Even before considering modern battle, we sense that the only real armies are those in which a well-considered, rational organization ensures cohesion throughout the engagement. The destructive power of weapons grows greater, and as a consequence the fighting disperses beyond the sight of the commander and even subordinate officers. The power of weapons increased, but man and his weaknesses remain the same. What is the good of an army of 200,000 if only 100,000 fight while the rest disappear in a hundred ways? Better to have 100,000 one can count on.[1]

The purpose of discipline is to make people fight despite themselves. It is naïve to say that there is any army worthy of the name without discipline. There is no army without organization, and every organization is deficient that neglects any means to make itself stronger by fostering solidarity among its soldiers. But the methods cannot be the same everywhere. Draconian

---

1. According to Victor Petit, this passage was inspired by du Picq's reading in the Bible of Gideon's miraculous victory over the Midianites when he was posted in Syria. This suggests that as early as 1860 du Picq was formulating ideas that would later find their way into *Battle Studies*. See Petit, 68–86.

discipline is not our way. Discipline is a social institution, derived from the virtues and defects of the nation.

Discipline cannot be commanded or created in a day or two. The commander must be absolutely confident of his right to command. He must be suited to command and proud of his command. This is what strengthens discipline in armies commanded by the aristocracy in certain armies.

The Prussians do not neglect powerful and vigorous auxiliaries, their homogeneity and cohesion as a body of troops. Hessian formations are composed in the first year of one-third Hessians, two-thirds Prussians, to reshape the particular esprit of troops in a country recently annexed. In the second year, two-thirds Hessian, one-third Prussian, and in the third year, all Hessian regiments are commanded by Hessian officers.

The Americans show us what will happen in modern battle to immense armies without cohesion. The lack of discipline, of traditional organization, and solidarity produced inevitable results: battles waged between concealed skirmishers at long distance, and for days, until some mistaken movement or perhaps moral exhaustion caused one or the other of the two forces to give ground.

In this American war, the melees of Agincourt are said to have returned (which really only means nothing but a melee of fugitives); but there was less close combat than ever.

Combat is far from natural to man. From the first day, we have tried to make it so and it continues. We can imagine that long-range weapons will force us back to fighting at close quarters, but we will simply run farther from the front. Primitive man, the savage, the Arab, is instability incarnate: the slightest breeze, a bit of straw, a shot, and he swerves in an instant. Civilized man in war (which is uncivilized) naturally reverts to these primal instincts.

With the Arabs, war is a matter of agility and trickery, and as hunting is his favorite pastime, the pursuit of savage beasts also teaches the pursuit of man. General Daumas regards the Arabs as cavaliers. What is more chivalrous than a night attack and slaughter of an encampment? (Just words.)

It is often held that war today is the most complex of all time, requiring erudition. But as long as man risks his skin in war it will be essentially a matter of instinct.

Ancient combat resembled a drill; there is no such resemblance in modern combat. This is most disconcerting to officers and soldiers.

Ancient battles were picnics for the victors, who lost nobody. Not so today.

Artillery had no role in ancient combat.

The invention of firearms has reduced casualties in battle; their improvement continues to reduce them every day. This seems a paradox, but numbers prove it, and reason—for those who can reason—shows it is inevitable.

Is war more lethal with the perfection of weapons? No. Man is capable of only a certain amount of terror: beyond that, he runs from battle.

At Pharsalus, the fighting lasted four hours. Caesar struck his camp, which is done in the morning, then formed for battle, then the battle, etc. And he says his troops were fatigued because the battle lasted until noon, which indicates he thought the battle was long.

The Middle Ages (Froissart): the knights in the battle of the Thirty[2] were armed for dismounted combat, which they preferred in a serious affair, that is to say, in a confined space. There was a halt, a pause in fighting, when the two sides were fatigued, exhausted. The Bretons, at this pause, were twenty-five against thirty. The battle had lasted up to the pause without a casualty. Without Montauban, the fighting would have ended with complete and mutual exhaustion and no further losses, because the greater the fatigue, the less strength for piercing the armor. Montauban was both a felon and a hero; a felon because he acted disloyally; a hero because if the Bretons had not gained an advantage by the pause, he would have been killed when he joined the English formation alone. At the end, the Bretons lost four dead, the English eight, four of whom were in their armor.

Explain how, under Turenne,[3] men stood much longer under fire than today. A simple explanation: man is capable of standing against only a certain amount of terror. Today, one must swallow in five minutes that terror which under Turenne took an hour. Here is an example:

With modern weapons, whose employment is well known, the instruction of the soldier is of little moment: it does not make a soldier. For example, the peasants of the Vendee, whose unity and not their individual training made them soldiers whose value could not be denied. Their unity was common among people of the same village, of the same commune, led in combat by their lords, priests, etc.

The greater the improvement of weapons, the more terrifying modern combat becomes, and the more difficult to preserve discipline.

---

2. The battle of the Thirty (March 27, 1351), for succession to the duchy of Brittany. As recounted by Froissart, each side picked thirty skilled knights to settle the claim. All of those who were directly engaged were killed or seriously wounded. In this telling, Montauban was the hero of the day.

3. Henri de La Tour d'Auvergne, Vicomte de Turenne (1611–1675), legendary marshal of France under Louis XIV. Acclaimed by Napoleon as the greatest military leader in history.

The less mobile the troops, the more lethal the fighting. Bayonet assaults are not so easily made, and morale is less affected, man fearing man more than death. One is astonished by the losses suffered by Turenne's armies without breaking. Were the losses accurately reported by the captains of the day?

Frederick[4] liked to say that three men behind the enemy were worth more for moral effect than fifty in front. The battlefield is far vaster today than in Frederick's time. The fighting is on more uneven terrain because the armies, more mobile, need not search for any particular ground.

The nature of ancient arms required close order whereas modern arms require open order, and they are so powerful that the discipline of opposing troops is often broken. What is to be done? Disperse the soldiers. Have them well acquainted with each other to ensure cohesion. Hold your reserves with draconian discipline to serve as a threat.

With modern weapons, the fighting is terrible and almost unbearable by the nervous system. (Who can say he has never been frightened in battle?) Discipline is more important as formations disperse, and lacking confidence in the materiel, discipline must arise from the knowledge of one's circle of comrades and from one's officers, who must always be present and visible. Who marches with the confidence of the rigid discipline and self-esteem of the Roman soldiers, when the struggle is no longer with man but with fate?

Today, when the range of artillery is much greater, there is more freedom of movement for the different arms. The apparent liaison between the arms is not as close, and this has an influence on morale. Cohesive troops have another advantage because they can be extended more widely and thus suffer fewer casualties. They will be in better spirits and more prepared for prompt action.

The more distant the terrain, the harder it is to judge. Thus scouting the terrain by skirmishers is even more necessary. (The Duke of Grammont neglected this at Nordlingen,[5] which is often forgotten.) This is another important reason skirmishers are needed.

The formation by ranks is a guarantee by discipline against the weakness of man in the face of danger. This weakness is greater today because the influence of weapons on morale is more powerful and the formation has the inherent lack of cohesion of the open order. However, the open order

---

4. Frederick II of Prussia (1712–1786), "Frederick the Great," a national and military leader of surpassing skill, credited with the establishment of Prussia as a leading power in Europe.
5. The battle of Nordlingen (1634), one of the climactic battles of the Thirty Years War; it led to the ejection of Sweden from the conflict and the intervention of France.

is necessary to reduce losses and permit the employment of weapons. Thus, today the rank is even more necessary for discipline (not for geometry) and doubly difficult to attain.

In ancient battle solidarity existed, at least among Greeks and Romans. The soldier was known to his commander and to his comrades. They saw that he fought.

In modern armies where victory costs as much as defeat, the soldier is more often replaced (in ancient battle the victor had no losses). The soldier is unknown to his comrades; he is lost in smoke, separated, floating in one direction or another, or fighting alone. Unity is no longer ensured by mutual surveillance. He falls, disappears, and who is to say it was from a bullet or the fear of going forward? The ancient soldier was never hit by an invisible weapon and could not fall so. The more difficult the surveillance, the individuality of companies, sections, squads becomes more necessary, and their ability to answer the roll call at all times should not be the least of their duties.

The ancients often avoided direct collision, so terrible were its results. In modern combat, there is never face-to-face fighting if one stands fast.

Day by day, close combat tends to disappear, replaced by long-range fighting and above all by the moral effect of maneuvers. Dispersion reminds us of the necessity for unity, which was absolutely indispensable in ancient battle.

Strategy, a game of leverage: the first strategist—and before Napoleon—was Horace against the three enemies, etc.

The expanse of the battlefield less than ever allows keeping formations together. The role of the general is much more difficult and many more chances are left to fate. Thus, the greater need for the best troops who best know their jobs, who are solid and tenacious, and who can reduce the risks of chance. They can hold out longer for support. The battles of soldiers are more difficult to determine, more difficult to sustain. A singular similarity, the value of the soldier, in battle at one league or battle at two steps: the essential element of success. Fortify the soldier with cohesion.

Battle is more important than ever. With the ease of concentration (by rail) and communications (the telegraph, etc.), strategic surprises (Ulm, Jena) are more difficult. All the forces of the country can be united, and as a consequence defeat becomes irreparable, disorganization greater and faster.

In modern combat, in our time, the melee really exists more than in ancient battle. This seems paradoxical; it is nevertheless true if the melee is taken as a mixed-up affair where it is infinitely difficult to see clearly.

Man, in the combat of our days, is a man who, hardly knowing how to swim, is suddenly thrown into the sea.

The good quality of troops will more than ever secure victory.

As to the value of troops, consider the value of troops with cohesion and that of new troops; the Zouaves of the Guard or Grenadiers at Magenta, and the 55th at Solferino.[6]*

Thus, nothing should be neglected to make the battle order stronger, man stronger, etc.

2. Moral Elements in Combat

When we contemplate in complete safety, after dinner, physically and morally content, on war, on combat, we are alive with the noblest enthusiasm and little connection with reality. However, how many, if taken in just that moment, would be ready to pay with their lives within the hour? Or march for days, for weeks, to arrive at the hour of battle? Or on the day of battle could they wait for the minutes, the hours to pass? If they are honest, they will confess how much the physical fatigue and anguish that precedes the action will be morally attenuated, how much less willing they are to fight than the month before, when they arose from the table in such a generous mind.

The nature of the heart is as variable as fortune. Man recoils in apprehension of *danger in any effort in which he cannot see a chance of success*. There are some lone characters of iron temper who resist, but they are swept away by the greater number (Bismarck).

Examples show that if a withdrawal is forced, the army is discouraged and takes flight (Frederick). The brave heart does not change.

Real bravery, born of duty, does not know panic and is always the same. The bravery that arises from hot blood pleases the Frenchman more. He understands it; it appeals to his vanity; it is part of his nature. But it is fleeting, and it fails him at times, especially when there is nothing for him to gain by doing his duty.

The Turks are full of passion in the advance. They carry their officers with them, but they retreat with the same zeal, abandoning their officers.

Uninspired troops like to be led by their shepherds, while steady troops like to be guided, with their leaders alongside them or behind. With the

---

6. *See Appendix II.

former the general is mounted at the front; with the latter, the commander is the manager.

Warnery[7] did not like officers leading charges. He thought it useless for them to die before the others. He did not place them in front and his cavalry was good.

General Leboeuf[8] did not approve of the proposal for platoon leaders to advance into battle at front and center of their platoons. He fears that when the captain falls the rest will be demoralized. What should be done? Leboeuf must have known that if the commander is not at the head of his troops they will advance with less confidence, that with us the officer is almost always in front. Practice is stronger than any theory; therefore, fit theory to it. In column, place the platoon commanders on the flank where they can see clearly, etc.

Terror: the Turks in the Polish Wars. What made the Turks so powerful in their wars with Poland was not their real strength but their ferocity. They massacred all who resisted; they massacred even without the excuse of resistance. Terror marched in front of them, destroying the courage of their enemies. The necessity to win or submit to extreme peril prompted cowardice and submission for fear of being defeated.

Turenne said, "you tremble, body, etc." The instinct of self-preservation can make the strongest tremble, but they are strong enough to withstand their emotion without losing their heads or their composure. Fear among such men never becomes terror, and it is obscured by the preoccupations of command. He who cannot resist his heart being seized by terror should never think of becoming an officer.

The soldiers themselves have emotion. The sense of duty, discipline, pride, the example of their commanders, and above all their composure sustain them and stop their fear from becoming terror. Their emotion never allows them to aim, or to more or less adjust their fire, and often they fire into the air. Cromwell knew this very well when he said, even though his troops were dependable, "Put your trust in God and aim at their shoelaces."

What is altogether true is that bravery does not at all exclude cowardice, selfish scheming, horrible, we might even say infamous sometimes.

The Romans were not men of talent, but of discipline and tenacity. We have no idea of the Roman military spirit, which ours does not resemble.

---

7. Carl-Emanuel von Warnery (1719–1786), an acclaimed Swiss cavalryman in the service of Frederick the Great as a commander of hussars during the Seven Years War. A prolific military writer, memoirist, and critic of Frederick.

8. Edmond Leboeuf (1809–1888), French general, marshal of France in the Second Empire, and minister of war at the outbreak of the Franco-Prussian War.

A Roman general who had no more composure than our own would have been lost. We have incentives in decorations, medals, that would have made a Roman soldier run the gauntlet.

How many men in the presence of a lion have the courage to face him, to decide to defend themselves, then do it? In war, when terror seizes you, it is like the lion, you flee trembling and allow yourself to be killed. How then, are so few among the brave absolutely brave? Alas! Gideon found 300 out of 300,000 and was pleased.

Napoleon said that "two Mameluks could hold off three Frenchmen, but 100 French horsemen were not afraid of 100 Mameluks; 300 always won against an equal number; 1,000 fighting 1,500, so great is the influence of tactics, of maneuver." In ordinary language, so great is the moral influence of solidarity created by discipline and made possible and effective by organization and mutual support. Without solidarity, properly formed men who individually are less valuable than a third will fight those who are better than them individually. Everything pertains to organizing an army. Consider how this simple quotation by Napoleon encompasses all the parts morale plays in combat. Convince the enemy that he lacks support, that he is isolated, cut off, overextended, turned, and so on (a thousand ways to convince him he is isolated); his men, his squadrons isolated, his battalions, his brigades, his divisions, and you win. And if his organization does not provide mutual support, there is no need for maneuver; the attack is enough.

How is it that men who do not fear death, who are ready for it at any time, Orientals, Chinese, Tartars, Mongols, and who are resigned to it always, cannot stand before the armies of the West? Deficient organization. The instinct of self-preservation that at the crucial moment dominates them absolutely is not checked by discipline. But then, we have often seen fanatic Western people, full of the belief that death in battle leads to a heroic and glorious resurrection, superior in numbers, break before discipline. If attacked straightforwardly they are crushed by their own weight, and in close combat the knife is better than the bayonet, but then there is instinct.

What makes the soldier capable of obedience and direction in action is the sense of discipline; his respect for and confidence in his leaders; his confidence in his comrades; his fear of their reproaches and revenge if he abandons them in danger; his need to follow others when they go forward without shaking any more than they do—in a word, esprit de corps. Only organization can develop these qualities. Four men equal one lion.

One comment: army organizations and tactical formations on paper are always decided from the mechanical viewpoint, neglecting the essential coefficient, morale, and they are almost always wrong.

Esprit de corps is formed in war. War becomes shorter and shorter and more and more violent. Build esprit de corps in advance.

Comradeship is not enough to make good troops. A good general spirit is required. Every idea should be about combat and not calmly going through drills without understanding their application. Once a man knows how to use his weapon and obey commands, only a few more exercises are necessary (to remind those who have forgotten) and then marches and maneuvers are required.

The technical training of the soldier is not the most difficult. He should know how to use and service his weapon, know how to move right and left, forward, to the rear, to charge, and to march with full pack, all at command. But this does not make the soldier. The Vendeans, who know little of this, were tough soldiers.

It is absolutely necessary to change the instruction, to reduce it to the minimum necessary and eliminate all the superfluities with which peacetime staff burden it every year. Knowing the essential well is better than knowing a little about many things, many of which are useless. Teach this the first year, then that the second, but the essential from the outset. Moreover, instruction should be simple to avoid the boredom of long drills that disgust everybody.

Here is a significant phrase in the list of the causes for the victory of the Prussians over the Austrians in 1866, by Colonel Borbstaed[9]: "It was . . . because every man, being well trained, knew how to act promptly and confidently in all phases of the battle." It is all here, everything.

To be held in a building every instant, every second, every minute of the day, under a not too intelligent supervision is indeed to be exasperated. The soldier counts the hours before he can escape. The sailor, no. This incessant supervision lowers the morale of both the watcher and the watched. What is the reason for this supervision that has long been more than that on ship? Was that not good enough?

3. Material and Moral Effect

The effect of an army, of one formation on another, is both moral and material. Material action on troops lies in destructive power, the moral effect lies in the fear it inspires.

---

9. Karl Borbstaed, Prussian army colonel, military writer, author of studies on both the Austro-Prussian and Franco-Prussian Wars.

In battle, two moral actions, even more than two material actions, are opposed: the strongest wins. The winner often loses more by fire than the loser. The moral effect does not come only from the real, effective power of destruction. It comes above all from its presumed, threatening power, present in the form of reserves threatening to resume the fight, of troops who appear on the left or the right, from a resolute frontal attack.

Material effects are greater as weapons are improved, as the men know better how to serve them, and as the men are more numerous and robust and, in case of success, can carry on longer.

With an equal power of destruction, inferior even, he will win who has the resolution to advance, by the dispositions and movements of troops, by always threatening his adversary with new material action; who takes, in a word, command of moral action. Moral action inspires fear; it must be changed into terror to prevail.

When confidence is placed in the superiority of material action, essential for keeping the enemy at a distance, it can be overturned by the resolution of the enemy. If he advances without regard to your superiority over the means of destruction, the morale of the enemy rises as yours falls. His morale dominates your own; you flee. Entrenched troops break in this way.

At Pharsalus, Pompey and his army depended on a cavalry corps to turn and take Caesar's rear in battle. The army of Pompey was moreover twice as strong. Caesar parried the enemy's blow, and his enemy was demoralized by the failure of the action he counted on. He was beaten and lost 15,000 men put to the sword (while Caesar lost 200), and as many prisoners. One can cite an infinity of such examples.

Even by marching forward you can challenge the enemy's morale, but your objective is to dominate him and force him to retreat in the face of your superiority. It is certain that everything that reduces the enemy's morale increases your own resolution to advance. Therefore, adopt a formation that allows your skirmishers, your agents of destruction, to support you by their material action and so reduce that of the enemy.

And armor, in reducing the material effect that one can suffer, reduces as well the dominating moral effect of fear. One can easily understand how much moral effect armor adds to cavalry. You feel that an armored enemy will succeed in reaching you.

It should be observed that when a soldier awaits an attack at bayonet range (something extremely rare), and the attacking soldier does not falter, the first does not defend himself. This is the massacre of ancient combat.

Against men without imagination, who remain cool and thus retain the ability to think in danger, the moral effect will be the same as the material effect. The simple act of attack does not succeed against such people, such as in Spain and at Waterloo. They should be destroyed, and we are better at this because of our skill in the use of skirmishers and above all our cavalry. But they should not be treated, unless they come to think of themselves so, as a precious jewel that must be guarded against injury. There should be little of it, but good.

"Seek and you will find" is not the ideal but the best method that exists. For example, in maneuvers skirmishers, who have some effect, are ordered back to the ranks to open fire that never killed anybody. Why not put your skirmishers in front? Why sound trumpets that they neither hear nor understand? That they do not is fortunate, for every captain has a different call sounded. For example, at Alma,[10] the retreat, etc.[11]*

The great superiority of Roman tactics lay in their constant search for ways to combine physical and moral effects. Moral effect passes; physical effect does not. The Greeks searched for dominance. The Romans sought to kill, and kill they did, and followed the better path. Their moral action was supported by solid, deadly swords.

We know from examples the value of morale to a nation at war. Pichegru's[12] treason had a great influence at home and we were beaten. Napoleon returned, and victory with him. But we can do nothing without good troops, even with a Napoleon. Consider Turenne's army after his death: it remained excellent despite the discord and inefficiency of the two commanders as in the defensive retreat across the Rhine. Note, the regiment in Champagne attacked in front by the infantry and was taken in the rear by the cavalry. One of the prettiest actions in the art of war.

Man, in modern battle, which is conducted at such long distance between combatants, has come to have a horror of man. He fights only to protect

---

10. The battle of Alma (September 20, 1854), the first battle of the Crimean War between the Anglo-French coalition and the Russians. The Allies' reluctance to pursue the outnumbered Russian defenders permitted the Russians to prepare their defenses of the fortress of Sebastopol.

11. *See Appendix II.

12. Jean-Charles Pichegru (1764–1804), French Revolution general, important commander in the invasion of the Netherlands. Later, as commander of the Army of the Rhine, he expelled the Austro-Prussian army from Alsace, returning home to great acclaim. He turned against the Revolution in 1795, served as president of the Council of Five Hundred, was arrested after the coup d'état, and was deported to French Guiana. He escaped and returned secretly to France, where he conspired against Napoleon. Eventually arrested for treason, he died in prison under suspicious circumstances.

himself or if forced to by some fortuitous encounter. Even more, one may say that he pursues the fugitive only for fear that he will return and fight.

Guilbert[13] says that shock actions are infinitely (infinite taken in its mathematical sense) rare. Guilbert reduces to nothing, by reasoning from practical observations, the mathematical theory of shock by one massed body of troops upon another. The physical energy is nothing, in effect. The force of morale that animates the attacker is all. Moral power comes from one's sense of the enemy's resolution. The battle of Amsterdam was said to be the only one in which a line actually stood against a bayonet attack. Even the Russians broke under the moral impulse before the physical. They were disconcerted, wavering, completely upset, hesitant, when the collision occurred. They waited long enough to receive the strikes of the bayonets, even of rifles (in the back, as at Inkerman[14*]).[15] This done, they took flight. Those who are calm and strong-hearted have all the advantage of fire; but the moral force of the attacker demoralizes the defender. He is fearful. He does not set his sights; he does not even aim. His lines are shattered without defense, indeed unless his cavalry—waiting in formation, horsemen a meter apart and in two ranks—does not break first and destroy all cohesion.

With good troops, if an attack is not prepared, there is every reason to believe it will be repulsed. The attacking troops suffer from material action more than the defenders. The defenders are in better order, fresh, while the attackers are in disorder and have already suffered a loss in morale after a certain amount of destruction. The superior morale that comes of offensive movement may be more than compensated for by the good order and cohesion of the defenders, while the attackers have suffered losses. The least demonstration by the defense demoralizes the attack. This is the secret of the English infantry against the French in Spain, and not their fire by ranks, which was just as ineffective as ours.

The more confidence one has in his methods of defense and attack, the more demoralized, disconcerted to see it in a moment insufficient to stop the enemy. Confident use of the modern improved firearm is still limited, with the present organization and actual use by men armed with carbines effective at only point-blank range just as before. It follows that bayonet charges (in which thrusts with the bayonet never happen) have, in our own

---

13. Jacques Antoine Hippolyte, Comte de Guibert (1743–1790), French general and leading military theoretician, author of the classic, and prescient, *Essai generaux de tactique* (1770).

14. *See Appendix II.

15. See also n. 25, below.

day, a greater moral effect, and victory will come to he who retains the most order and *élan*. These two qualities, which we neglect too much, and the willingness and intelligence to sustain a firm control over troops in immediate support, will give us hope to take and hold what we take. Therefore, do not neglect destructive action before employing moral action. Use skirmishers up to the last moment; otherwise no attack succeeds. Thus, against the rapidity of actual fire (harassing fire, but harassing fire multiplied by the rate of fire) no attack can succeed.

And it must be that this moral force is a terrible thing. Here is a formation advancing against another; it only has to stay calm, ready to take aim, every man fixed on the man in front of him. The attacking force comes within range, deadly range. It halts to fire or not, but all the same it will be a target for the other formation that awaits it, calm, ready, certain of its effect. The whole first rank of the attackers falls, shattered. The rest, discouraged by their reception, disperse right away, before any sign of an advance on them. Is this what happens? Not at all! Confronted by the moral momentum of the attacker, the defenders are anxious. They fire into the air if at all. They scatter immediately in the face of the attackers, who are even encouraged now that the first shots have been fired, and they quicken their pace to avoid a second volley.

The British troops, it is said by those who fought them in Spain and at Waterloo, are capable of the required coolness. I doubt it nevertheless. After they fire, they quickly advance. Otherwise, they might have fled. In any case, the English are stolid people with little imagination, who try to be rational in all things. The French, with their nervous irritability, their vivid imagination, are incapable of a similar defense.

I think, in truth, that anyone who believes he could stand under a second volley is a man without any idea of battle (Prince de Ligne[16]).

History provides many examples of troops who stood like walls, who could not be moved or pushed, who stood patiently under the heaviest fire, and who retired *with haste* when the general ordered a retreat (Bismarck).

The maneuvers of the cavalry, like those of the infantry, are menaces. The most menacing win. A formation of ranks is a menace, and more than a menace. A force engaged is not under the control of its commander. I know

---

16. Charles-Joseph, prince de Ligne (1735–1784). Belgian soldier and author, veteran of the Seven Years and Russo-Turkish Wars, adviser to Joseph II, Emperor of the Holy Roman Empire, and intimate of Catherine the Great of Russia. A favorite in the courts and salons of Enlightenment Europe.

what it can do. It acts; I can gauge the effect of its action. But a force in formation is under control; I know it is there, I see it, feel it. It can be ordered in any direction. I feel instinctively that it alone can surely reach me, attack me on the right, on the left, penetrate a gap, turn me. It troubles me, this threat. Where will it fall next?

The formation in ranks is a threat, a serious threat, which at any instant may be put into effect. It imposes a terrible dread. In the heat of battle, a formation does more to secure victory than those who are actually engaged, whether or not they exist in reality or only in the enemy's imagination. In indecisive combat, he wins who can show, and merely show, battalions and squadrons in good order. The fear of the unknown!

From the taking of the entrenchments at Fribourg[17] to the bridge at Arcola,[18] to Solferino,[19] there is a multitude of heroic feats, of positions taken by frontal attack, which mislead everyone from generals to civilians, which always lead to the same mistakes. It is time to inform these gentlemen that the entrenchments at Fribourg were not taken by frontal attack, nor the bridge at Arcola (see the correspondence of Napoleon I), nor was Solferino.

Lieutenant Hercule took fifty cavalry through Alon, ten kilometers on the Austrian flank at Arcola, and the position that halted us for three days was evacuated. The evacuation was for strategic, if not tactical, moral effect. General or soldier, man is the same.

Depending on the morale of the enemy, demonstrations should be made at a greater or lesser distance; that is to say, the methods of battle should vary with the enemy, and a fitting method should be employed in each case.

We have discussed and shall discuss only the infantryman, for in battle (ancient or modern) he suffers most. In ancient battle, if he is defeated, he stands at the mercy of the victor. In modern battle, the man on horse moves quickly through danger, while the infantryman must walk. He even has to halt in danger, often and for long periods. He who knows the morale of the infantryman, which is put to the hardest test, knows the morale of all combatants.

---

17. The battle of Freiburg (August 3, 5, and 9, 1644), an unsuccessful, sanguinary attempt by Turenne to capture the Bavarian city in the closing campaign of the Thirty Years War.

18. The battle of Arcola, August 15–17, 1796, during France's War of the First Coalition against Austria.

19. The battle of Solferino (June 24, 1859), between Napoleon III and Emperor Franz Joseph I of Austria. Decisive battle of the Franco-Italian War, and the last battle in which monarchs commanded all the armies engaged.

4. The Theory of the Strong Battalions

Today, we are preoccupied by numbers. Napoleon was (see his strength reports). The Romans did not come to this; their preoccupation was in seeing that everyone fought, while we assume that everyone present on the day of battle, in an army, a division, a regiment, fights. Right there is the error.

The theory of the strong battalions is a disgraceful theory. It depends not on the quantity of courage, but on the quantity of human flesh. This is contrary to the soul. Orators great and small who speak of military matters today speak only of masses. War is made by enormous masses, and so on, and so on. And in the masses the individual man disappears. One sees only the numbers, and yet today as ever, quality alone produces real results. The Prussians were victorious at Sadowa[20] with experienced soldiers, united, and inured to discipline. We can make such soldiers in three or four years today, because the material training, indeed, is not so different.

Caesar found legions that were inexperienced, not yet good soldiers, though they had been formed nine years.

Austria was beaten because her troops were conscripts, of poor quality.

Our projected organization will give us 400,000 good soldiers, but all our reserves will be without cohesion if they are thrown into any old organization on the eve of battle. From afar, these may be impressive, but up close they are reduced to 50 or 25 percent who really fight. Wagram[21] was not very well done; it called for desperate efforts that for once had a moral effect on an impressionable enemy, but this time only. But, again?

The Cimbrians show[22]* that man has not changed.[23] Who today is braver than them? And they did not have to face artillery or rifles.

In the beginning, Napoleon found an instrument, an army possessed of good battle methods, and in his best battles the fighting followed these methods. He himself ordered (or so it is said, for he gave a false account at

---

20. Also known as the battle of Koniggratz (July 3, 1866), Prussia's decisive victory in the Seven Weeks War between Prussia and Austria.

21. The battle of Wagram (July 5–6, 1809), Napoleon's decisive victory against the Austrian army commanded by Archduke Charles. The largest battle fought in Europe up to that time, the Austrian defeat led to the dissolution of the Fifth Coalition, Austria's alliance with Great Britain.

22. *See Appendix II.

23. A reference to the Roman Consul Gaius Marius's victory over the Cimbrians at the battle of Vercellae in 101 B.C., as described by Plutarch.

St. Helena) the methods employed at Wagram, at Eylau, at Waterloo, and engaged enormous masses who had no material effect. But it consumed a frightful number of men and created a disorder that, once they had been unleashed, did not allow them to rally and resume the battle. Barbaric methods (in the Roman sense), amateurish, if it were permitted to say such a thing of the man; a method that could not succeed against talented, seasoned troops, a kind of thinking (d'Erlon's[24] corps at Waterloo) that lead to disaster.

With luminous clarity, Napoleon saw only the goal, and on this day his impatience (or omnipotence leading to impatience), or the perhaps lack of experience and knowledge of his officers and soldiers, impeded his continued employment of real attack tactics; he completely sacrificed the material effect of infantry and even that of cavalry to the moral effect of masses. In ancient battle, victory cost much less than with modern armies, and the same soldiers served longer in the ranks. At the end of Alexander's campaigns, when he had soldiers sixty years old, he had lost only 700 men by the sword. Napoleon's system was more feasible with the Russians, who congregate, naturally mass together, but are not effective, as at Inkerman.[25]

What did Napoleon I do? He reduced the role of men in battle and depended instead on action by masses. There is no chance for us, the instruments, to be glorious.

Masses of infantry, masses of cavalry toward the end of the Empire, marked a tactical degeneracy as a result of the erosion of their elements and of lowering the standards of morale and training. And as the Allies understood and adopted our methods and our doctrines, Napoleon thought to try something new (or so old that it seemed new) to achieve surprise, but surprise one day only, until the enemy recovered: an act of desperation permitted only by the great power he saw slipping away from him.

When misfortune and a sacrifice of *cannon fodder* overcame him, Napoleon reverted to practicality, no longer blinded by his great power. His supreme good sense, his genius eclipsed the *mania to conquer* at all costs, and we have the campaign of 1814.

---

24. Jean-Baptiste Drouet, Comte d'Erlon (1765–1844), French field marshal under Napoleon, commander of the Armée du Nord at Waterloo.

25. The battle of Inkerman (November 5, 1854); Allied victory over the Russians during the Crimean War that opened the way to the siege of Sebastopol. Deemed a "soldier's battle" because fog on the battlefield defied any exercise of troop command and control.

General Ambert[26] says, "Without military traditions, almost without command, these confused masses (the American armies) struck as men struck at Agincourt and at Crecy." At Agincourt and at Crecy,[27] few were struck, but were struck a lot; these battles were immense slaughters of French by the English and other French, who did not suffer much themselves. How, except in disorder, did the American battles resemble these butcheries with the knife? The American combatants engaged skirmishers at a distance of leagues. The general has been carried away by his fondness for phrase-making.

Victory is always with the strong battalions, and for good reason. If sixty determined men can rout a battalion, one must find these sixty men. One may find only as many as the enemy has battalions (note Gideon's 300 out of 30,000, one out of a hundred). Who knows if it would not be better, under the circumstances, to fight at night?

5. Combat Methods

Ancient battle was fought in a restricted space. The commander could see his entire force. Seeing clearly, his observations should have been clear; instead, in many these are obscure, lacking details, so that we are obliged to supply them. In modern combat, no one knows what occurs or what has occurred except from results. Narrations cannot enter into details of execution.

Feats of arms are curious to read, recounted by the victors (so-called) and the vanquished. One cannot tell which is truthful, if either, disguised with great aplomb, without knowing of the politics of the war that may pervert the facts for disciplinary, moral, or political reasons. (Sommo-Sierra.)[28]

The companies were all commanded by captains, but it is difficult to estimate the losses because they all cheat, they all lie. Why?

In modern narratives, French accounts and foreign accounts of the same event are so different the facts bear no resemblance to each other. What is

---

26. Jean-Jacques Ambert (1765–1851), veteran of the American Revolutionary War and French Revolutionary War. Division commander in the Army of the Rhine and Moselle during France's War of the First Coalition.

27. The battles of Crecy (August 26, 1346) and of Agincourt (October 25, 1415), both decisive English victories over the French.

28. The battle of Sommo-Sierra (November 30, 1808), in which Napoleon's army forced a passage in the mountain range north of Madrid, leading to the capture of the city a few days later.

the truth? Only the results (such as the casualties on both sides) can say, if they can be had, and they are quite instructive.

Under Turenne, I believe, there was not the same degree of national pride that obscured the truth. The troops in both armies were often from the same nation.

If national vanity and national pride were not so sensitive about recent events and so passionately debated, numerous examples could be drawn from our last wars, from us or from the Allies. But who can speak of Waterloo without passion, with impartiality, without being ashamed? A victory at Waterloo would not have advanced our affairs. Napoleon attempted the impossible, and the impossible was beyond the reach of genius. After a terrible struggle against English solidity and tenacity, a struggle in which we could not subdue them, the Prussians appear. We would have done no better had they not, but conveniently for our pride, they did. They were engaged, and then the rout began, not among the troops engaged, but among those facing the English, who were exhausted perhaps, but no more than their enemies. This was the moral effect of the attack on their right, where they had expected reinforcements. The right followed the movement, and what a movement!

Why do not the experts recognize the facts and try to formulate combat methods that conform to reality? It would reduce a little the disorder that troubles men who are not warned of it when they jump from the frying pan into the fire. Two officers I could mention, one of them very brave, who said, "Leave the soldiers alone before the enemy; they know better than you what has to be done." This is a fine example of French confidence that the soldiers know better what is to be done. Especially *in a panic*, one supposes!

Long ago the prince de Ligne justified battle formations, above all the famous oblique order. Napoleon decided the question. All discussion of formations is pedantry. But there are reasons of morale for the power of order by echelon.

We cannot believe the incredible difference between practice and theory. A general, a thousand times on the battlefield, when asked for guidance, gives this order: "Go there, Colonel." The colonel, a man of good sense, asks, "Will you explain, my general? What point shall I guide on? How far should I go? Who is on my right? On my left?" The general: "Advance on the enemy, sir. That is enough. Why the hesitation?"

"But, my general, what are my orders? The area is large. If you do not know where to send your troops and how to guide them, to ensure they understand where they are to go, to give them guides if required, what kind of general are you?"

What is the method for taking a fortified work, or a line? We have none! Why not prescribe that of Marshal de Saxe?[29] Ask several generals how they would do it? They will not know.

Always, there is a mania, an impatience to know the results without thinking of the means. However, it is the general's role to judge the best moment for attack and in knowing how *to prepare* for it. We took Melegnano[30] without artillery or maneuver, but at what a price! At Waterloo, the farm at Hougoumont resisted us all day, cost us dearly, and transformed us into a mad mob until Napoleon sent, as he should have done at the beginning of the attack, eight mortars to demolish and burn the chateau.

A rational and well-conceived method of combat, even if not prescribed but still known by all, is enough (with discipline) to make good troops. The Portuguese infantry in the Spanish War who were taught combat methods by the English almost rivaled the English infantry. Today, who has codified a method? Who has a traditional method? Ask the generals. No two will agree.

However, we have a method, or rather a manner, that accords with the national temperament: skirmishers in a great flock. But this is nowhere codified, and before the campaign it is derided and for good reason, because it quickly becomes a flock of lost sheep, without dogs or shepherds. Thus, troops arrive on the battlefield entirely innocent of reality, and all the leaders, all the officers, are confused, disoriented. Often we meet generals who have lost their divisions, their brigades, staff officers who have lost both their generals and their divisions. (And although this is more easily understood, many company officers who also have lost their commands). A serious matter, one that may cost us much in a prolonged war while the enemy gains experience. We may hope that experience will prompt us, not to change the principle, but to modify in a practical way our common tactics of *escaping by advancing*. (The brochure by the prince of Prussia shows that, without having fought us, the Prussians understand our methods.)

There are men such as Marshal Bugeaud who are born warriors by virtue of their character, spirit, intelligence, and temperament. They commend and show by their example, as in Colonel Bugeaud's engagement in 1815 at the bridge at l'Hopital, tactics wholly in keeping with their national and

---

29. Maurice, Count of Saxony (1696–1750), marshal of France, renowned professional soldier, adventurer, and author of the classic work on the art of war, *Mes Reveries*.

30. The battle of Melegnano (June 8, 1859), an unnecessary rearguard battle during the Second War of Italian Independence, initiated by the Austrians while retreating from their defeat by the French at Magenta.

personal characters.[31] Note Wellington and the Duke of York among the English. But the execution of tactics such as Bugeaud's required officers who are similar, at least in their courage and decisiveness. All commanders are not of their caliber. Therefore, prescribed tactics that accord with national character are required, tactics that may guide the ordinary officer without demanding he possess the extraordinary ability of Bugeaud. These prescribed tactics would serve an officer as the perfectly clear and well-defined tactics served commanders of the Roman legion. The officer could not depart from them without failing his duty. Of course, they will not make him an exceptional leader, but except in case of utter incapacity they will keep him from making inane blunders. Nor will they keep officers of Bugeaud's talent from using their abilities. On the contrary, prescribed tactics will help them by placing men under their command who are prepared for details of battle that will not take them by surprise.

This method need not be as absolutely dogmatic as Roman tactics. Our manner of combat is too variable. But some clear rules, informed by practice, would prevent gross mistakes by incompetents (such as allowing skirmishers to disappear after the formation's first rank fires and in their withdrawal, dragging the first rank with them). They would also permit useful, timely adjustments by men of coolness and decision.

Prescribing such tactics would reply to those (and the number is great) who claim that everything is improvised on the battlefield and can find no better improvisation than to abandon the soldier.

We must therefore find a method that controls just this behavior in our soldiers, who advance by flight (such as the Vendeans) or, if you like, *escape by advancing*, or if they are caught by surprise, flee to the rear just as quickly.

Invention is needed less than verification, demonstration, and organization of proper methods; to verify, observe better. To demonstrate, experiment and describe better. To organize, disperse better (remembering that cohesion means discipline). I do not know who put matters this way, but it is truer than ever in this day of invention without an atom of practical thought.

Very few among us reason or understand reason, very few are cool. The effect is negligible in the confusion of the mass. It is lost in numbers. It follows that above all we need a method of combat sanely thought out in advance,

---

31. Bugeaud's defensive battle at the Savoyard village of l'Hopital, in which with 1,750 soldiers he defended the bridge over the River Arly against an Austrian force of 10,000, was actually fought *after* he and his command received news of Napoleon's defeat at Waterloo.

and it must acknowledge that we are not passive, obedient instruments, but very nervous and restless people who wish to finish things quickly and to know beforehand where we are going. It must recognize that we are a very proud people, but people who would cower if we were not seen, and who consequently must always be seen and act in the presence of our comrades and of the officers who observe us. Thus, the necessity to organize the company solidly. (It is the infantryman on whom combat exerts the most violent impression; therefore, he must be the most firmly supported.) Solidarity is created by a mutual, long-standing relationship between all the company's components.

Have no combat methods that require commanders without fear, of high intelligence, with good sense, esprit, etc.; you will always be disappointed. Bugeaud's method was excellent for him, but it is clear that in the fighting at the bridge at l'Hopital his battalion commanders did not help. Had he not been there, all would have been lost, and he alone, present everywhere, executed resolute attacks that no one else could have. His system (always attack, even on the defensive, and fire and take cover only when not attacked) was rational, given his mentality and the situation, but in executing it he assessed his officers and soldiers himself and was mistaken. No dogmatic principles can be drawn from his method or from any other. Man is always the same. He cannot command ability and resolution. Two methods: which one the commander chooses depends on his troops and himself.

Tactics is and always has been the art, the science of making men fight with maximum energy, which alone can arm an organization against fear.

Those who agree this is the result of mathematics are wrong. It is the dominant science of war, because combat is only the final goal. To get to the truth, the point of departure is that fear of defeat, it is self-regard, it is the great mass of numbers, and the lack of intelligence about a thing they cannot feel. However, there is an element of truth beyond this, and it is the basis of all true tactics. Discipline is part of tactics, its absolute foundation as the Romans believed; they were more intelligent than the Gauls, but not braver.

To start with: battalions of four companies, four platoons, in line or column. The order of battle: two companies deployed as skirmishers, two companies in reserve under command of the battalion commander. The skirmishers will provide the destructive action, which should be directed by the battalion commander, but usually is not. Nothing will be accomplished by the skirmishers beyond 600 paces. They will never, never, never be neatly placed in front of their battalions, calm and composed, after an advance, even if only at maneuvers. The battalion commander should be skillful enough to direct his skirmishers. The battalion, half-engaged, the other half at the ready, should remain under his command as far as possible. In the advance, the officers and soldiers fret if they are not directed; but when the fighting gets hot, they have to see their commander, to know that he is near. It does not matter if he has no initiative, or is incapable of giving an order. His presence creates a belief that direction exists, that orders exist, and that is enough.

When the skirmishers meet resistance, they retire to the ranks. The role of the reserves is to support and reinforce the line, and above all, by a charge to cut the enemy's line. Then they fall back and the skirmishers move forward again if the advance has resumed. Then the second line, the battalions in line or column, the formation that covers it best. Cover the infantry before they engage; cover them as much as possible and by any means; take advantage of the terrain; make them lie down. That was the English method of the defense of heights, used in Spain and at Waterloo. One bugle call for each battalion should sound calls. What else is needed?

Many pompous generals would scream in protest like eagles were it suggested they take care to protect second-line battalions or first-line troops who were not engaged, but this is merely a sane measure to keep good order without the slightest hint of cowardice.[32]* With breech-loaded weapons, skirmishers on the defensive almost always fire from a prone position. They are made to stand with difficulty, either for retreat or advance. This makes the defense more tenuous.

---

32. *It is true that there are recommendations in training camps and in publications, but in maneuvers they are ignored in the madness for alignment, and in that other mad desire of generals to interfere in matters which do not concern them.

II

Infantry

1. Masses—Deep Columns

Now we want to explain the force created by the material effect of a column attack and by mass action in general. Today, we may read this singular rationale for attack by battalions in close columns:

> A column cannot stop instantly without a command. Suppose your first rank stops at the instant of shock; the twelve ranks of the battalion that follow would run into it, pushing it forward. Experiences have shown that beyond the sixteenth rank the push of the ranks from the rear have no effect on the front rank; it is completely absorbed by the fifteen ranks already massed behind the first rank. To do the experiment, march at charging pace and command a halt to the first rank without warning the rest. The ranks will collide with one another unless they are careful, or unless, anticipating the command, they unconsciously check their march.

But in a real charge, all your ranks are alert, restless, anxious about what is happening at the front, and if it stops there will be a *movement to the rear, not the front.* Imagine a good battalion, imperturbable and poised, thrown at full speed against the enemy, at 120 paces a minute. Today, they would advance against a rate of fire of five rounds a minute! And if at this last moment the front rank halts, it will not be pushed as the *theory* reads, it will be thrown into confusion. The second rank will arrive to collide with the first, and so on. We should conduct an experiment on the training ground to determine how far this crashing over cardboard figures would extend.

But physical impulsion is only a term, for if the front rank halts it will let itself fall and be trampled rather than give in to the pressure that pushes it

74

forward. For those who have seen, felt, experienced modern infantry combat, this is what happens and demonstrates the error of physical impulsion, a mistake that moves commander after commander in the Empire—such is the power of routine and prejudice—to order attacks by close column, attacks that dissolve into absolute disorder without the commander's intervention. So here is what happens: a battalion fresh from their barracks marches in light order, its subdivisions plainly separated by four paces, controlled by their noncommissioned officers. But if the terrain is slightly uneven, if the guide does not march with mathematical precision, the battalion in close order becomes a flock of sheep in the twinkling of an eye. But wait, our battalion is 100 paces from the enemy. What happens then? No one will ever see this today with rifles, or anything else.

If the battalion has marched resolutely, if it is in good order, it is ten-to-one that the enemy has already withdrawn without further delay. But if the enemy does not falter? Then, modern man against fire loses control of himself. The instinct of self-preservation controls him absolutely. There are only two ways of evading or allaying the danger: escape or assault. Now, regardless of how small the space or how brief the time that separates us from the enemy, instinct asserts itself. We quickly advance, but we rush prudently, letting the most aggressive ones, the bravest ones, move ahead. But it is absolutely true; as we close with the enemy, the less organized we are. Farwell to the theory of pressure. And if the first rank is stopped, the ones behind slow down rather than push, and even if the first rank is pushed, it will itself relent rather than advance. There is no question, it is a fact. There is pushing, but for those fleeing. (Note the fighting at Diernstein.)[33]

Today more than ever the rout begins in the rear, which is affected even more than the front.

Mass attacks are incomprehensible. Not a tenth was ever successful and none could ever withstand a counterattack. One can only explain them by the lack of confidence by the general in his troops. Napoleon expressly condemns such attacks in his *Memoires*, and he never ordered them. But when good troops were used up, and when the generals do not think they can make determined attacks in tactical formations with inexperienced troops, they regress in desperation to the mass formations from the infancy of the art.

---

33. The battle of Diernstein (November 11, 1805), in which, during the War of the Third Coalition, a French division found itself trapped between two Russian columns on the north bank of the Danube. The division was rescued but at the cost of very high casualties on both sides.

If you persist, if you press on, your force will vanish as if a magician were waving a wand, or a kitten drowning in a stream.

But the enemy does not stand. The moral pressure that advances before you is too strong to withstand. Otherwise, those who stood and aimed even with empty rifles would never see the charge approach them. The first rank of the attacker would sense death and no one would want to be left in the first rank. Therefore, the enemy never stands, because if he does it is you who flees, and this always nullifies the shock. The enemy is no less anxious than you are, and when he sees you approach the same question is whether to run or to advance. And then *the question is between two moral impulses.*

This is the instinctive reasoning of every soldier, every officer: "If these men wait for me to close to point-blank range, I am dead. I may kill, but I will certainly die; at the mouth of a cannon the ball cannot miss. But if I can frighten them, they will run away and I can shoot them and bayonet them in the back. Let's try." So comes the test, and at some stage of the assault, perhaps only at two paces, one of the two forces turns away and gets the bayonet in the back. (We always imagine fully charged weapons, but in fact that takes too long.)

Shock is only a word. The theories of de Saxe, of Bugeaud, "close with the enemy and with fire at close quarters. That kills the most people and the victor is the one who kills most," are not founded on fact. No enemy awaits you if you are resolute, and never, never, never are two equal resolutions face to face. All nations, everyone, know that the French have never met anyone who resisted a bayonet charge.

The English in Spain, marching resolutely against French charges in column, always won. The English were not frightened by the mass. If Napoleon had remembered the defeat of the giants of the Armada by the small English ships, he might not have ordered d'Erlon's columns forward.

Blücher,[34] in his instructions to his troops, recalled that the French had never withstood the resolute march of attacking Prussian columns.

Suvorov's[35] tactics were no better, but his battalions in Italy drove us at the point of their bayonets.

---

34. Gebhard Leberecht von Blücher, Fürst von Wahlstatt (1742–1819), Prussian field marshal who, having retired after a distinguished career, was recalled to active service at the age of seventy-one to command Prussian forces opposing Napoleon at Waterloo. Blücher's timely attack on Napoleon's right flank helped to turn the battle in the Allies' favor.

35. Aleksandr Vasilyevich Suvorov, Count Rimniksky (1729–1800), renowned Russian general, who was said to have never lost any of his sixty battles during his nearly fifty years of service. The last *generalissimo* of the Russian empire.

All the nations of Europe say no one stands before a bayonet charge made by us, and with good reason. The French do not oppose a bayonet attack more than anyone else. Everyone believes that their attacks are irresistible, that their advance will frighten the enemy into retreat, and whether the bayonet is fixed or in the scabbard does not matter.

In antiquity it is said that young troops were anxious if anyone advanced upon them in tumult and in disorder, but that old troops saw signs of victory. At the commencement of a war, all troops are young. Our impetuosity drives us to the front like fools . . . the enemy takes flight. If the war continues, everyone becomes seasoned, and the enemy is not troubled when standing before troops charging in disorder because he knows and feels that they are moved as much by fear as by resolution. Only good order impresses the enemy in an attack, because it indicates real resolution. That is why it is necessary to establish good order *at the outset and keep it to the very end*, and that is why it is unwise to increase the pace prematurely, because you become a flock of sheep and leave so many men behind you will not reach your objective. The close column transforms you in advance into a flock of sheep, in which officers and soldiers become a mob with no way to support each other. Therefore it is necessary to continue in order so that the noncommissioned officers enforce unity, and everyone advancing is observed, in the open. In closed columns man marches unobserved and for the least reason will lie down or fall behind. That is why it is always best to keep your skirmishers in front or on the flanks and never recall them when near the enemy. That creates a counter-current that carries away your men. Let your skirmishers be. They are your lost children. They know best when they should rest, and so on.

In sum, there is no shock of infantry against infantry. There is no physical impulse, no force of mass. There is only *the impulsion of morale*, and no one denies that this moral impulsion is greater the more one feels supported, that it has a greater effect on the enemy if it threatens him with more men. It follows, therefore, that the column is more valuable in the attack than the deployed order.

One might conclude from what we have said in this long note that moral pressure, which always leads to flight before a bold attack, prevents any infantry from holding out against a cavalry charge; indeed, never against a determined charge. But the infantry must fight when it is not possible to get away, and until they are completely demoralized, absolutely terrified, the infantry knows this. All infantrymen know it is foolish to run away from cavalry when the rifle is infallible at point-blank range, at least from the rider's point of view. It is true that every really bold charge should succeed, but whether the man is on foot or horseback, he is always man. On foot he only has himself to convince; on horseback he must force man and beast to advance against the enemy. And mounted, it is easy to take flight. (Remark by Varnery.)

We have seen that in an infantry mass those in the rear of the formation cannot push those in front unless there is greater danger in the rear. The cavalry has long understood this. It attacks in column at double-distance rather than half-distance to avoid the horrible, inert confusion of an inert mass. And yet, so seductive is the mathematical reasoning that cavalry officers, especially the Germans, seriously propose attacking infantry by deep masses so that units in the rear might push those in front, following the proverb, "one nail drives another." What does one say to those who talk such nonsense? Nothing, except, "always attack us this way."

Real bayonet attacks occurred in the Crimea (Inkerman).[36]* They were made by a smaller force against a larger one, and the power of mass had no effect in such cases, for we saw it was the mass that recoiled, fell back even before the shock, so that those who charged resolutely merely struck and fired at the backs of those retreating. But these examples show men confronting the enemy face to face at a distance at which one can close without hesitation or running out of breath. These are chance meetings. One party is not yet demoralized by fire; he must strike or retreat. Close combat does not exist. At close quarters, we see the ancient carnage when one force strikes the backs of the other.

Columns have an absolute moral effect and are threatening formations.
. . .

You have long denied the value of the mass impulse of the cavalry. You have renounced forming it in deep ranks although cavalry has speed that would produce more of a push on the front when it stops than the last ranks of the infantry would impose on the front. Yet you believe in the mass effect of infantry!

When ancient mass formations advanced, they did not lose a man and no one took to the ground to avoid fighting. Momentum persisted until the time to stop; in modern formations, among the French especially, the march can continue, but the formation loses men while marching under fire. Today, above all in France, man resists the use of his life in this way. The Frenchman wants to fight, to strike blow for blow. If he is not permitted,

---

36. *See Appendix II.

this is what happens. It happened to Napoleon's mass formations. Consider Wagram, where his mass was not repulsed. Of 22,000 men, 3,000 to 1,500 reached the position, and they certainly did not seize the position; it was taken by the material and moral effect of 100 pieces of artillery, cavalry, and so on. Were the 19,000 missing men disabled? No. Seven out of twenty-two, a third, an enormous proportion, may have been hit, but what became of the 12,000 absent? They had fallen to the road, pretended to be dead so as not to continue. In a mass so confused by the column of deployed battalions, observation is impossible, and nothing is easier than dropping out by inertia; nothing more common.

This happens to *all* troops in the advance, under fire, in any formation. The number of men falling out, giving up at the least opportunity, is greater if the formation is less well formed and the scrutiny of officers and comrades is more difficult. In a battalion in closed column, temporary desertion is enormous; one half of the men drop out in this way. The first platoon is mixed up with the fourth. They are truly a flock of sheep. No one has control over the action since they are all intermingled. Even if the position is carried by the initial momentum, the disorder is so great that if it is counterattacked by four men, it is lost.

The morale of such masses is fully described in Caesar's battle against the Nervii, Marius against the Cimbri.[37]*

2. Skirmishers–Supports–Reserves–Squares

It is quite singular. The cavalry has a clear tactical method, and except for the shirkers, it knows how it will fight. The infantry? None.

Our infantry no longer has combat tactics; the soldier's initiative commands all. The First Empire had confidence in both the morale and pliancy of mass formations. Today, the soldier bridles at the passivity of masses; they fight as skirmishers instead, or else go forward to the front of the flock, three-fourths of whom seek cover even while en route if the fire is serious. The first method, only slightly better than the second, is bad enough without iron discipline and combat methods studied in advance and every day by means of practical exercises to keep up strong reserves. These should be left in the hands of the commanders, the officers, to employ as support

---

37. *See Appendix II.

troops, to prevent panics, and to intensify the moral effect of a march on the enemy, of threats to the flank, and of the deadly work of the skirmishers.

Today, when firearms are so deadly, so effective, a unit that closes up for combat is a unit in which morale is failing.

Practical maneuver is possible only with a good organization, otherwise it is no more useful than a passive mass or a rabble in the attack.

In ancient combat, the soldier responded to his commander. But today, when formations are open, the soldier cannot answer or even be directed. Thus, it is necessary to engage in action at the last possible moment and to ensure that the officers in command understand exactly what is wanted, the objective, and so on.

In modern combat, we lose control of the infantryman when he scatters, and then we say, a soldier's war. Wrong, wrong. Instead of scattering to infinity, deal with this matter by increasing the number of rally points and strengthen the companies, then the battalions, then the regiments. . . .

Fighting in open order under Turenne was not possible or imaginable. The majority of the soldiers were not held under close command, in formation, and they fought badly, usually from cover. (Note the Americans.)

The organization of Marshal de Saxe's legion shows how singular was his propensity for shock action over action in which firepower predominated.

The maneuvers, parades, shooting, etc., at Potsdam were not the tactics of the old fox Fritz (his secrets were timeliness and rapidity of movement), but they were widely believed to be, and still are. For all their parades and mathematics, the Prussians eventually took up the best practices. The Prussians themselves were beaten by Frederick's tactics at Jena,[38] but since then they have been the first to take a practical course, while we in France are still imitating the Potsdam drills.

The greater number of generals who fought in the last war, who were in real battles, advocate large bodies of skirmishers, well supported, because our men have such a tendency to collect themselves in such groups in defiance of their commanders. It is said they would not fight otherwise.

A number of writers and military men call for large bodies of skirmishers because they are now dictated by the necessities of war. Ask them to explain this mode of action and you will see that all this talk of skirmishers

---

38. The battle of Jena, also known as the battle of Jena-Auerstadt (October 16, 1807), a major engagement of the Napoleonic War in which the French army shattered the obsolete Prussian army and required Prussia to sign the Peace of Tilsit (July 1807), which reduced Prussian territory by half.

is nothing but a euphemism for absolute disorder. They have tried to fit the theory to the facts. Large units of French skirmishers *under fire* is an absurdity. The terrain and the intensity of action severs initiative and direction from the commanders, who leave their men to form small groups among themselves.

Weapons are meant to be used. The best formation for material effect in attack or defense is that which permits the easiest and most lethal use of weapons; this is in the dispersed, thin line. The whole science of combat is therefore the happy combination of the open order (and it is relative, depending on the enemy, the terrain, and his morale), dispersed to achieve destructive effect, and a good disposition of troops in formation to serve as support and as reserves so as to complement by moral effect the material action of the lead troops. On the other hand, the thin line is only possible under strict discipline, a solidarity that the men attain from pride, a pride that exists only among those who know each other well, who have esprit de corps, and a company spirit. (There must be an organization that encourages company unity by creating a real sense of identity.)

Self-esteem is without question one of the most powerful motivations of our soldiers. They do not want to be seen as a coward in the eyes of their comrades. They advance to distinguish themselves. But after an attack, the rank (not the formation of the drill ground but the one formed by rallying to the commander and advancing with him) no longer exists because an advance under fire is inherently disarranged. The confused men (and officers as well) are no longer watched over and sustained by their comrades or their commanders; their self-esteem deserts them and they cannot hold on. The least counterattack routs them.

The evening's experience should always serve the day after, but because the next day never repeats the evening, the counsels of experience cannot be applied. When confused battalions exchanged fire at 200 paces for some time (with weapons inferior to ours), men on the wings of the formation took flight. Therefore, experience said, let us reinforce the wings, and so the battalion was placed between two elite companies. But combat methods were transformed. The elite companies were then reassembled into an elite corps of companies, and the battalions were weaker than before without them. Suppose that combat in open order is the norm, and companies of light infantrymen being essentially skirmishers, the battalion is once more no longer supported. In our day, using deployed battalions as skirmishers is no long possible, and after all, one of the essential reasons for picked companies is to strengthen the battalion.

Of the Guard, we read in the brochure, who saved the French army on the Berezina[39] and at Hanau?[40] The Guard, it is true. But aside from the elite troops, what was the French army then? Droves, not troops. Abnormal times, abnormal feats. The Berezina, Hanau, they prove nothing today.

With rapid-fire infantry arms today, the advantage lies with the defense, complemented by offensive movements executed at opportune times.

Everyone screams for rapid fire (even if it is quite as ineffective as in the days of the muzzle-loaders), which is four or five times faster. Everyone says this is why cavalry charges against unbroken infantry are impossible. What, then, about infantry charges?

Attacks in deep masses are no longer seen; they are not wise and never were. To attack with a line in column of battalions, with large intervals and covered by a thick line of skirmishers when the artillery has prepared the way, is all very well. People with common sense have never done otherwise, but a thick line of skirmishers is essential. I think that is the crux of the question.

But enough. It is simple prudence for the guns to prepare the infantry engagement by a momentary exchange of fire with the artillery of the enemy infantry. If that infantry is not commanded by an imbecile (as it sometimes is), it will avoid that particular exchange that would break it up even if it is not under direct fire. All things being equal, both infantries suffer equally in the artillery duel. The proportion does not vary, however complete the artillery preparation. One infantry must always close with the other under rapid fire from troops in position, and this kind of fire is always (today more than ever) to the advantage of the defense. Ten men advance toward me from 400 meters; with old weapons I have time to kill only two before they reach me; with rapid fire, I have time to kill four or five. Morale does not increase when danger has run its course, but rather the opposite is true. The eight survivors in the first case might reach me; in the second case, the remaining five or six certainly will not.

If the commander keeps pace he can be seen, the file closers can see, and the platoon can see what lies ahead. Falling by the wayside always happens, but less often in open order because men are easily recognized. As the

---

39. The battle of the Berezina (November 25–29, 1812); the fiercely contested crossing of the Berezina River by Napoleon's Grand Army in full retreat from Russia.

40. The battle of Hanau (October 30–31, 1813); a minor battle between the remnants of Napoleon's Grand Army in the aftermath of his disastrous defeat at the battle of Leipzig, in which the forces of the Sixth Coalition attempted—and failed—to block Napoleon's line of retreat to France.

companies know each other better, and as the officers and men are more dependable, there will be fewer stragglers.

It is difficult if not impossible to make French infantry employ fire before charging. If it fires it will not charge because it continues to fire. (Bugeaud's method of advancing while firing is good.) It is therefore necessary to have skirmishers who only fire effectively, and troops in formation who push the skirmishers along as they advance to the attack.

The soldier wants to be occupied, return shot for shot. Put him in a position to act immediately, on his own initiative, and whatever he does, you will not have lost your authority over the man.

At drill, the officers and noncommissioned officers should tell the private again and again and again: "This is meant to serve you under these circumstances."

Generals and field officers ought to tell officers the same. Only this can make a trained army like the Roman army. But today, who among us can explain page by page the use of anything ordered by our tactical regulations except the school of the skirmisher? "Forward," "retreat," and "by the flank" are the only practical movements? Why not port arms in the left hand? Why not ordinary pace? Why not fire on command in the school of the battalion? Because it serves well enough in the company, but in a battalion, never.

Everything leads to the belief that combat with modern weapons will be, in the same period of time, more lethal than in ancient combat. The flat trajectory of the projectile has greater range; the rate of fire is four times greater; more men will be put out of action in less time. While weapons become more deadly, man does not change; his morale permits only so much even as greater demands are made on it. Morale is overcome more quickly, reaching its greatest tolerance, propelling the soldier toward the front or the rear. The role of the commander is to maintain morale when it is under maximum tension, to direct movements in which the men instinctively execute and engage while in great danger.

Napoleon said that in combat the role of the skirmishers is the most exhausting and the most dangerous. Under the Empire, as now, heavily engaged infantry units rapidly dissolved into skirmishers, and this action was decided by the moral agency of those who were not engaged, under control, capable of moving in any direction and acting as a great threat to an enemy already shaken by the destructive action of the skirmishers. The same is true today, but the more powerful the weapons, the more imperative that they be employed. The role of the skirmisher is preeminently the destructive role, and it is forced on every unit seriously engaged by the greater moral pressure that causes men to disperse sooner.

Commanders in chief imagine organized battalions firing on the enemy and *do not include the employment of skirmishers in their training*. This is a mistake, because they are necessary in training and everywhere. Organized ranks are more difficult than ever to employ. General Leboeuf employed a very practical formation when going into battle: by platoons, which advance to the line of engagement in echelon, and can fire even if they are engaged as they move. There is always the same predisposition to crowd together even when a battalion is moving. But it is a mistake to confuse movement of units in detail with those of an army. The Emperor Napoleon III does not dictate the use of skirmishers in even terrain, but every officer who does not know how to use them in some way should be *broken*.[41]

The role of the skirmisher becomes more and more predominant. He should be all the more observed and directed as he is used against more lethal weapons and is thus more disposed to slip from all control, from all command. It is in these conditions of combat that formations are proposed that deploy skirmishers 600 paces in advance of battalions and that assign the commander the task of observing and directing (with six companies of 120 men each) troops dispersed over an area of 300 by 500 paces at least. To advance skirmishers 600 paces ahead of their battalion and to expect they will remain there is the work of the unobservant.

There has been a constant preoccupation to integrate the commander with the skirmish line. Leaders have been seen spreading an entire battalion in front of an infantry brigade or division so that the skirmishers, under one commander, might better follow general directions. This method, barely workable in training maneuvers and indicating a complete lack of practical sense, reveals this preoccupation. The authors of these new drills go too far. They assign immediate command of the skirmishers in each battalion to the battalion commander who must lead them and his battalion at the same time. This expedient is more practical than the other. It abandons all thought of an impossible general control and assigns special direction to the right hands. But the commander is too far away and has to see to the work of his battalion on line, or when combined with other battalions of the brigade or division, as well as the particular conduct of his skirmishers. The more difficult and confused the engagement becomes, the simpler and clearer the roles of each should be. Skirmishers need more control than

---

41. That is, demoted.

ever so they can do their part. The battalion commander should be entirely occupied with the skirmishers, or with his line. There should be smaller battalions, half the number in reserve, and half as many skirmisher battalions. The line of skirmishers will then become steadier.

The commander of the second line of troops should occupy himself completely with his battalion.

The battalion of six companies is now too unwieldy for one man. Create battalions of four companies of 100 men each. This is certainly quite enough, considering the lethal power that each of the four companies place in the hands of one man. Even at that, he will be pressed to maintain and direct the action of these four companies under the fire of powerful modern weapons. He will be pressed to observe them in modern combat, when the intervals between the men in line are so much greater because of these weapons. With a unified battalion of 600 men I would do better against a battalion of 1,000 Prussians than with a battalion of 800, 200 of whom immediately slip from my control.

Skirmishers have a destructive effect; formations a moral effect. Training maneuvers should prepare for actual combat. In these maneuvers, at the decisive moment of attack, why should you lessen the moral anxiety and the destruction of the enemy by retrieving your skirmishers? If the enemy keeps his own skirmishers ahead and marches behind them, you are lost, because his moral supremacy is enforced by the violent action against which you have so kindly disarmed yourself.

Why call back your skirmishers? Is it because they get in the way of your columns, dense bayonet charges? Whoever advances such reason has never been in combat. At the last moment, at the supreme moment when you are 100 or 200 meters from the enemy, there is no longer a line. There is a daring advance; your skirmishers are your last resort. Let them charge as they choose. Let them be overtaken or pushed forward by the mass. Do not recall them. Do not give them an order they cannot execute, except maybe falling back to form a defensive line. In such moments, everything hangs by a thread. Is it because your skirmishers would interrupt your fire by ranks on command? Do you believe in firing under the pressure of approaching danger, before the enemy? If the enemy is wise, he certainly advances behind the skirmishers, who kill men in your ranks and are made confident by the sight of your skirmishers disappearing in front of them. These skirmishers will certainly take cover after they have unmasked your front. In that position they will easily cause you losses, and you are subjected to their lethal effect and their moral effect in advancing against you. Your ranks become confused. You cannot hold the position. There is only one way of holding it, and that is to advance, and in order to do that it is necessary at all costs to avoid firing before advancing. Once firing begins, no one advances farther.

On the training ground, we always believed in opening and ceasing fire by command. Opening battalion fire with modern arms is the beginning of disorder, the moment when the battalion begins to escape the control of its commander. Even in training, after a lively little drill, after a movement, battalion commanders cannot control fire.

But we never get within 200 meters of the enemy, it is said; that a frontal attack never succeeds. Both! Let us attack the flank. But a flank is always more or less covered; men are put there, more or less ready for an attack. It is necessary to storm these men.

With rapid fire, today more than ever, there are other possibilities of fire, with some coolness, besides the fire of skirmishers.

Rapid firing has reduced six ranks to two ranks. With steady troops who do not need the moral support of a second rank behind them, one rank is enough today. In any case, we can receive an attack in two ranks.

By dictating fire on command, in attempting to reduce the role of the skirmishers (Camp Châlons under General Leboeuf,[42] conversation with the Emperor) instead of making it predominate, you are siding with the Germans. We are not suited for that kind of game; if they adopt fire by command it is just one more reason to find another method. We invented, discovered the skirmisher. He is forced on us by our men, our arms. He must be organized.

In battle, in firing by two ranks, the men congregate in small groups and become disoriented. The more space they have, the less disorder.

By force of circumstances also, the first two ranks must be even thinner. All the bullets fired by the second rank are lost. The men should not touch; they should be far apart, and when the second rank fires from position at the right moment they should not be directly behind the first rank. The men should be echeloned behind the first rank. It is necessary to make this firing as effective and as easy as possible. I do not wish to challenge the experiences of the firing range, but I wish to put them to practical use.

---

42. General Leboeuf commanded the camp at Châlons in 1868; it was established in 1857 by Napoleon III and was the site of the French army's annual maneuvers (as well as a place to showcase his troops). After the Franco-Prussian War the camp was made into a permanent training establishment.

It is evident that modern weapons are much more lethal than old ones; the morale of the troops will therefore be much more severely shaken. The influence of the commander over the combatants immediately engaged should be greater. If it seems rational, have the colonels engage in the action, with the battalions of their regiment in two lines. One battalion serves as skirmishers; the other battalion stands ready to aid the first. If you do not wish to use the colonels in this way, put all the battalions of the regiment in the first line and eventually use them as skirmishers. This will inevitably happen anyway, so do it yourself at the first opportunity.

The need to replace ammunition so quickly used up by the infantry requires engaging infantry by units, who can be relieved by other units after the ammunition supply is expended. Because skirmishers are exhausted quickly, engage entire battalions as skirmishers, assisted by entire battalions as supports or reserves. This measure ensures good order. Do not throw all four companies of the battalion into the fight immediately. No. The battalion commander must guard against throwing everyone into the fight until the extreme limit of the possible.

There is a mania among us, which can be seen in our training camps, for *completely* covering a battle front, a defended position, by skirmishers without any intervals between different battalions. With what result? First, at the *beginning of the action*, a waste of men and ammunition; then, how to reinforce them?

Cover the front everywhere? You can see clearly in the distance, so where is the advantage? Leave very wide intervals between your deployed companies. We are no longer only 100 meters from the enemy when we commence firing. We are not likely to see the enemy dash into the intervals by surprise. Your skirmisher companies at wide intervals begin the fighting, the killing. As the advance companies move forward, the battalion commander follows with his formed companies, covered as much as possible. He lets them go on. If the skirmishers are engaged, he observes. If the commander wishes to reinforce his line, if he wants to oppose an enemy who attempts to advance into an interval, if he has any reason for doing it, in a word, he rushes new skirmishers into the interval. Certainly, these companies have more dash, if dash is needed, than skirmishers already in action. If they pass the first skirmishers, it is no harm because there you have echelons already formed. The skirmishers who are engaged, seeing support, can be launched forward more easily.

Moreover, the companies launched into the intervals are a surprise for the enemy. That is something to be considered, because if there is fighting in place, the intervals in the skirmish lines are a good place for bullets. Furthermore, these companies are still in the hands of their commanders. The present method of reinforcing skirmishers (I am speaking of the practical method of the battlefield, not that of theory), a company, starting from behind engaged skirmishers, without a place to deploy, does not have anything better to do than mingle with the skirmishers. This doubles the number of men, but it also creates disorder, prevents the control of the commanders, and breaks up regularly constituted groups. Closing up the intervals to make places for new arrivals is good for the drill ground, or good before or after the fighting, but it *never* works *during* battle.

Certainly, no interval can be maintained precisely; it will open, it will close, according to the fluctuations of the fighting. But at the first moment when it can be kept, is not the moment of sharp fighting. It is the moment of the engagement, of contact, of feeling out the situation. Being able to find a place in which to advance is essential. Suppose you are on a plain, for a maneuver always begins on flat terrain. In extending a new company the wings of the others will be reinforced, the men naturally supporting the flanks of their comrades. The individual intervals will close to make room for the new company. The company will always have a well-established core, a rallying point for the others. If the interval has vanished there is always time to resort to the emergency method of doubling the front ranks. But one must never forget, whatever happens, to preserve good order.

We cannot resist our obsession with closing intervals between battalions, as if we were still in the day of the pikemen when, indeed, it was possible to pass through an interval! Today, fighting is done at ten times the distance, and the intervals between battalions are not weak points. They are covered by the fire of the skirmishers, as well as fire from the rest of the front, and beyond the sight of the enemy.

Skirmishers together with masses, these are the formations for poorly trained French troops. With training and solidarity there would be *skirmishers and formation in battalion columns at most.*

Troops in close order can only have a moral effect in an attack or in a demonstration. It you want to produce a real effect, use musketry, and for this it is necessary to form a single line. The action of the line has purely a moral effect. Whoever counts on their material, effective action against steady, cool troops is mistaken and beaten. Only skirmishers do damage. Aimed fire would do more if properly employed.

When you march to attack a position, begin the charge at the latest possible moment, when the commander judges he can reach the objective without being winded. Until then, it has been possible to march in rank, that is, under the control of the officers (the rank not being the mathematical line, but the portion under the hand of the leader, under his eye). But with the charge comes confusion. Many stop; fewer if the charge is brief. They take cover and will rejoin only if the attack succeeds, if they rejoin at all. If the charge is too long the men will stop and take a breath, and then the dash is broken, shattered. At the order "Advance!" very few will start. Ten chances to one the attack will fail, become a joke, with cries of "Forward with fixed bayonet!" [with] none advancing except some brave men who will be killed uselessly. The attack vanishes on the slightest demonstration of the enemy—an unfortunate word, a mere nothing. . . .

Absolute rules are nonsense because the conduct of every charge is an affair requiring tact, so that we can say at the beginning, "there is a way," and there is a way. Conduct it as the cavalry charge is conducted: have a rear guard of noncommissioned officers, of the most reliable ones, in each battalion to gather the men, to closely follow the charge at a walk and to collect all those who have lain down to avoid marching or because they are out of breath. The rear guard could consist of a small platoon of crack shots of the sort we need in each battalion. The charge ought to be made at a proper distance, otherwise it vanishes, evaporates. The commander who begins it too soon has either lost his head or does not want to take the objective.

Reserving the line infantry for *support* is the inverse of what should be done. The least solid, the most impressionable, are thus ordered on the road stained with the blood of the strongest. We place them, after the moral agony of waiting, face to face with the terrible destruction and mutilation of modern weapons. If antiquity had need of steady troops in support, we have an even greater need of them, because death in ancient combat was not as horrible as in modern combat where the flesh is mangled, slashed by artillery fire. Few were wounded in ancient combat except in defeat. This is the reply to those who want to begin an action with chasseurs, Zouaves, and so on.

General or mere captain, he who employs everyone in storming a position can be sure of seeing it taken by an organized counterattack of four men and a corporal.

For control and real responsibility in formations from companies to brigades, troops in support should be from the same company, the same battalion, the same brigade, as the case may be. Each brigade should have its two lines, each battalion its skirmishers, and so on.

The system of keeping a reserve for independent action as long as possible after the enemy has used his own should be applied from top to bottom;

each battalion should have its own reserve, each regiment its own, firmly under control.

More than ever, the supporting forces, the reserves, should be protected. The power of destruction increases; morale remains the same. The strain on morale, more violent than ever, should be as brief as possible, because the power of morale has not increased. The masses, the reserves, the second and first lines, should be protected and sheltered even more than the skirmishers.

Squares are broken sometimes by cavalry, pursuing skirmishers into the square. Instead of lying down, the skirmishers rush blindly to their refuge whose unity they paralyze and disrupt. No square can hold out against determined cavalry—but!

The infantry square is not a matter of mechanics, a result of mathematical reasoning; it is a matter of morale and nothing else. It is certain that a platoon of four ranks, two facing front and two facing the rear, its flanks guarded by the extreme files that face the flank, and directed, supported by noncommissioned officers placed in a fifth rank inside the rectangle, powerful in its appearance and its firepower, is invulnerable to cavalry. However, this platoon will prefer to be part of a larger square; it will think itself stronger because of numbers, and indeed it will be since this feeling of strength is felt throughout the formation. This feeling is power in war.

Those who calculate the destructive power of infantry only by volume of fire would have it deploy in line against cavalry. They do not think that although such a formation is supported and maintained, and although such a formation may seem to prevent flight, the very impetus of the cavalry charge will break the deployment before the shock arrives. Clearly, if the charge is badly executed, whether the infantry is steady or not, it will never reach its objective. Why? For reasons of morale and no other the soldier in a square feels stronger than when in line. He feels himself protected from the rear and has nowhere to escape.

3. Firing[43]

Breech-loading weapons such as the carbine are easily misused. The fashion today is to use small entrenchments to protect the battalions. As old as pow-

---

43. *See also Appendix I.

der, but no matter; it is good. On one condition, however: that from them one can fire usefully.

Now look at these two ranks crouched in the cover of a small trench. Simply follow the direction of the shots, or even the trajectory of the burst of flame. You will be convinced that, under these conditions, simple horizontal firing is a fiction. In a second, there will be wild firing because of the *lightheadedness*, the crowding, the vexation in the two ranks, and then everybody tries to find the best possible cover. Goodbye, firing.

We want to save ammunition, to use weapons as efficiently as possible, but the official recommendation of fire by ranks means falling back on useless firing at random. Marksmen are wasted, placed where it is impossible for them to fire well.

If we have a weapon that fires six times faster than the old weapon, why not profit by it to cover a given space with six times fewer riflemen than before? Riflemen with more space will be less confused, will see more clearly, will be more easily observed (which may seem strange), and fire more effectively than before. Moreover, they will use six times less ammunition, and that is the most important question. Always conserve ammunition, that is to say, among those troops not yet engaged. Reserves must be held out. Hard to manage, perhaps, but not as hard to manage as firing on command.

What is the use of firing by ranks? On command? It is impracticable against the enemy (except for the occasional cavalryman on lookout, it is a joke!). Of two ranks? Only the first rank can fire horizontally (the only thing to order). The second rank can only fire into the air with knapsacks preventing them from raising their arms higher than their elbows. (Learn from the campaigns of the English, the Prussians, the Austrians.) Could the packs be not so thick or wide? Have the first rank be open and the second be like a checkerboard, and have firing against cavalry be the only firing executed in line.

One line will be better than two, because it will not be impeded by the one behind it. Only one kind of fire is practicable and efficient, that of a single rank. This is the fire of skirmishers in close formation.

The king's order of June 1, 1776, reads (p. 28), "Experience in war having proved that three ranks fire standing, and the intention of his majesty being to prescribe only what can be executed in front of the enemy, he orders that in firing, the first man is never to put his knee on the ground, and that the three ranks fire standing at the same time." (This same order includes instructions on target practice, etc.)

Marshal Gouvion Saint-Cyr[44] affirms that it is no exaggeration to say that one-fourth of the men are put out of action by the third rank. This estimate is not high enough if it refers to a unit composed of recruits like those who fought at Lutzen and Bautzen.[45] The marshal cites the astonishment of Napoleon when he saw the great number of men wounded in the hand and forearm. Napoleon's surprise is singular. How ignorant were his marshals' inability to explain such wounds! Chief Surgeon Larrey,[46] by examining the wounds, exonerated our soldiers of the accusation of self-inflicted wounds. The observation would have been made sooner, had such wounds been numerous before. That they had not can only be explained by the young soldiers of 1813, keeping instinctively close in their ranks in order to fire. Or perhaps, in 1813, these young men might have been permitted to fire a longer time so as to keep them in their ranks, and not often permitted to act as skirmishers for fear of losing them. Before, firing by ranks must have been more rare, and fire action must have declined almost entirely to the use of skirmishers.

Fire on command assumes a composure that, had any troops possessed it, would have them mowing down battalions like cornstalks. But it has been known for a long time, since Frederick, since before Frederick, since the first rifle. Allow the troops to judge the range calmly, and allow them to take aim together so they do not upset or hinder one another. Let each one see clearly and, on a signal, let them fire all at once.

Who the hell do you want standing against such people? But, did they adjust their fire in those days? Not so accurately, perhaps, but they knew how to fire waist-high, to shoot at the feet. They knew how to do it; I do not say they did. Had they known, there would have been no need to remind them

44. Laurent, Marquis de Gouvion Saint-Cyr (1764-1830), marshal of France, minister of war (1815 and 1817-1819), veteran of the Napoleonic Wars, responsible for the reform of the French army following Napoleon's defeat. France's École spéciale militaire de Saint-Cyr is named in his honor.

45. The battle of Lutzen (May 2, 1813) and battle of Bautzen (May 20-21, 1813) were attempts by Allies during the War of the Sixth Coalition to prevent Napoleon from taking Leipzig. Although Napoleon remained in possession of the field after these battles, his losses forced him to agree to a temporary truce with Russia and Prussia (the Armistice of Pleischwitz). The respite permitted both sides to recover and re-equip, but the Sixth Coalition was the greater beneficiary of the pause in fighting.

46. Dominique-Jean, Baron Larrey (1766-1842), pioneering military surgeon who served under Napoleon in all his campaigns from Egypt to Waterloo. He is credited with the introduction of field hospitals, field ambulances, and first aid on the battlefield. A founding member of the Académie de Médicine.

so often. Note Cromwell's favorite saying, "Aim at their shoelaces," and that of officers of the Empire, "Aim at the height of the waist." In a study of battles, of the expenditure of bullets, no such terrible results are shown. If this means of destruction was so easy to achieve, why then did not these worthy people recommend it instead? (Words of Gouvion Saint-Cyr.)

Security alone creates cold-bloodedness under fire.

In minor operations, how many captains are capable of commanding their fire and maneuvering calmly?

A singular matter: You hear in military lectures firing by rank against cavalry seriously recommended, even though not a colonel, not a battalion commander, not a captain requires the execution of this fire while maneuvering. The soldier always initiates the firing, and he is ordered to fire almost before he aims to prevent him from firing without command. Yet he ought to feel that when he is aiming, with his finger on the trigger, that the shot does not belong to him but to the officer. He should be able to allow the soldier to take aim for five minutes, if advisable, examining, changing positions, and so on. When aiming, he should always be ready to fire at the target designated without ever knowing whether his commander will order him to fire.

Fire on command is not practicable in the face of the enemy. That is not the question; it would depend on the coolness of the commander and the *obedience* of the soldier. The soldier is much more amenable to direction.

The Austrians had fire on command in Italy against cavalry; did they use it? They fired before command, an irregular fire, fire by file, with inaccurate results.

Fire on command (firing at will is a commander's dream) while under enemy fire is impossible, an illusion. For reasons already noted, and for this reason: closed ranks are incompatible with firearms because of the wounding by following ranks. In closed ranks, with two lines elbow to elbow, a man who falls throws ten others into complete confusion. There is no room for those who fall, and however few, the disorder immediately turns the two ranks into a collection of small, confused groups. If the troops are young, they become a disordered flock before any demonstration. (Caldiero, Duhesme.[47]) If the troops are steady, they will make space for themselves,

---

47. General Guillame Philibert, first count Duhesme (1766–1815), commander of the French army's 4th Division at the battle of Caldiero against the Austrian army during the War of the Third Coalition. Duhesme was killed at Waterloo in command of the Young Guard Division of the Imperial Guard. Author of *Essai historique de l'infanterie légère* (1806).

they will make way for the bullets. They will disperse as skirmishers with small intervals. (Note the Grenadier Guards at Magenta.)[48*]

With very open ranks, more room, men who fall are seen by fewer other men, and he drags no one down when he falls. The moral impression on his comrades is not so great, and their courage is less impaired. Too, with rapid fire everywhere, with ranks spaced so that no one is in front of anyone else, at least horizontal fire is permitted. In closed ranks, fire is hardly permitted in the first rank, whose ears are deafened by the shots from the men behind them. With a rate of fire of four or five shots a minute, one line is certainly more solid than two, because there is half as much firing, and it is more than twice as likely to be horizontal fire than in the two-rank formation. Of course, sustained fire even with blank cartridges would be enough to prevent a successful charge. With slow fire, two ranks alone would be able to keep up a continuous fusillade. With rapid fire, a single line fires more than two lines with old weapons and, therefore, suffices as a fusillade.

Two closed ranks, while good for marching, are never suited for firing in place. While on the march, we like a comrade at our side; when exchanging fire, we imagine lead entering our body and prefer to be relatively isolated, with space around us. Breech-loading weapons do strange things to the head; generals can be found who say rapid firing will bring back fire on command as if there was ever such a thing. They will say rapid fire will bring back firing by volley, which will permit a clear view. These men do not have an atom of practical sense.

It is strange to see a man of practical ideas on most things like Guibert, giving a long dissertation, showing that officers of his day were wrong in aiming at the middle of the body—that is, aiming low—saying that this is ridiculous to anyone who understands the rifle's trajectory. Those officers were right; they revived the recommendations of Cromwell, because they knew that in combat the soldier naturally fires too high because he does not aim, and because the shape of the rifle when it is brought to the shoulder tends to keep the muzzle higher than the breech. Whether that is the reason or something else, the fact is indisputable. In Prussian drill, it is said, all the bullets hit the ground at fifty paces. With the arms and the manner of fighting of those days, the results in battle would be magnificent.

But at Mollwitz,[49] the Austrians had 5,000 taken out of action, while the Prussians had 4,000.

---

48. *See Appendix II.

49. The battle of Mollwitz (April 10, 1741), an early engagement in the War of Austrian Succession, in which superior Prussian training in drill and musketry saved the day from

Why begin the movement to fire from the horizontal position if the barrel is heavier; moving the rifle from the vertical to fire is deadlier.

4. Marches–Camps–Night Attacks

Although infantry should always fight in thin formation, dispersed, it does not follow they should be kept in that order. Battle order can only be kept in column, and it is necessary to be in control of one's men as long as possible because, once engaged, they no longer belong to you.

A closed mass is not suitable for marching formation—even in a battalion for a short distance. The heat generated by a closed column is intolerable, like a room without circulation. A formation at half-distance is better.

This formation makes it possible to quickly deploy the column into battle order in the event of necessity or surprise. The trailing half-division can be brought up, arms at the ready, and act as skirmishers or as a reserve for the first line as it engages.

At Leuctra,[50] Epaminondas reduced the depth of his men by one-half to form square phalanxes of fifty by fifty men. He needn't have bothered, because the Lacedaemanian right was at once thrown into disorder by its own cavalry, which was posted in front of it. The superior cavalry of Epaminondas not only ran over the enemy cavalry but also the infantry that followed it. The infantry of Epaminondas, coming in the wake of his cavalry, finished the work. Turning to the right, Epaminondas's left took the flank of the Lacedaemonian line. Also threatened in its front by the advancing echelons of Epaminondas, this line became demoralized and took flight. Perhaps this fifty by fifty formation was formed in order to present a front of fifty that could move in any direction. At Leuctra, it simply moved to the right against the enemy's flank and in reverse. . . .

Moving through thick woods is generally done in close column. There is never any opening up of the formation, with subsequent closing on the far side of the woods. The result is as confused as a flock of sheep. . . .

In a march through mountains, difficult, a bugler should be placed on the left, under the orders of an intelligent officer who can call a halt when

---

Frederick the Great's mistakes, including his premature flight from the battle. Afterward, he vowed to never again abandon his troops when they were engaged.

50. The battle of Leuctra (371 B.C.), in which the Boetian army under Epaminondas defeated a Spartan army under King Cleombrotus and established Theban hegemony in Greece. Said to have been the origin of the tactic of the attack by "oblique order," later used to great effect by Frederick the Great.

the line needs ordering. The right responds, and if the place has been correctly judged the order of the formation is preserved. Stay in ranks; if one man falls out, others follow. Do not permit men to leave the ranks without requiring them to rejoin.

In the rear guard, it is always necessary to have pack mules just in case; without this precaution, time can be lost, and in difficult places time is lost every day.

In camp, organize your fatigue parties in advance; send them out in formation and under escort.

General instructions should be given to the convoy, and the chief baggage-master ought to supervise it (which is rarely done).

Furnishing mules to officers and replacing them when they are lost or sick is a mistake. The officer overloads the mule and the State loses more than it realizes. Convoys are endless because of overloaded mules and stragglers. If given money to buy a mule the officer uses it economically because it is his. If mules are issued individually to officers instead of money, the officer will care for his beast for the same reason. But it is better to give money only, and if the officer is not well cared for on the march he has no claim against the State.

Always, always take draconian measures to prevent pillage from the beginning, because once it begins it is difficult to stop.

Infantry units are never left alone. There is no reason to regard infantry officers as inept. They are in position. That is good, but the other battalions are not established on absolutely the same line, with absolutely equal intervals. Ten moves are made to achieve the exact alignment according to regulations on camp movements. Yet naming a guide battalion might answer well enough and still be according to regulations.

Why are not night attacks used more today, at least on a grand scale? The great front that armies occupy makes their employment more difficult, and requires troops with a special aptitude for this kind of surprise (Arabs, Turks, Spahis), or absolute reliability. However, with a system of guides, men whose knowledge of terrain is sometimes so astonishing, whose eye for distance is unerring, who can find their way at night through places they have only seen by day, one could move with certainty. These are simple means, rarely used, for moving a body of troops through even the blackest nights. They are even a means of assuring the fire of a gun at night on a given point with as much precision as in plain day. . . .

III

Cavalry

1. Cavalry and Modern Weapons

It is said that cavalry is finished, that it cannot fight in battles with modern weapons. Isn't the infantry affected as well?

Examples from the last two wars prove little: in a siege, in a country that is disputed, one does not employ the cavalry and thereby forfeits its audacity, which is almost its only weapon.

The usefulness of cavalry has always been suspect because it is expensive; it is seldom used because it is expensive. The economic question is paramount in time of peace, and when we overvalue certain men they are not slow to agree and guard themselves against being reduced. Look at staff officers who (with rare exception) are never reduced, even when the general himself is.

With new weapons the role of the cavalry certainly has changed less than any other arm, although it is the arm we worry about most. The cavalry has only one doctrine, the *charge*. Cavalry versus cavalry is always the same; against infantry the same again. Today as always, the cavalry knows it can only attack infantry that has been torn apart. (We must dispense with epic legends that are always false, whether they concern the cavalry or the infantry.) The doctrine for infantry versus infantry says even less: there is a complete anarchy of ideas. There is no doctrine for the infantry.

With the destructive power of modern weapons, which force you to slow down if not halt, advancing under fire is almost impossible, and the advantage is with the defense. This is so evident only a madman would dispute it. What is to be done? Halt, snipe, and cannonade at long distance until ammunition runs out? Perhaps. But it is certain that this situation makes maneuver necessary. More than ever, maneuver at long distance is required

97

to force the enemy to shift, to abandon his position. What maneuvers faster than the cavalry? There is its role.

The far-reaching advancement of weapons allows only individual action in combat, dispersed. It also allows the effective use of mass action beyond enemy range, of maneuver on the enemy's flanks or rear in such force that he is threatened.

Can cavalry maneuver on the battlefield? Why not? It can move quickly and above all beyond the range of infantry fire if not artillery fire. Maneuver being a threat, a great moral threat, the cavalry general who knows how to use it can contribute importantly to success. He can arrest the movement of the enemy, who wonders what he will do next. He forces the enemy to assume a formation that holds him under artillery fire for some time, above all that of the light artillery if the general knows how to use it. He adds to the enemy's demoralization and can then rejoin his command.

Rifled cannons and precision rifles do not change cavalry tactics. These weapons, as the word "precision" indicates, are only effective when all the conditions of combat, all conditions for targeting and ranging, are ideal, and if they are not, their effect is impaired. Precision fire at a distance against moving troops is impossible, and movement is the essence of the cavalry. Rifled weapons fire at them of course, but they fire on everyone.

In sum, cavalry is in the same condition as anyone else.

What is the response to this argument? The infantrymen do not have to march under fire to take a position since weapons have improved? The cavalryman is not of the same flesh? Does he have less heart than the infantryman? If one can march under fire, cannot the other ride under it? When the cavalryman cannot gallop under fire, the infantryman cannot march under it. Battles will consist of exchanges of rifle fire at long range by concealed men. The battle will end only when ammunition is spent.

The cavalryman rides through danger. The infantryman marches, and that is why (if he learns, as he probably will, to keep his proper distance) the cavalryman's role will never be diminished by the perfection of long-range fire. An infantryman will never succeed alone. The cavalryman will threaten, create diversions, anxiety, scatter the enemy's fire, and even get to close quarters if he is properly supported. The infantryman will act as usual, but more than ever he will need the support of the cavalry in the attack. He who knows how to use his cavalry with audacity will inevitably be the victor. Even though the cavalryman is a larger target, long-range weapons will paralyze him no more than anyone else.

The most probable result of modern artillery will be to increase the dispersion of the infantry and even of the cavalry, who can begin in skirmisher formation at a distance and concentrate as it closes on the objective. It will be more difficult to command (but this is to the advantage of the French).

The consequence of improved ballistic weapons for the cavalry are the same for the infantry (there is no reason it should be otherwise): men will flee at a greater distance than before, and only that.

Since the Empire, opinion in the European armies is that the cavalry has not given the service expected of it, for the reason that neither we nor the others have had true cavalry generals. That is, it seems, a phenomenon that is produced every thousand years or so, more rarely than true infantry generals. To be a *good general*, infantry or cavalry, is infinitely rare, like the good of anything. The profession of the good infantry general is as difficult, perhaps even more difficult, than that of a good cavalry general. Both require composure, but it comes more easily to the cavalryman than to the foot soldier, who is more directly *engaged*. He requires steady judgment and a feeling for the moral and physical forces affecting the soldier who is more tested than the cavalryman.

The cavalry general necessarily sees less clearly. His vision has limits. Great cavalry generals are very rare, and Seydlitz[51] could not repeat his prodigies in the face of modern weapons. But there is always room for improvement; a great deal of improvement, I believe.

Under the Empire we did not have a great cavalry general who knew how to maneuver masses. The cavalry was used like a blind hammer, striking heavily and not always accurately, and it suffered immense losses. Like the Gauls, we place a little too much faith in "advance, advance, no methods." But methods do not impede the "advance." They prepare the effect and make it more certain and less costly to the attacker. We all have a little Gallic brutality. (Note Melegnano [sic],[52] where the force of artillery and the threat of a turning maneuver around a village were ignored.) What rare things are infantry and cavalry generals!

A commander must combine resolute bravery and impetuosity with prudence and composure. Difficult!

The broken terrain of European fields no longer permits, we are told, the use of long lines, of great masses of cavalry. I do not regret it. I am

---

51. Frederich Wilhelm, Baron von Seydlitz (1721-1773), Prussian general of cavalry under Frederick the Great during the Seven Years War. Credited with creating a cavalry whose tactical precision and skill equaled that of the Prussian infantry.

52. The battle of Marignano (September 13-14, 1515), French King Francis I's victory over the Swiss in the War of the League of Cambrai that led to the ejection of Swiss forces from northern Italy, a battle in which Swiss pikemen and halberdiers opposed French artillery and heavy cavalry. The last offensive campaign of the Swiss Confederation beyond its borders.

struck more by the picturesque effect of these hurricanes of cavalry in the accounts of the Empire than with the results they obtained. It does not seem that the results were commensurate with the apparent force of the effort and the real grandeur of the sacrifice. And, indeed, these enormous hammers are hard to handle; they do not possess the sure direction of a weapon well in hand. If the blow is not true, recovery is impossible, and so on. However, the terrain no longer permits the concentration of cavalry in great numbers, a compelling reason for reorganization that dispenses with all others.

Even so, other reasons given in the ministerial statement of 1868, on the cavalry service, seem excellent to me. It is certain that the *expansion of the battlefield* along with the advancement of arms, and the confidence that immediate cavalry support gives to the infantry and artillery, *require* cavalry in sufficient strength for effective action in each division.

I think, therefore, that a regiment of cavalry should be at the disposal of a division commander, and regardless of the lessons from the training centers, they cannot change my conviction of the merit of this arrangement in the field.

2. Cavalry against Cavalry

Cavalry fighting, even more than that of the infantry, is a matter of morale.

Consider first the morale of man to man cavalry combat. Two cavalrymen ride against each other. Will they steer their horses head to head? Their horses would collide, and for what? Both would be dismounted, in danger of being crushed in the crash or in the fall of their mounts. Each rider relies on his strength, on his skill, on the suppleness of his mount, on his personal bravery. Thus he does not want a blind collision, and he is right. They halt face to face, side by side, to fight man to man; or they pass each other, thrusting with saber or lance; or each tries to wound the other's leg and dismount him so. But as each strikes the other, he tries to keep out of the way himself. He does not want a blind crash that cancels out the fighting. The ancient battles, the cavalry fighting, and the rare cavalry engagements of our own time show us nothing else.

Discipline, maintaining the cavalry in ranks, has not changed the instinct of the rider. The rider in line is no more willing to meet the shock of collision than the isolated man. There is a terrible moral effect in an advancing mass; if one cannot escape to the left or right, combatants, man and horse, halt. But only the bravest troops of equally high morale, equally well led, are swept along. These conditions are never found on both sides, so it never happens. Forty-nine out of fifty times, one side will hesitate, bolt, break into disorder, and turn away from the resolution of the other. Three-fourths of the time this will happen at a distance, before they can see each other's eyes. Often they will drawn closer, but there is always the halt, the recoil, the swerving of horses, and the disarray that exposes fear and hesitation, reducing the shock and setting them to instant flight. The resolute assailant does not have to slow down; he has not been able to pass through the obstacles and uproar of enemies, attempting to turn about without being thrown into disorder himself. But this disorder is that of victory, of the "advance," and a good cavalry does not trouble itself; it rallies while advancing on, while those who have broken have fear at their heels.

But on the whole there are few losses because the engagement, if there is one, is a momentary affair. It proves that in an action of cavalry against cavalry only the defeated lose men, and he generally loses very few. Combat against infantry alone is the truly deadly struggle. Equal numbers of little chasseurs have routed heavy cavalry. How could they have done so if the others had not given way to their resolution? The question, thus and always, is *resolution*.

Cavalry losses from fire and sickness are always much less than those of the infantry. Is it because cavalry is the aristocratic arm? This explains why in long wars the cavalry improves much more than the infantry.

As there are few losses between cavalry and cavalry, so there is little fighting.

Hannibal's Numidians, the Cossacks of the Russians, inspired true terror by the alarms they raised incessantly. They exhausted themselves by killing without fighting.

Why is the cavalry handled so badly? (It is true the infantry is handled no better.) Because its role is all movement, all morale, of morale and movement together, so that movement alone without any charge or shock action is enough to drive the enemy to retreat and, if followed closely, into a rout. That is the result of the speed of the cavalry when led by one who understands.

Without exception, all writers on cavalry will tell you that the charge pushed home and the shock at top speed have never existed. Always, before the collision, the weaker turns about if there is not a face-to-face check. What then becomes of MV^2? If this famous MV^2 an empty word, why then crush your horses under giants, forgetting that in the formula besides M there is V^2. In a charge, there is M, there is V^2, there is this and that.[53] THERE IS RESOLUTION, and I believe nothing else counts.

Cohesion and unity impart force to the charge; to explain, alignment is impossible at a fast gait when the fastest pass the others. Only when the moral effect has been produced and one can fall upon a disordered enemy turning about should the gait be increased. Cuirassiers charge at a trot. This calm aplomb frightens the enemy into an about-face, and then the enemy's back is charged at a gallop.

They say that at Eckmühl,[54] for every French cuirassier who fell, fourteen Austrians were struck in the back. Was it because they had no back plate? It was because they had exposed their back to the blows.

Jomini[55] speaks of charges at a trot against cavalry at a gallop. He cites Lasalle, who used the trot and who, seeing cavalry approach at a gallop, would say, "there are lost men." Jomini insists on the effect of shock. The trot permits the compactness that the gallop breaks up. That may be true, but the effect is moral above all. A troop at the gallop sees a massed squadron advancing toward it at a trot. It is surprised at first by such coolness, by the superior *material impulsion* of the gallop, but there are no intervals, no gaps[56*] to penetrate in order to avoid the shock that overcomes men and horses. There is more openness in the attack at a gallop, and if some go on to the end, three-quarters of the enemy have already tried to avoid collision; there is complete disorder, demoralization, flight; and then begins the chase at the gallop.

---

53. An expression of kinetic energy, or the energy an object possesses by virtue of its velocity; a concept whose origin is attributed to the French mathematician Gaspart-Gustave Coriolis, whose *Théorie mathématique des effets de jeu de billard* was published as a text in 1835 in Paris by Carilian-Goeury, and thus conceivably available to Ardant du Picq while a student at Saint-Cyr.

54. The battle of Eckmühl (April 21–22, 1809), a decisive battle in the War of the Fifth Coalition, in which Archduke Charles of Austria at first took Napoleon's forces by surprise but was ultimately defeated.

55. Antoine-Henri, Baron de Jomini (1779–1869), French general whose writings on military theory and history made him the best known of all military critics in the nineteenth century. Ultimately, his prominence as a military theorist was eclipsed by the Prussian military theorist Carl von Clausewitz.

56. *Concerning gaps: at the battle of Sempach 1,300 badly armed Swiss opposed 3,000 Lorraine knights in phalanxes. The Swiss attack in formation was ineffective and they were threatened with envelopment. But Arnold von Winkelreid created a gap; the Swiss penetrated and massacre ensued.

The charge at a trot requires confidence and steadiness of the commander and soldier alike. Only the experience of combat can ensure that all have these qualities. But this charge, depending on its moral effect, will not always succeed. It is a matter of surprise. Xenophon[57] recommended the use of surprise in his advice on cavalry operations, the use of the gallop when the trot is customary, and vice-versa. "Because," he writes, "agreeable or terrible, the less a thing is foreseen, the more pleasure or fright does it cause. This is nowhere seen better than in war, where every surprise strikes terror even in the strongest."[58]*

As a general rule, the charge is made at the gallop; it makes a flashy impression, intoxicating for man and horse alike, and it is made at the distance that ensures success whatever it may cost in men and horses. That is why the regulations want the charge to begin close up, and for this reason. If the troopers waited until the *command*, they would always succeed. But the men are possessed, and because of pride and fear they charge too soon against ordinary troops and have caused more charges to fail than succeed. Keeping the men under control until the command to "charge," and seizing the precise moment for this command, are both difficult and fleeting, demanding an energetic leader and a keen eye when three out of four men no longer see anything. Good cavalry leaders, good squadron leaders, in general are very rare. Real charges are just as rare.

Genuine shock no longer exists. The moral impulsion of one of the adversaries in advancing always overturns the other, perhaps from afar, perhaps a little closer, and if "a little closer," one of the two troops would already be defeated before the first saber cut and would break up to escape. With genuine shock, all would be thrown into disarray. A real charge by one or the other would cause mutual extermination, and in practice the victor hardly loses anyone.

Observation alone demonstrates that cavalry does not close with cavalry; its lethal fights are only those against the infantry.

Even if one waits firmly, the horse will always want to escape, to avoid the collision. If the trooper goes too soon, so does the horse. Why did Frederick like to see his center close ranks before the assault? As the best guarantee against the instincts of man and horse.

---

57. Xenophon (ca. 430 B.C.–350 B.C.), generally regarded as one of the first historians; renowned for his many works depicting ancient Greece. His *Anabasis* (The March Up Country), recording the long retreat home of Greek mercenaries after their defeat by the forces of the Persian King Artaxerxes II at Cunaxa, is one of the early classic works of military history.

58. *See Appendix II.

Frederick's cavalry ordinarily had only insignificant losses, the effect of resolution.

Man always wants to be distracted from approaching danger by movement. If left to themselves, cavalrymen who go at the enemy would begin at the gallop for fear of not arriving, or arriving exhausted (subject to carnage, as what happened with the Arabs in 1864 against General Martineau's cavalry[59]). Rapid movement dispels anxiety; it is natural to wish to reduce it. But the leaders are present; their experience and the regulations require advancing slowly, then to accelerate progressively so as to arrive at maximum speed: the walk, then the trot, then the gallop, then the charge. But it takes a sharp eye to estimate the distance, the nature of the terrain, and, if the enemy approaches, the point at which to meet them. The nearer the approach, the greater the pressure on morale in the ranks. The question of how to arrive at the moment of maximum speed is not only a mechanical one, since indeed one never collides. It is a moral question. One must sense the exact moment when the men's anxiety requires the intoxication of a headlong, charging gallop. An instant too late, anxiety takes the rein to act on the horses; the start is not clean, some evade by staying behind. An instant too soon, the speed of the charge, the animation, the intoxication of the charge, are exhausted. Anxiety takes the reins again, the hands act instinctively, and even if the start was unimpeded, the arrival is not.

Frederick and Seydlitz were content when they saw the center of the charging squadron three and four ranks deep; it was as if they understood that with this compressed center the leading lines could not escape to the left or right and were forced to continue straight ahead.

To advance in a rush like battering rams, even against infantry, both men and horses should be watered and fresh (consider Ponsonby's[60] cavalry at Waterloo). If there is contact between cavalries, the shock is so reduced by the hands of men, the rearing of horses, the swinging of heads, that both sides come to a halt face to face.

The gallop is certainly necessary to carry man and horse to the supreme moment before attacking the enemy, before putting him to flight.

---

59. Émile-Philippe Martineau des Chesnez (1819–1884), French officer commanding the *Chasseurs d'Afrique* in Algeria who later became a general officer commanding the 6th Division in the Franco-Prussian War.

60. Major General Sir William Ponsonby (1772–1815), British general, veteran of the Peninsular campaign who commanded the Union Brigade at the battle of Waterloo; killed by French lancers when he and his dragoons outran their charge against the French.

Charges at the gallop of three or four kilometers presume one has horses of bronze.

Because morale is not studied, and because historical narratives are always taken literally, every age complains that cavalries are no longer seen charging and fighting with the sword, that too much caution dictates running away instead of directly engaging the enemy.

These complaints have been made ever since the Empire, both by us and the Allies. But this has always been true. Man was never invulnerable. The charging gait has almost always been the trot. Man does not change. Even the combats of today are more lethal than in the lamented days of chivalry.

The retreat of the infantry is always more difficult than that of the cavalry; that is simple. A cavalry repulsed, returning in disorder, is a predictable, almost ordinary event. It rallies at a distance; it often reappears with advantage. One can almost say that experience shows that is its role. An infantry that is repulsed, especially if the action has been heavy and the cavalry rushes in, is often disorganized for the rest of the day.

Even authors who say that two squadrons never collide will tell you continually: the force of the cavalry is in the shock. In the terror of the shock, yes. In the shock, no. It lies only in resolution. It is a mental and not a mechanical affair.

Never give cavalry officers and men mathematical demonstrations of the charge. They are good only to shake confidence, because mathematical reasoning shows that mutual shock never happens. Show them the truth. Lasalle[61] with his always-victorious charge at the trot guarded against similar reasoning, which might have shown him mathematically that a charge of cuirassiers at a trot could be routed by a charge of hussars at the gallop. He simply told them: "Go resolutely and be sure that you will never find a daredevil sufficiently determined to engage you." It is necessary to be a daredevil to go all the way to the end. The Frenchman is one above all, because he is a good trooper in combat, and when his commanders are themselves daredevils he is the best in Europe. (Note the remarks of Wellington, a good judge.) And if his commanders use their heads, no harm is done. The formula of the cavalry is R (Resolution) and R, and always R, and R is greater than all the MV^2 in the world.

---

61. Antoine-Charles-Louis, Comte de Lasalle (1775-1809), French cavalry commander, known for his dashing successes in the Napoleonic wars from the Peninsular campaign until his death in the battle of Wagram. Known in the French army as the "Hussar general."

An important aspect of the pursuit of cavalry by cavalry: the pursued cannot halt without handing himself to his pursuer. The pursuer can always see the pursued, and if the latter stops and tries to come about the pursuer can take him by surprise first. If he alone stops, two pursuers may rush him, for they see ahead and naturally attack whoever tries to come about. With an about-face, danger confronts the pursuer once more, and the pursuit is often motivated by the fear that the enemy will turn about. The important fact that, once in flight all together, the enemy cannot come about without risking surprise and being overtaken makes the flight continuous. Even the bravest flee until they put some sufficient distance between them and the enemy, or some other circumstance such as cover or supporting troops permits a rally and return to the advance. In this case, the pursuit may turn into a flight.

This is why all cavalry insists on attacking on an equal front, because if with a broad front the enemy gives way, the wings may attack it and make it the pursued instead of the pursuer. The moral effect of resolution is so great that the cavalry, breaking and pursuing a more numerous enemy, is never surprised by enemy wings. However, the idea that one may be taken from behind by forces whom one has left on the flanks so affects the resolve that the impulse for an attack under these conditions is rare.

Why does Colonel A_____, who believes in the pressure of the rear ranks on the first, not want a deep formation for cavalry? It is because he really believes that only the first rank can act in a cavalry charge, and that this rank is not pushed, or speeded up, by those from behind.

There is a debate about the advantage of one or two ranks for the cavalry. Again, this is a matter of morale. Let there be freedom to choose, and under varying circumstances of confidence and morale, one or the other will be adopted. There are enough officers for either formation.

The cavalry tends to advance farther than the infantry and as a result it exposes its flanks all the more. The cavalry thus needs more reserves to cover its flanks than infantry does. It needs to protect its pursuit and support it because it is almost always attacked on its return. Even more than with infantry, victory belongs to those whose last reserves remain intact. Those with reserves are always able to take the offensive. Adhere to that, and no one can stand before you.

With enough space, the cavalry can rally quickly. In deep columns, it cannot.

The engagement of cavalry lasts only an instant; it must be reformed quickly. With a roll call after each sortie, it escapes control of the commander less than with the infantry, which once engaged has little respite. There should be a roll call for cavalry and for infantry after every advance, at each pause. There should be roll calls at drill and on field maneuvers, not that they are necessary but in order to become accustomed to them. Then the roll call will not be forgotten on the day of action, when very few think what should be done.

In the tumult and speed of cavalry action, man slips loose from observation more easily. In our battles, his action quickly becomes separate and rapid. The cavalryman should not be left to himself too much because it is dangerous. Troops in action should be frequently reformed and called to roll. It would be a mistake not to do so. There might be ten to twenty roll calls a day. The officers and soldiers would then have a chance to demand an accounting from each, and they might demand it the next day.

Infantry today, once in action (and the action lasts), slip away from the control of their officers. This is because of the inherent disorder of battle, because of the lack of roll calls, which cannot be held while in action. Thus, control can only be in the hands of his comrades. The infantry in modern war has the greatest need for cohesion.

The cavalry always fights poorly and very little. This has been true from antiquity, when the cavalryman was of superior caste and ought to have been braver.

All troops, cavalry or infantry, should scout and reconnoiter as soon as possible the terrain on which it will act. Condé forgot this at Neerwinden.[62] The 55th forgot it at Solferino.[63]* Everyone forgets it. And from the failure to use skirmishers and scouts comes mistakes and disasters.

The cavalry has a rifle for special service. Take care that this exception does not become the rule. We have seen at the battle of Sicka,[64] after the first encounter was spoiled by a lack of dash by a regiment of the *Chasseurs d'Afrique*, who, after departing at the gallop, paused to shoot. In the second attack, General Bugeaud himself took the lead to show them how to charge.

---

62. The battle of Neerwinden (March 18, 1793), fought during the War of the First Coalition, in which French revolutionary forces commanded by Charles Dumouriez were defeated by Allied forces under the command of Prince Coburg. General Dumouriez's subsequent defection to Austria prompted the French republicans to impose strict political control and draconian penalties on generals who were found wanting in the field.

63. *See Appendix II.

64. The battle of Sikkak (June 6, 1836), Abd-el-Kadir's first, disastrous attempt to meet General Bugeaud's French regulars on equal terms of orthodox warfare. After this defeat, Abd-el-Kadir resorted to hit-and-run attacks; over the next five years, this approach largely succeeded in confining French forces to coastal Algeria.

A young colonel of light cavalry asked for rifles. Why? Because I can reconnoiter the village from afar (700 or 800 meters) without losing anyone. Most decidedly, the carbine makes everyone lose common sense.

The role of the light cavalry means that sometimes they will be captured. One cannot get news of the enemy without getting close to him. If one man in a patrol escapes, that is sufficient; even that fact is instructive. The cavalry is valuable and no commander wants to break it, but it is only by breaking it that he can get results.

Some authors think that the role of the cavalry is to skirmish or to fight dismounted. So they advance by holding the bridle? This is absurd. If the cavalryman fires, he will not advance. The African incident proves that. Better to give the cavalryman two pistols than a carbine.

The Americans, in their vast country, used cavalry wisely by sending it on distant forays to cut communications, raise resources, and so on. What role their cavalry had in battle is not known. The cavalry raids in the American war were a war against wealth, public works, a war of destruction against riches, not of men, and one that entailed few losses and caused few. The cavalry is always the aristocratic arm that loses little, even if it risks much. At least it seems to risk all, which is something. It must have daring, and daring is not so common. But the most insignificant infantry engagements in equal numbers cost more than the most brilliant cavalry raids.

3. Cavalry against Infantry

Cavalry knows how to fight cavalry, but how it fights infantry is something not one cavalry officer in a thousand knows. Perhaps not even one. They go forward happily, in complete ignorance.

A military man, a veteran of our great wars, recommends a charge against the infantry's flank, horse after horse, as infallible. The cavalry would make contact on the left, ride around to the front, and come about so as to strike from the right. This cavalryman is right; such charges should produce excellent results, because the cavalry can only strike to the right, and in this way every cavalryman can strike. Against ancient infantry such charges would have been as effective as our own. This officer saw with his own eyes excellent examples in the wars of the Empire, and I do not doubt either his facts or his deductions from them. But for such charges there must be officers who inspire absolute confidence and dependable, experienced soldiers. There must be an excellent cavalry, composed of veterans of long wars, officers and men of firm resolution. So it is not surprising that examples of this sort of action are very rare. They always will be. They need a single leader for a charge, and when they are about to make contact, the leader falls back into the formation, thinking that there is more safety in the mass than in acting alone. Everyone is willing to charge but only if everyone does. It is a matter of belling the cat.

The attack in column on infantry has a greater moral effect than a charge in line. If the first and second lines have been repulsed, but the infantry sees a third line charging through the dust, they will wonder, "When is this going to stop?" And they will be shaken.

An excerpt from Folard: "Only a capable officer is needed to get the best results from a cavalry that has confidence in its movement, which is known to be good and vigorous, and also is equipped with excellent weapons. Such cavalry will break the strongest battalions, if its leader has sense enough to know its power and courage enough to use this power."

Breaking is insufficient, and it is a feat that is far too costly unless the whole battalion is killed or taken prisoner, or, at least, if the cavalry is not followed by other troops assigned to this task.

At Krasno, August 14, 1812, Murat, at the head of his cavalry, could not break an isolated body of 10,000 Russian infantry who kept him at bay with fire. He retired peacefully across the plain.[65]

The 72nd was upset by cavalry at Solferino.

Since antiquity, the lone infantryman has had the advantage over the lone cavalryman. There isn't the shadow of a doubt in ancient narratives. The cavalry fought only the cavalry. He threatened, harassed, and troubled the infantry, but he did not fight him. He slaughtered him when he was put to flight by other infantrymen, or at least scattered him so the light infantry could slaughter him.

The cavalry, in the hands of someone who knows how to use it, is a terrible accessory. Who can say that Epaminondas, without the Thessalonian cavalry, would have defeated the Spartans three times?

Gradually, rifle and cannon fire deafen the soldier, fatigue overcomes him, he is rendered inert, and he no longer heeds commands. If enemy cavalry arrives unexpectedly, he is lost. Cavalry conquers merely by appearing. (Bismarck or Decker.)

---

65. One of several engagements following Napoleon's crossing of the Dneiper River as a prelude to the capture of Smolensk during the invasion of Russia. Not to be confused with the later battle of Krasnoi on November 18-21, during Napoleon's retreat from Moscow.

Modern cavalry, like ancient cavalry, has a real effect, but only on troops already broken, on infantry engaged with infantry, or on cavalry disorganized by artillery fire or frontal demonstration. In these circumstances, their action is certain to produce great results. You may fight all day and lose 10,000 men, and the enemy just as many, but if your cavalry pursues, you may take 30,000 prisoners. The cavalry's role is less chivalric than its reputation and appearance, less so than the infantry. It always suffers fewer losses. Its greatest effect is the effect of surprise, and that is how it achieves such astonishing results.

What formation should infantry, armed with modern weapons, adopt to guard against flank attacks by the cavalry? If one fires four times as fast, and if that fire is sustained, one needs only a quarter as many men to defend a position against cavalry. Defense might be secured by placing small groups of men a rifle shot apart on the flanks. But these troops must be dependable, free of concern about what goes on behind them.

4. Armor and Armaments

The need for armored cavalry is demonstrated by moral observation.

Concerning cuirassiers and morale: at the battle of Renet [Renty] in 1554, Tavannes, a marshal, had with him an armored company, the first ever seen. Supported by several hundred fugitives who had rallied, he placed himself at the head of his company and threw himself on a column of 2,000 German cavalry who had just broken the infantry and cavalry. He chose his time so well that he broke and carried away these 2,000 Germans, who fell back, and broke the 1,200 light horsemen supporting them. A general flight ensued, the battle won.

"The decadence of the cavalry," General Renard[66] says, "led to the disappearance of the square battle formation of the seventeenth century." It was not the decadence of the cavalry, but the development of rapid fire infantry weapons. When cuirassiers break through, they serve as examples, and others emulate them and try once more to break through themselves.

Why cuirassiers? Because they alone, now and always, charge to the very end.

---

66. Bruno Renard (1804–1879), Belgian army lieutenant general and military historian. Author of *Considérations sur la tactique de l'infanterie en Europe* (Paris: J. Dumaine, 1857).

The cuirassiers need only half the courage of dragoons to charge to the end, because the armor increases their morale by one-half. But as the cuirassiers have as much natural courage as the light infantry (for they are men all the same), is it proper to expect more from them?

One kind of cavalry only? Which? If all our men could wear the cuirass and at the same time do the fatiguing work of the light cavalry, if all our horses could carry the cuirasses, I would say there should be only cuirassiers. But I do not understand why morale should be lightly discarded so as to have only one cavalry with the cuirass.

A cavalryman fully armored, and his horse partly so, can charge only at a trot.

General Ambert once wrote that cavalry covered itself with masses of armor rather more like anvils than cuirasses, and in those days it was the essential arm. Heart, spirit, and speed have a value beyond that of mass. (I leave aside mathematical theories that seem to me to have little to do with matters of combat.) I would choose the best men in the army to wear the cuirass, big-chested, red-blooded, strong and fast, a *foot cavalry*, and I would form a regiment of light chasseurs for each of our divisions. Man and horse, these regiments would be more robust and active than our present cuirassiers. If our armored cavalry is worth more than any other army's because of its aggressiveness, this cavalry would be worth twice as much. It is objected: "How would these men of small stature get into the saddle?" I would reply, "They will manage." This objection, which I do not accept, is the only one that can be made against the organization of a light armored cavalry, a formation made essential by the advancement of firearms. The remaining men in the chasseur battalions should then return to the infantry, which has long wanted to reclaim them, and the hussars and dragoons dismounted as required would also be well received.

Concerning the sword thrust: it is more deadly than the cut. You do not have to lift your arm; you plunge. But the cavalryman must be persuaded by his officers that in their experience (when, in peacetime?) parrying a vertical cut is tricky. This is not easy. But in this as in much else the advantage goes to the brave. A cavalry charge is above all a matter of morale; in its methods, its effects, it is the same with an infantry charge. All the stages of a charge (the walk, trot, gallop, charge, and so on) have a basis in morale, for reasons already advanced.

Roman discipline and character demanded tenacity. The ability to endure fatigue, a good organization ensuring support, produced that tenacity against which the bravest could not stand. The Gaul's exhausting fencing and great sweeps of the sword could not last long against the Romans' skilled and less tiring thrusting.

The Siks [Sikhs] of M. Nolan[67] (armed with dragoon sabers they sharpened themselves) preferred the cut. They knew nothing of fencing and they did not train. They said a good saber and a willingness to use it was enough. True, true.

There is always a question about the lance and the saber. The lance requires cavalrymen of skill and vigor, together with a steady mount, and good training, because fencing with a lance is more difficult than with a sword, especially when it is not so heavy. Is not this the answer to the question? No matter what is done, no matter what method is used, one should always remember that our wartime recruits are sent into squadrons as into battalion with hasty, incomplete training, and if you give them lances most of them will just have sticks in their hands, whereas a straight sword at the end of a strong arm is both simple and terrible. A short trident spear, with three short points just long enough to kill but not to go through the body, would remain in the body of a man and carry him along. The cavalryman who delivered the blow would recoil; he would be upset by the blow itself. But the dragoon must be supported by the saddle, and as he held the shaft he would not be able to disengage the fork that has pierced the body some six inches. No cavalry of equal morale could stand against a cavalry armed with such forked spears.

For beginners in mounted fencing, as between forks and lances, *the fork would replace the lance*. But the fork!!! It would be *ridiculous, not military*!!!

With the lance one always calculates without the horse, whose slightest movement diverts the lance just so much. The lance is an arm frightful even to the mounted man who uses it properly. If he spears an enemy at the gallop he is dismounted if he continues to hold the lance now in the body of the enemy.

Cavalry officers and others who look for examples in *Victories and Conquests*, in official reports, in Bazancourt,[68] are too naïve (hard to get at the

---

67. Captain Lewis Edward Nolan (1818–1854), British army officer, riding master, author of the highly regarded *Cavalry: Its History and Its Tactics* (London: Thomas Bosworth, 1854); remembered now as the officer who conveyed the order that launched the Charge of the Light Brigade at Balaclava during the Crimean War. Nolan was the first casualty of that charge.

68. César Lecat Bazancourt (1810–1865), French novelist and historian. Author of *The Expedition to the Crimea to the Capture of Sevastopol–Chronicles of the War in the East* (Paris: Amyot, 1856) and *The Italian Campaign, 1859: Chronicles of the War* (Paris: Amyot, 1860).

truth). In all these matters of war, we accept the last example we have seen, and now we want lances that we do not know how to use, which frighten the cavalryman himself, and pluck him from the saddle if he spears anyone. We want no more cuirasses, we want this and that, and we forget that the last example offers only a limited number of instances that relate to the matter in question.

According to Xenophon, it appears that it was not easy to throw the dart from horseback, and he recommends obtaining as many men as possible who know how. He recommends leaning well back to keep from falling from the horse in the charge. On reading Xenophon, it appears there was much falling from the horse.

It is clear that the use of a saber in combat is as difficult as that of the bayonet. The handling of the musket is also difficult (isn't this seen in the use of the regulation arms by the Spahis?). There is only one serious thing for the cavalryman: a good seat. He should be mounted for hours at a time every day, as soon as he joins the formation. If men who knew horses were drafted, and if they were made cavalrymen, the practical training of most of them could be quickly done. I do not mean the routines of the stable. Drills on foot, between periods of mounted drill, could be done briskly, freely, without pedantry, faster every day. Such drills would train cavalrymen much more quickly than today's methods.

A dragoon horse on campaign carries one day's food of 308 pounds; without food or forage, 277 pounds. How can such horses carry this and be fast?

Always look at the end, not the means. Make a quarter of your cavaliers into muleteers, a quarter of your horses into pack animals. That way you will secure for the remaining three-quarters unquestioned vigor. But how will you make up these pack trains? You will have plenty of wounded horses after a week of campaign.

IV

Artillery

If artillery had no greater range than the rifle, we could not risk separating them so far from their support, as it would have to wait until the enemy was only 400 or 500 paces to fire. But with its increase in range, supports can be placed farther away.

With longer ranges of modern artillery, and the greater freedom of movement among all arms, they need not be positioned side by side for mutual support.

The greater the artillery range, the easier it is to concentrate fire. Two batteries 1,500 meters apart can concentrate on a target 1,200 meters in front and between them. Formerly, they had to be too close together and the terrain did not always permit concentration.

Too, do not position artillery immediately behind or to the side of the infantry, as is done three-fourths of the time in training maneuvers. Instead, conceal the infantry on the left or right well behind without worrying too much, and let the artillery call for support if the gun is in danger. Why should infantry be placed too close, and as a result demoralized, forfeiting the greatest advantage we French have in defense—defending ourselves by advancing, with morale intact—because we always take losses when we halt. There is always time to come to the aid of the guns, and skirmishers can be quickly moved between them. The skirmishers between the guns will have nothing to fear from enemy cavalry, and even being engaged by their infantry would not be so terrible. The skirmishers can take cover behind the guns and fire at an enemy approaching in the open.

Guilbert, I believe, said that artillery should not worry whether it was supported, that it should fire up to the last moment, then abandon the guns, which supporting troops may or may not recapture. The supporting troops should not be too close. It is easier to defend guns, even to take them back, by advancing on an enemy scattered among them, better than defending them by standing fast and sharing in the artillery's casualties. (Note the English in Spain; the absurdity of artillery with infantry platoons in train.)

Artillery in battle has men group around fixed rally points, the guns, dispersed, each with its own commander and cannoneers, who are always the same. Thus, there is a roll call each time the guns form as a battery. Artillery carries its men along; they cannot straggle or slip away. If the officer is brave, his men rarely desert him. In all armies, it is certainly in the artillery that the soldier can best do his duty.

As General Leboeuf tells us, four batteries of artillery can be maneuvered, not more. Here it is exactly: four battalions is enough command for a colonel; a general has eight battalions. He receives orders: "General, do so and so." He orders: "Colonel, do so and so." So in the absence of regulations for exercises of more than four battalions, you can exercise and drill as many as you like.

V

Command, General Staff, and Administration

There is no lack of carefree generals who are never worried or harassed. They are never bothered about anything: "I advance. Follow me," and off the columns march in incredible disorder. Were ten raiders to fall shouting upon the column, this disorder would dissolve into a rout, a disaster. But these gentlemen never contemplate such an eventuality. They are lucky. They are the great men of the day—until the instant some disaster overtakes them.

It is no more difficult to work with cavalry than with infantry. Some military writers think a cavalry general should have the wisdom of the phoenix. The perfect one should; so should the perfect infantry general. Man on horse or foot is always the same. But the infantry general rarely has to account for his casualties, which may have been because of faulty or improper handling. The cavalry general does. (Why? We shall leave aside the reasons.) The infantry general has six chances for real fighting to every one for the cavalry general. There are two reasons why, at the commencement of a war, more initiative is found in infantry than cavalry generals. General Bugeaud may have made a better cavalry general than an infantry general. Why? Because he was decisive and resolute. The resolution of the infantryman needs to be firmer than that of the cavalryman. (Why? Numerous reasons, mostly prejudice.)

In sum, the morale of the infantryman is always more fatigued than that of the cavalryman; and I think that a good infantry general is rarer than one of cavalry. Moreover, the resolution of an infantry general must last longer than only a moment; it must last for a long, long time.

Good artillery generals are common. Why? They are less concerned with morale than with materiel. They have less need to concern themselves with the morale of their troops, because *combat* discipline is better among them than in the other arms (which is demonstrated elsewhere).

Brigadier generals should be in their prescribed places, etc., etc. Very good, but most of them are not and never are. They were required to be in their places at the battle of Moscow, but, as they had to be ordered there, it is clear they were not accustomed to it. They are men, and their rank, it seems to them, should reduce rather than increase their risk. And so, in the action of an engagement, where should they be?

When one holds a high rank, general-in-chief, even division commander, a great deal of activity escapes him, and only a strict conscientiousness aided by perceptiveness will allow him to avoid this handicap. It extends to those about him, to his chiefs of service. These gentlemen live well, sleep well; surely, this is true of everyone! They have picked well-bred horses; the roads are excellent! They are never sick; the doctors must be exaggerating sickness. Something happened because of monstrous negligence, as we often see in war. With a good heart and a full belly, they exclaim, "But this is a shame! It cannot be! It is impossible!" And so on.

Today there is a tendency whose cause must be sought, a tendency that is of ancient vintage, which is aided by the *mania of command,* inherent in the French character, of encroachment from top to bottom by the commander on his subordinates. The result is the diminishing of the subordinate officers' authority in the minds of their soldiers. This is a grave matter, because only by firm authority and prestige can subordinate officers maintain discipline. The tendency is to oppress subordinates, to impose upon them in all matters the views of the superior; not to admit honest mistakes; to reprove them as faults; to make everyone down to the lowest private feel there is only one infallible authority. A colonel, for instance, sets himself up as the sole authority possessed of judgment and intellect. Thus, he erases all initiative from his subordinates and reduces them to a state of inertia owing to their lack of self-confidence and fear of being reproved. How many generals before a regiment think only of showing how much they know? With cheeks puffed out, they depart, proud of having . . . attacked discipline.

The firm hand that directs so much disappears in an instant. All subordinate officers up to this moment have been held with too strong a hand, which has detained them in a position that is not natural to them. All at once, they are like a horse always held on a tight rein, whose rein is loosened or missing. They cannot in an instance recover that self-confidence that has been gradually taken away from them without their wishing it. In such a moment, the situation becomes difficult, and the soldier very quickly senses that the hand that holds him vacillates.

A false principle: "Ask much to obtain little." A source of mistakes, an attack on discipline. One ought to obtain what one asks. It is only necessary to be reasonable and practical.

To continue, one is astonished by the lack of foresight in three out of four officers. Why? Is there anything so difficult about looking forward a little? Are three-quarters of the officers therefore more beast than thinker? No! Their egotism, often frankly acknowledged, allows them to think only of who is looking at them. Perhaps they think of their troops by chance, or when they have to. Their troops are never their preoccupation, and so they do not think of them at all. A major in command of a unit in Mexico, on his first march in an arid country, began without full canteens, perhaps with no canteens at all, without any provisions for water, as one might do in France. No officer in his battalion called this omission to his attention, nor was more foresighted. In this first march, because of his complete lack of foresight, half of his command died. What he demoted? No! He was made a lieutenant colonel.

Officers of the general staff learn to *order*, not to command. "Sir, I order," a popular phrase, is customary to them.

The bad luck is not that there is a general staff but that it has achieved command, for it has *always commanded* for the commander, it is true, and never obeyed, which is its duty. It commands in fact, so be it! But all the same it is not supposed to.

Is it the quality of the general staff or of the combatants that makes armies? If you want good soldiers, do everything to excite their ambition for improvement, so that intelligent people with a future will not disdain the line and elect to serve in it. The line gives you high command, the line only, and very rarely the staff. However, the staff does not die very often, and that is something. Do they say that military science can only be learned in the general staff schools? If you really want to master your profession, enter the line.

Today, no one knows anything unless he knows how to show off, to banter. A peasant knows nothing. He cannot even cultivate the soil, but the agriculturist from the bureau is a farmer emeritus, and so on. In the same way, is it then believed that there is ability only in the general staff? There we find the aplomb of the scholar, of the pedagogue who has never practiced the science in the books (false science when it concerns matters of war).

But knowledge of the profession, real knowledge? No. Knowledge of the regulations? Yes. Knowledge of the possible? No. Knowledge of fighting? No.

Slower promotion in the general staff as compared to the line might make many men of intelligence, of head and heart, pass the general staff by and enter the line to make their own way. To be in the line would not then be a brevet of imbecility. But today when general staff officers rank the best of the line officers, the latter are discouraged and, rather than submit to this, all who feel themselves fitted for advancement want to be on the general staff. So much the better? So much the worse. Promotion is warranted only by battle.

How administrative illusions, in politics or elsewhere, falsify conclusions drawn from fact!

In the Crimea, 100 percent of the French operated upon succumbed, while only 27 percent of the English died. That was attributed to the difference in temperament! The great cause of this discrepancy was the difference in medical care. In the Crimea, our newspapers accepted the self-satisfied and self-glorified statements provided by our own command, which showed the sick being treated by the Sisters of Charity. The fact is that our soldiers had neither sheets, nor mattresses, nor changes of clothes in the hospitals; that three-quarters or more lay on moldy straw on the ground in tents. The fact is that such were the circumstances under which our sick were infected, some 25,000 to 30,000, with typhus after the siege; that thousands of pieces of medical equipment were offered by the English to our quartermaster-general, which he refused. Everyone *knew he would refuse.* To accept this equipment was to admit he did not have it, as he should have. Indeed, according to newspaper and quartermaster reports, he did have it. He had twenty-five beds per hospital, so he could say, "We have beds!" (The hospitals each have 500 or more patients.)

These gentlemen are annoyed if they are called Jesuits. While our soldiers were in hospitals with nothing at all, so to speak, the English sick had large tents, well ventilated, cots, sheets, even nightstands with bedpans. And ours had not even a drinking cup! People were healed in the English hospitals. They might have been in ours, before they died—which they usually did.

It is true that we had typhus and the English did not. That is why our men, in tents, had the same care as in our hospitals, and the English the same care as in their hospitals.

Read the war reports of our quartermaster and then go without warning to verify them *in the hospitals* and the magazines. Have them verified by summoning and questioning the heads of department, but question them carefully, without dictating the answers. In the Crimea, in May of the first year, our men were no better than the English who complained so much. Who has dared to reveal that from the time they entered the hospital to the time they left—dead, wounded, or cured—through fifteen days of cholera or typhus, our men lay on the same planks, *in the same shoes, the same underwear, shirts, and clothing* they arrived with? Living putrefaction, itself enough to kill healthy men. The newspapers sang the praises of the admirable French command. In the second winter, the English *had no sick,* fewer than in London. But to the eternal shame of the most perfect command in the world, and that of our generals, no less than our administration, all were full of devoted solicitude to meet the needs of the soldier. That is an infamous lie and known as such, we hope.

The Americans have set an example: the good citizens have gone themselves to see how their soldiers were treated and provided for them on their own. When, in France, will good citizens lose their faith in the army's management, the best in the world? When will they, confident, do spontaneously, freely, what this management cannot and never will do?

The first thing to fall apart in an army is its administration. The simplest foresight, the least sign of order, disappears in a retreat. (Russia-Vilna.)

In the Crimea and more or less everywhere, the doctor's visit was without benefit to the sick. It was to keep up his spirits, but it could not be followed by care because of the lack of personnel and resources. After two or three hours of rounds, the doctor was exhausted.

The aid stations of a sane country should be able to care for one-fifth of the army's strength at the least. Today's hospital staff should be doubled. It is quickly worn down, and it should have time not only to visit the sick but also to care for them, feed them, treat and dress them, and so on.

VI

Social and Military Institutions; National Characteristics

The admiration of man for the great spectacles of nature is the admiration of force. In the mountains it is mass, a force, that impresses him, strikes him, makes him admire. In the calm sea, it is the mysterious, terrible force that he perceives, that he senses in this enormous mass of liquid; in the angry sea, force again. In the wind, the storm, the vast depth of the sky, it is again the force.

All these astounded man when he was young. He has now grown old, he knows them. Astonishment is now admiration, but it is always the sense of formidable force that compels his admiration. The admiration for the warrior is. . . .

The ideal of the primitive man, of the savage, of the barbarian, is the warrior. The higher people rise in moral civilization, the more this ideal recedes, but with the public everywhere the warrior is and for a long time will be the ideal. It is because man loves his own force and valor. When that force and valor find other means of expression, or at least when the public is shown that war does not offer their best examples, that there are truer and more elevated exemplars, this ideal will give its place to a higher one.

Nations and states are alike in their sovereignty by virtue of their existence, recognize no superior jurisdiction, and call upon force to adjudicate their differences. Force alone decides, not whether might was right, but as the weaker bows to necessity until the next round (Prudhomme[69]*). Gregory VII's[70]* conception is very easy to see here.

Armies are toys (in peace) in the hands of princes. If princes know nothing of them, which is the usual way, they disorganize them. If they do understand them, like Prussia, they prepare their armies for war.

The Prussian aristocracy and the king of Prussia, feeling overwhelmed by democracy, have replaced the popular passion for equality among their people with a passion for domination over other nations; easily done when crowned by success, for man is merely a friend of equality but a lover of domination. He is easily persuaded to take the shadow for the substance. They have successes, and they are forced to perpetuate their system for fear of being dismissed as useful members of society and as mere warlords. Peace is the death of the nobility, and nobles do not want it; they foment rivalries among nations, rivalries that alone justify their existence as war leaders (and later in peace). This is why the military spirit is dead in France. The past cannot be resurrected. In the spiritual as well as the physical world, what is dead is dead. Death comes only with the exhaustion of the elements, the conditions that are necessary for life. This is why the war with Prussia is the continuation of the Revolutionary wars. This is why, if we were winning, we would find arrayed against us the aristocracies of Austria, Russia, and England. But as we are defeated, democracy spreads throughout Europe, protected by the security that victory awards to the victors. This process is slower but surer than the quick work of war, which slows only for a moment the spread of democracy within the countries themselves. Democracy then does her work with less chance of being deterred by the rivalry between us. Thus we are nearer to the triumph of democracy than if we had been the victors. French democracy wants to live and is right to do so, and she does not want to do so at the expense of national pride. Because she will be surrounded for a long time by societies dominated by the military, by the nobility, she must have a dependable army. And as the military spirit in France is waning, it must be replaced by well-paid noncommissioned and commissioned officers. Good pay establishes position in a democracy, and

69. *Louis-Marie Prudhomme (1752-1830), a well-known French journalist and historian of his day; a Royalist, he was jailed several times for his opposition to the Revolution and criticism of Napoleon. Among his several works, in 1799, he published a two-volume list of names known to him who were executed during the Reign of Terror.

70. *Gregory VII (1025-1085), one of the leading popes in the medieval church, who instituted a broad range of reforms aimed at asserting papal supremacy over the secular political world of his day.

today no one turns to the army because it is poorly paid. Let us have well-paid mercenaries. With good pay good men can be secured, thanks to the old warrior strain in the race. This sacrifice is necessary for our security.

The soldier, in our century, is a merchant: this much of my flesh, of my blood, is worth so much. So much of my time, so much of my affections, etc. It is a noble profession, however, perhaps because man's blood is noble merchandise, the noblest of transactions.

M. Guizot[71] says, "Get rich!" That may seem cynical *to prudes* but it is true. Those who reject it and today speak so condescendingly, what do they advise? If not by words, they counsel the same thing, and example is more contagious. Is not individual wealth, but wealth in general, the avowed goal of all, democrats and others? Let us be rich; that is to say, let us be slaves to the needs that wealth creates, and so on. . . .

The Invalides[72] in France are superb exhibits of pomp and ostentation. I wish that their founding had been based on ideas of justice and Christianity and not purely on military-political considerations, but the results are disastrous to morality. This collection of weaklings is a school of depravity, where the invalided soldier loses in vice his right to respect.

Some officers want to transform the regiments into permanent schools for officers of all ranks: two hours a day on legislation, the military art, and so on. There is little taste for military life in France, and this would lessen it. The leisure of army life attracts three out of four officers, laziness if you like. This is the objective fact. If you make an officer into a schoolboy all his life he will send his profession to the devil if he can, and those who can will generally be those who have received the best education. An army is a monstrous thing, but as it is necessary there should be no surprise that extraordinary steps must be taken to maintain it, such as offering in peacetime little work and a great deal of leisure. An officer is a kind of aristocrat, and in France we have no finer ideal of aristocratic life than one of leisure. That is not proof of the highest ideals or of the firmest character, but what is to be done?

It does not follow that, because the military spirit is lacking in our nation (and officers are more difficult than ever to recruit in France), we will not have to go to war. Perhaps the opposite is true.

---

71. Francois Pierre Guillaume Guizot (1787–1874), politician and historian; foreign minister and prime minister of France under Louis Philippe. Perhaps best known today for the exhortation du Picq quotes above.

72. *Hôpital des Invalides*, a retirement home in Paris for veterans and hospital for wounded soldiers.

Is it not patriotic to say this? The truth is always patriotic. The military spirit died with the French aristocracy in 1789, died because it had to, because it was exhausted, at the end of its life. That which dies no longer has the spark of life. Those who are merely sick can return to health. But can that be said of the French nobility? An aristocracy that dies, dies always by its own fault, because it no longer does its duty, because it fails, because its functions are no longer of any value to the state, because there is no longer any reason for its existence in a society intent on suppressing its functions.

After 1789, with patriotism menaced, the natural feeling for self-protection revived the military spirit in our army and in our nation. The Empire advanced this sentiment and made the defensive military spirit into one of offense and used it with greater effect until 1814 or 1815. The military spirit of the July Revolution was an act of nostalgia, a relic of the Empire, a form of opposing the government by liberalism instead of democracy, and not by the military spirit, which is essentially conservative.

There is no military spirit in a democratic society, where there is no aristocracy, no military nobility. A democratic society is antipathetic to the military spirit.

The military manner was unknown to the Romans. At home, no distinctions were made between military and civil service. They were one in the same. I believe the military manner dates from the day the profession of arms became a private profession, from the time of the bravos, the Italian *condotierri*, who were more terrifying to civilians than the enemy. When the Romans said "*cedant arma togae*," they did not refer to civil officers and soldiers. The civil officers were soldiers when called; professional soldiers did not exist. "Let arms yield to the toga," as translated.

Machiavelli cites a proverb: "War makes thieves and peace hangs them." The Spanish in Mexico, which has been in revolt for thirty years, are more or less thieves. They want to continue their profession. Civil authority is no longer recognized, and obedience to it would be regarded as shameful. One can understand the difficulty of organizing a *peaceful* government in such a country. One half of the country would have to hang the other half, and the other half does not want to be hanged.

We are a democratic society, and we grow less and less military. The Prussian, the Russian, and the Austrian aristocracies, who alone sustain the military spirit in those countries, regard our democratic society as a threat to their existence. They are our enemies, and they will continue to be until they are extinct, until the Russian, Austrian, and Prussian states become democratic. It is a matter of time.

The Prussian aristocracy is a young aristocracy that has not been corrupted by wealth, luxury, and the servility of the court. The Prussian court is not a court in the luxurious sense of the word. Therein lies the danger.

Meanwhile, Machiavellianism not being unknown to aristocrats, these people appeal to German chauvinism, to German patriotism, to all the passions that incite the jealousy by one people of another. All this for masking, under the guise of patriotism, their fear for themselves as an aristocracy, as a nobility.

The real threat of the day is czarism, stronger than the czars themselves, which calls for a crusade to suppress Russia and its immoral race of slaves.

It is time we understood the weakness of mob armies, that we remember the illusion of the first armies of the Revolution that were spared immediate destruction by the indecision of European cabinets and armies. Consider the Jacobins[73] of all eras, who have everything to gain and cannot hope for mercy; are they not examples? Since Spartacus,[74] have they not always been defeated? Certainly, Spartacus and his men were terrible individual fighters, gladiators who fought to the death, prisoners, barbarian slaves enraged by their loss of liberty, fugitive slaves, none of whom could hope for mercy. But discipline and command were improvised and could not impose the firm discipline, centuries old, drawn from the social institutions of the Romans. They were defeated. Time, a long time, is required for leaders to acquire the habit of command and confidence in their authority, to give soldiers confidence in their leaders and in their comrades. It is not enough to order discipline; the officer must have the will to enforce it vigorously; it must make the soldiers fear it more than they fear the enemy's blows.

How did Montluc[75] fight in an aristocratic society? He shows us, tells us. He marched at the head of an assault, but in difficult spots he places a soldier in front of him, a soldier whose skin was not worth as much as his own. He had not the slightest doubt or shame about doing this, and the soldier did not protest because the propriety of it was unquestionable. You,

---

73. Jacobins: the best known, and most notorious, of the radical political clubs of the French Revolution, now commonly associated with the Reign of Terror after the establishment of the revolutionary dictatorship in 1793.

74. Spartacus (111 B.C.-71 B.C.), Thracian gladiator who was one of the leaders of a slave uprising against the Romans in the Third Servile War.

75. Blaise de Lasseran-Massencôme, Seigneur de Montluc (1502-1577), marshal of France who began his military career as a private archer and man-at-arms in Italy under King Francis I. Author of *memoires*, detailing his fifty years of service to the crown—the "soldier's bible," according to Henry IV.

officers, try that in a democratic army, such as we have begun to have, such as we shall later have!

In danger the officer is no better than the soldier. The soldier is ready to advance, but behind his commander; furthermore, his comrades' skin is no more precious than his own, so they must advance as well. This preoccupation with equality in danger, which seeks equality only, causes only hesitation and not resolution. Some fools may rack their brains, trying to close in, but the rest will fire from a distance. Not that this will reduce losses; far from it.

Italy will never have a truly strong army. The Italians are too civilized, too cultured, too democratic in a certain sense of the word. The Spaniards are the same. We may scoff, but it is true.

The French are indeed worthy of their fathers, the Gauls. War, the most solemn act in the life of a nation, an act of utmost justice, is for them a light matter. The Good Frenchman lets himself be carried away into the wildest enthusiasm, inflamed to commit the most ridiculous feats of arms. He defines the word "honor" in his own certain way. He launches an expedition for no good reason, and good Frenchmen who do not understand why disapprove. But soon blood is spilled, and justice and good sense require that this should stain those who are authors of this unjust enterprise. But chauvinism! "French blood has been spilled, honor is at stake!" And so, for a ridiculous glory, millions in gold and men are sacrificed to an unknown cause.

Where does this tendency come from, this facility for war that characterizes the good citizen, the public, who are not called on to participate personally? (The military, except for those seeking promotion or a pension, are not so easily swayed; but even they are called to duty.) It derives from the poetry that envelops war, the fighting, that with us ten times more than others have the power of exciting enthusiasm among the people. It would be a service to humanity in our nation to dispel this illusion, to show what combat is: a terrible comedy, indeed, and a comedy no less for the blood that is spilled. The actors, heroes in the eyes of the crowd, are only poor souls torn between fear, discipline, and pride. They play a game of advance and retreat for hours without ever meeting, closing with, or even seeing the other poor souls, the enemy, who are just as fearful but caught up in the same web of circumstance.

What conditions are required to organize an army in a country in which there is at once a national as well as a provincial spirit? This is France, in which there is no longer a need for uniting national and provincial feeling by blending the soldiers. In France, will the motive of pride that comes of organizing units from particular provinces be useful? The character of our troops derives from the fusion of various elements, which is to be considered. The composition of our heavy cavalry, a group of men from the northern provinces and Germans, should perhaps be examined.

French sociability creates cohesion more quickly than could be created among troops of other nations. Organization and discipline do the same, but with a proud people like the French, a rational organization united by French sociability can often obtain results without employing the coercion of discipline.

Marshal Gouvion Saint-Cyr said, "Experienced French soldiers know, and others ought to know, that French soldiers once committed to the pursuit of the enemy will not return to their formation unless forced back into it by the enemy. During this period of time they must be considered as lost to the rest of the army."

At the beginning of the Empire, officers trained in the wars of the Revolution by incessant fighting possessed great firmness, which no one would ever wish to purchase at such a price. But in our modern wars the victors often lose more than the vanquished (apart from the temporary loss of prisoners). Losses exceed the resources in capable men and discourage the exhausted, who appear to be quite numerous, as well as those adept in avoiding danger. We lapse into disorder. The Duke of Fezensac,[76] testifying in another time, shows us what also happens in our own day. Moreover, today we rely only on mass action, and at that game, despite clever stratagems, we must lose all, and do.

French officers are not so firm, but they have pride. In the face of danger they lack composure, are disconcerted, breathless, hesitant, forgetful, and can think of no way out except to cry, "Forward! Forward!" This is one reason why handling a line is difficult, especially since the African campaigns, when so much is left to the initiative of the soldier.

---

76. Raymond-Aymery-Philippe-Joseph de Montesquieu Fezensac (1784–1867), French general of the Napoleonic Wars. Descended from a distinguished and venerable family, he enlisted as a common soldier at the age of twenty and rose to the rank of lieutenant general; distinguished in military service from the German campaign of 1805 to the end of the Empire. One of the circle of Napoleon's aides-de-camp during the Russian campaign, after which he wrote a journal that was published in 1860. His journal and memoirs served as one of the sources for Charles Minard's innovative graphic representation of the Russian campaign, *Carte figurative des pertes successives en hommes de l'Armée Française dans la campagne de Russie, 1812–1813.*

The formation in ranks is thus an ideal that cannot be met in modern war but toward which we should work in any case. But we are turning away from it, and then, when habit loses its grip, natural instinct reclaims its empire. The remedy? An organization that creates solidarity by the mutual acquaintance of all, top to bottom, which makes possible the mutual observation that has such power over French pride.

[There are two sorts of wars.] A larger war, that in open country, on the plain, and a small war of posts, in broken terrain; in the larger war, without posts, we should be lost. Marshal de Saxe knew us well when he said that the French were best in a war of position. He recognized the lack of solidarity in the ranks.

Within rifle range the ranks tend to disperse. You hear officers who have been under fire say, "When you approach the enemy, the men disperse as skirmishers despite you. The Russians group under fire, the huddling of sheep joined by fear of discipline and danger." There you have two modes of conduct under fire, the French and the Russian.

Why do the French, in singular contrast to the Gauls, scatter under fire? Their natural intelligence, their instinct under pressure of danger, causes them to deploy. The Gauls, who, seeing the firmness of the Roman ranks, made their first rank unbreakable by chaining themselves together. This prevented the advantage they had not perceived in the Roman line, the replacement of the wounded and exhausted with fresh men. This accounted for the firmness that seemed so striking to the Gauls. The ranks renewed themselves.

The Gauls' method must be adopted. Rather than the draconian discipline of the Roman soldier who was followed by the fear of death, we must adopt the soldier's method and try to instill order in it. How? By French discipline and an organization that permits it.

Broken, covered country is well suited for our methods. The Zouaves at Magenta could not have done so well on another kind of ground.[77]* Above all, with modern weapons, the terrain for the advance must be limited in depth.

How much better modern weapons suit the impatient French character! But also how necessary it is to guard against this impatience and to keep supports and reserves under control.

It should be noted that German or Gallic cavalry was always better than Roman cavalry, which could not stand against it even though better armed.

---

77. *See Appendix II.

Why? Because decision, impetuosity, even blind courage have more chance with cavalry than with infantry. Defeated cavalry is the least brave cavalry (our cavalry should take note!). It was easier for the Gauls to have good cavalry than it is for us, as fire did not bother them in the charge.

The Frenchman has more qualities of the cavalryman than of the infantryman. Yet French infantry appears to be of greater value. Why? Because on the battlefield, the use of cavalry requires exceptional decision, and if the French cavalryman is unable to prove his worth, the fault lies with his commanders. The French infantry has always been defeated by the English infantry. The English cavalry has always turned bridle before the French cavalry. Is it because our cavalrymen were older and more experienced than our infantrymen? This does not affect us only. If it is true for our cavalrymen, it is also true for English cavalrymen. The reason is that on the battlefield the role of the infantryman opposing a solid adversary requires more composure and nerve than does the role of the cavalryman. It requires tactics founded on an understanding of our own national character as well as our enemy's. Against the English, our faith in the charge that is implanted in our brains was completely betrayed. The clash of cavalry against cavalry is much simpler. French confidence in the charge makes for good fighting cavalry, and the Frenchman is better at this role than any other. On the battlefield, it is understood that because they move faster than the infantry, the cavalry charge, which has its limits, is better preserved when they engage with the enemy.

The English have always turned bridle before our cavalry. This shows that, though they were strong enough to stand against our infantry, they were not strong enough to stand before the stronger impetus of our cavalry.

We should be much better cavalrymen than infantrymen because the essence of a cavalryman is a fearless impetuosity. The cavalry commander should use this trait without hesitation while guarding against its shortcomings. The attack is always, even on the defensive, evidence of resolution and displays a moral ascendancy. Its effect is more immediate with the cavalry because they move much more quickly, and their moral effect has less time to be attenuated by reflection. To ensure that the French cavalry is the best in Europe, a really good cavalry, it only needs one thing: to conform to the national temperament, to dare, to dare, and to advance!

One of the singular anomalies of French discipline while on the march, especially on campaign, is that the means of repression for derelictions becomes illusory, impractical. In 1859, there were 25,000 soldiers absent without leave in the army in Italy. The soldier sees this right away, and indiscipline ensues. If our customs do not permit draconian discipline, let us replace that moral coercion by another. Let us ensure cohesion by the mutual acquaintanceship of men and officers; let us call French sociability to our aid.

With the Romans, discipline was most severe and most rigidly enforced in the presence of the enemy. Today, why should not the men in our companies enforce discipline and punishment themselves? They alone know each other, and keeping up discipline is so much in their interest that it should discourage skulking. The 25,000 men in Italy who absented themselves all wear the Italian medal. They were discharged with certificates of good conduct, which should be awarded by the squad only. Instead of that, discipline must be obtained somehow, and the officer is burdened with it. He above all has to uphold it, and he is treated without regard for his dignity. He is made to do the work of the noncommissioned officer. He is used at pleasure, and so on.

The cohesion that we want in units from squad to company need not be feared in other armies. We cannot develop it to the same degree and by the same methods of other armies. They are not constituted as we are. Their character is different. The individuality of our squads and companies comes from the makeup of our army and from French sociability.

Is it true that the rations of men and horses are actually insufficient in campaign? A singular economy! To not increase the soldier's pay by five centimes! It would improve his fare and avoid turning the officer into a trader in vegetables in order to properly feed his men. Yet millions are squandered each year on uniforms, baubles, shakos, etc.!

If a large army is needed, it should cost as little as possible: simplicity in all things, down to all sorts of *plumes*! Fewer amateurs! If there is less embarrassment, too bad! There is no such thing as a beautiful sailor. Insignificant and boring details abound while vital details of proper footgear and instruction (target instruction always) are neglected. The question of campaign uniform is solved by adopting jackets and capes and by abolishing headquarters companies; this silliness has escaped everyone. Our current uniforms need tailors; jackets and capes, no.

Appendix I
Memorandum on Infantry Fire[1]

1. Introduction

It seems that the history of infantry fire is not so very clear, even though in Europe today firepower is almost the only means of destruction employed by that arm.

Napoleon said, "The only practicable fire in war is fire at will." And yet, after a declaration by one who knew, there is still a tendency to employ fire at command as the foundation of infantry battle tactics.

Is this correct? Is it not? Only experience can reply. Experience may be acquired, but nothing in the profession of war is forgotten as quickly as experience. So many things could be done, beautiful maneuvers executed, ingenious combat methods conceived in the offices or in training camps! Nevertheless, let us hold on to the facts.

2. Succinct History of the Evolution of Firearms, from the Arquebus to Our Rifle

The arquebus used before the advent of powder produced the idea for the model of our firearms. Thus the arquebus marked the transition from the ancient weapons firing missiles to the new weapons firing bullets.

The barrel was retained to direct the projectile, and the bow and string were replaced by a powder chamber and means of ignition.

This made a simple, light weapon, easy to load, but the small-caliber ball fired from a very short barrel, and the small charge allowed for a penetration only at a very short distance.

---

1. Written in 1869.

The barrel was lengthened, the caliber increased, and a more efficient but less convenient weapon was the result. It was impossible to fire the weapon from the aiming position and withstand the recoil.

To reduce the recoil a hook was attached to the barrel to anchor on some fixed object at the moment of discharge. This was called the *hook arquebus.*

But using the hook was possible only in certain circumstances. To give the weapon a resting point on the body, the stock was lengthened and inclined in order to sight while *standing or kneeling.* The soldier also had a fork for support of the barrel.

In the musket that followed, the stock was again modified and rested against the shoulder, and the firing mechanism was improved as well.

In the original, the weapon was fired by a lighted match, but with the musket the weapon became lighter and lighter, from the serpentine lock, the matchlock, the wheel lock, and finally the Spanish lock and the flint-lock.

The adoption of the lock and the bayonet made the rifle, which Napoleon regarded as the most powerful weapon that man possessed.

But the rifle, in its primitive state, had defects: it was slow to load, it was inaccurate, and under some conditions it would not fire.

How were these defects remedied?

To correct the weakness in loading, Gustavus Adolphus,[2] understanding the influence on morale of rapid loading and the greater destruction of rapid fire, invented the cartridge for muskets. Frederick, or someone in his time, replaced wooden ramrods with cylindrical iron ramrods. A conical funnel permitted quicker priming by allowing the powder to pass from the barrel into the firing pan. These last two refinements saved time in two ways, priming and loading. But it was the adoption of the breech loader that increased the rate of fire the greatest.

These modifications in weapons, all of which tended to increase the rate of fire, corresponded with the most remarkable military period in modern times:

Cartridges—Gustavus Adolphus

Iron ramrod—Frederick

---

2. Gustavus Adolphus (1594–1632), King of Sweden, founder of the modern Swedish state, and the greatest general and military innovator of the age. His intervention in the Thirty Years War forestalled the ambitions of the Hapsburg Empire for imperial authority over Europe and ensured the survival of German Protestantism. He was killed leading a cavalry charge against the forces of Wallenstein at the battle of Lützen.

Improved vent (*by the soldiers*), if not prescribed by competent orders—wars of the Republic and of the Empire.

Breech loading—Sadowa

Accuracy appeared to be less important than rate of fire for a long time (later we will see why). It is only today that the general use of rifling and of elongated projectiles has brought accuracy to a point that can hardly be surpassed. Also, the use of fulminate allows firing in any weather.

We have succinctly described the successive improvements in the perfection of firearms from the arquebus to the rifle.

Has the art of employing them made the same progression toward perfection?

3. *Progressive Introduction of Firearms into the Armament of the Infantryman*

The revolution, not in the art of war but in that of combat, caused by powder progressed slowly, along with the improvement of firearms. These weapons eventually became those of the infantryman.

Thus, under Francis I, the proportion of infantrymen carrying firearms to those carrying pikes was one to three or four.

At the time of the Wars of Religion[3] the number of arquebusiers and pikemen was about the same.

Under Louis XIII, in 1643, there were two firearms for every pike; in the war of 1688, four to one. Finally, pikes disappeared.

At first, men with firearms were independent of other combatants and fought like light troops in earlier times.

Later all the pikes and muskets were integrated with other elements of the main body of the army.

Eventually, all the pikes were placed in the center of the line and the muskets on the flanks; this became the common formation.

Sometimes the pikemen were placed in the center of their respective companies, the musketeers on the company flanks, formed abreast.

Or half the musketeers might be placed in front of the pikemen, half behind.

---

3. The Wars of Religion (1562–1598), the intermittent and often bloody conflict in France between Protestant Hugenots and Roman Catholics. The massacre of a Hugenot congregation at Vassey in 1562 ignited a civil war punctuated by several truces until the elevation of Henry IV to the throne and the subsequent Edict of Nantes guaranteed religious tolerance of the Hugenots.

Or again, all of the musketeers might be placed behind the kneeling pike-men. In these last two examples, firepower covered the entire front.

And finally, the pikes and muskets might alternate their places.

These combinations are found in all the treatises on tactics. But we do not know how these examples worked in fact, how these combinations were maintained in action, or whether they were actually used.

4. The Classes of Fire Employed with Each Weapon

When, in the beginning, a certain number of infantrymen were armed with primitive, long, and heavy arquebuses, the feebleness of their fire led Montaigne[4] to say, with the certainty of military authority, "Firearms have such little effect, except on the ears, that their use will be discontinued." Research is required to find any mention of their use in the battles of this era.[5*]

However, we find a rare piece of information by Brantôme,[6] writing of the battle of Pavia:

The Marquis de Pescani won the battle of Pavia with Spanish arquebusiers, in an irregular defiance of all regulation and tradition by employing a new formation. Fifteen hundred arquebusiers, the ablest, the most experienced, the cleverest, above all the most agile and devoted, were selected by the Marquis de Pescani, instructed by him on new lines, and practiced for a long time. They scattered by squads over the battlefield, turning, leaping from one place to another with great speed, and thus escaped the cavalry charge. By this new method of fighting, unusual, astonishing, cruel, and unworthy, these arquebusiers greatly hampered the operations of the French cavalry, who were completely lost. For they,

---

4. Michel de Montaigne (1522-1532), a leading philosopher of the French renaissance and renowned essayist.

5. *It is difficult to determine what method of fire—at command or at will—was employed, but what we find in the military writings of the best authorities from Montecuccoli to Marshal de Saxe is general resistance to the replacement of the pike by the rifle. All forecast the abandonment of the rifle for the pike, and the future proved them wrong. They ignored experience. They could not see that stronger than all logic is the instinct of man, who prefers long range to close fighting, and who, having improved the rifle, would not let it go but constantly improved it.

6. Pierre de Bourdeille, seigneur de Brantôme (1540-1614), French soldier and memoirist, veteran of the Wars of Religion, in which he fought on the Catholic side, including the siege of La Rochelle. His memoirs, published posthumously in 1740, ran to fifteen volumes.

joined together and in mass, were brought to earth by these few brave and able arquebusiers. This irregular and new method of fighting is more easily imagined than described. Anyone who can try it will find it is good and useful; but it is necessary that the arquebusiers be good troops, very much on the jump (as the saying goes), and above all reliable.

It should be remembered in considering the preceding passage that there is always very great difference between what actually happened and what is written (often by men who were not there, and God knows with what authority). But, in these lines of Brantôme we find the first example of the most destructive use of the rifle, as employed by skirmishers.

During the Wars of Religion, which consisted of skirmishes and the taking and retaking of posts, the fire of the arquebusiers was executed without order, individually, as described above.

The soldier carried the powder charge in a small metal box on a bandolier. A finer priming powder was carried in a powder horn; the balls were carried in a pouch. At the onset of fighting, the soldier had to load his piece and this was how he had to fight with the match arquebus. This was far from fire at command.

However, this would soon appear. Gustavus Adolphus was the first who tried to introduce method and coordination into infantry fire. The avid spirit of innovation followed in his wake, and there appeared, in succession, fire by rank, in two ranks, by subdivision, section, platoon, company, battalion, file fire, parapet fire, and formal fire at will, and so many others that we can be certain that all combinations were tried at this time.

Fire by ranks was undoubtedly the first of these; it will give us a bearing on all the others.

The infantry was formed in ranks six deep. To execute fire by rank, all ranks knelt except the last. The last rank fired and reloaded. The rank in front of it then rose and did the same, as did all ranks in succession. The whole sequence recommenced as before.

Thus, the first fire by formation was successively executed by rank.

Montecuccoli[7] said, "The musketeers are ranged six deep so that the last rank has reloaded by the time the first has fired, and takes up the fire again, so that the enemy faces continuous fire."

---

7. Raimondo Montecuccoli (1609–1680), Austrian field marshal and military reformer, leading commander opposing Gustavus Adolphus at the battles of Breitenfeld and Lützen. Master of the maneuver warfare of his age. Author of the military classic *Dell'arte militaire*.

However, under Condé and Turenne, we see the French army use only fire at will.

It is true that at the time fire was regarded as an accessory in battle. The infantry of the line, whose influence had grown since the exploits of the Flemish, the Swiss, and the Spaniard, was required for the charge and advance and they were armed with the pike.

In the most celebrated battles of the time, Rocroi, Nordlingen, Lens, Rethel, and the Dunes, we see the infantry operate in this way. Two armies, in straight lines, begin by cannonading each other, and both charged with their cavalry wings and advanced with the infantry in the center. The best and bravest infantry drove back the other, and often, if one of its wings was successful, finished by routing the enemy. Research into this period reveals no marked influence of fire. The tradition of Pescani was lost.

Nevertheless, firearms improved; they became more effective and tended to supplant the pike. The pike required the soldier to remain in rank and fight only in certain situations, exposing him to injury without exchanging blows. And, this is singularly instructive: the soldier had acquired by this time an instinctive dislike for the weapon, which condemned him to a passive role. This repulsion necessitated offering high pay and privileges in order to recruit pikemen. But even so, at the first chance the soldier discarded his pike for a musket.

The pikes gradually disappeared as they were replaced by the musket. The ranks were thinned to allow their use. The four-rank formation was tried, with fire by rank, by two ranks, standing, kneeling.

Despite these trials, we see the French army on the battlefield, notably at Fontenoy,[8] still using fire at will, in which the soldier broke ranks to fire and then returned to reload.

It can be stated, therefore, that despite numerous trials and attempts, no fire at command was attempted in combat until Frederick's time.

Already, under Wilhelm[9] the Prussian infantry was recognized for the rapidity and continuity of its fire. Frederick further improved the firepower of his battalions by reducing their depth. This fire, tripled by the speed of loading, was so heavy and violent it gave the Prussian battalions superiority over others of three to one.

The Prussians distinguished three kinds of fire: at a halt, in the advance, and in retreat.

---

8. The battle of Fontenoy (May 11, 1745), a major victory over the Pragmatic Allies by French forces under command of Marshal Maurice de Saxe in the War of the Austrian Succcession.

9. Frederich Wilhelm I (1688–1740), King of Prussia and elector of Brandenburg.

We know the technique of firing while halted, in which the first rank fires while kneeling. As for firing while marching, here is how Guilbert described and judged it:

> What I call marching fire, and which everyone who thinks about it must find as ill-advised as I do, is a fire I have seen used by some troops. The soldiers in two ranks fire as they march, but of course they move at a snail's pace. This is what Prussian troops call advancing fire, and it consists of combined and alternating volleys by platoon, company, half-battalions, or battalions. Those parts of the line that have fired advance at the double, and those who have not fired advance at the half step.

In other methods of firing, as we have said, the Prussian battalion was in three ranks, the first kneeling. The line delivered fire by salvo at command only.

Nevertheless, the complexities of executing the regulation of fire by salvo in three ranks did not concern Frederick's old soldiers. We shall see shortly how they executed it on the battlefield.

Whatever it was, Europe was infatuated with these techniques and dedicated themselves to adopting them. D'Argenson[10] provided for them in the French army and introduced fire at command. Two regulations appeared in 1753 and 1755, but in the war that followed, Marshal de Broglie,[11] who undoubtedly had as much experience and common sense as M. D'Argenson, prescribed fire at will. All the army was drilled in it during the winter of 1761–1762.

In 1764 and 1776, two new regulations superseded the old ones. The second prescribed firing at command in three ranks, all standing upright.[12]*

We now come to the wars of the Revolution with fire at command in the regulations, but which were not followed on the battlefield.

Since these wars, our armies have always fought as skirmishers. In the accounts of our campaigns, fire at command is never mentioned. It was the

---

10. Marc-Pierre de Voyer de Paulmy d'Argenson (1696–1764), French politician in the court of Louis XV. Appointed secretary of state for war during the War of the Austrian Succession, during which with Marshal de Saxe he initiated army reforms aimed at adopting the Prussian style of warfare. Among his reforms, d'Argenson founded the *École Militaire* in 1751.

11. Victor-François, second Duke de Broglie (1718–1814), marshal of France under Louis XV and Louis XVI. Secretary of state for war in the waning days of Louis XVI's reign.

12. *The danger resulting from this kind of fire led to the proposal to place the smallest men in the first rank, the tallest in the third.

same under the Empire, despite numerous trials at Boulogne and elsewhere. At Boulogne, fire at command was first tried by order of Napoleon. This technique, meant to be employed against cavalry—superb in theory—seems never to have been used. Napoleon himself says so, and the regulations of 1832—in which some traditions of soldiers of the Empire should be found—direct firing in two ranks or at will to the exclusion of all others.

According to our military authorities, on the advice of our old officers, firing at command did not suit our infantry, and yet it remained in our regulations. General Fririon[13] (1822) and Gouvion Saint-Cyr (1829) criticized this method, yet nothing was done. It remained in the regulations, but without being prescribed for any particular circumstance, except perhaps for parades.

When d'Orleans[14] created the chasseurs, fire by rank was revived, but neither in our African campaigns nor in the Crimea nor in Italy can any example of fire at command be found. In practice, it was considered unworkable.

But today, with the breech-loading rifle, once again some believed it was workable and took it up with new interest. Is it more reasonable now than in the past? We shall see.

5. Execution of Fire in the Presence of the Enemy;
Impractical Methods That Are Recommended or Ordered;
Use and Efficacy of Fire at Command

It appears incontestable that at the Potsdam maneuvers the Prussian infantry employed fire by salvo. The firing itself was executed with admirable precision. A discipline that we cannot impose kept the soldiers in place and rank. Sentences of almost barbaric severity were introduced into the military code: beatings, whippings, rages against the slightest faults. The noncommissioned officers themselves were subjected to blows with the flat of the sword. Yet all this was not enough on the battlefield. A complete rank of file-closers was also used to keep the men in their places.

---

13. Joseph Françoise Frinion (1771–1849), brigadier general of infantry in the Revolutionary and Napoleonic Wars.

14. Ferdinand Philippe, Duke of Orleans (1810–1842), heir to the House of Orleans, eldest son of King Louis Philippe I. Army officer, veteran of the early Algerian campaigns, founder of the *chasseurs à pied*; military reformer especially interested in the morale and welfare of the troops.

M. Carion-Nisas[15] says, "We saw these file-closers join their halberds by the hook to form a continuous line that could not be broken." Despite this, after two or three salvos (says General Renard, whom we believe more than charitable), no amount of discipline could prevent regular fire from degenerating into firing at will.

But let us look closer into Frederick's battles, for example, the battle of Mollwitz, in which success was attributed to fire at command, almost lost, and then won by Prussian salvos.

Historians tell us:

The Austrian infantry had opened fire against the lines of the Prussians, whose cavalry had been dispersed; it was only necessary to shake them to ensure victory. The Austrians still used wooden ramrods and fired slowly, while the Prussian fire was thunderous, five or six shots a minute from each rifle. The Imperial troops, surprised, disconcerted by the massed fire, tried to hurry, but in their haste broke many of their fragile ramrods. The confusion spread through the ranks, and the battle was lost.

But if we attend to the actual situation at the time, we see several things that did not happen in such an orderly fashion.

The fusillade began, and it was said to be long and deadly. The iron ramrods of the Prussians gave them an advantage over their enemies, whose ramrods were wooden, more difficult to handle, and easily broken. However, when the order to advance was given to the Prussians, the battalions stood fast; it was impossible to move them. The soldiers tried to evade the fire and hid behind one another, so that they were thirty to forty deep.

Here are men who, under fire, exhibit an admirable composure, an immovable solidity. Each moment, they hear the dead, heavy sound of a bullet striking; they see and feel, all around them, between their legs, their comrades fall and writhe, because the fire is deadly. They have in their hands the power to return fire, to return to the enemy the death that hisses and strikes about them. They do not take a false step; their hands do not close instinctively on the trigger. They wait, impassively, for their commander's order—and what commanders! These are the men who at the command

---

15. Henri Françoise Carrion-Nisan (1767–1841), French army dragoon officer, playwright, politician. Veteran of the Peninsular, 1813, and 1814 campaigns. Secretary-general of the Ministry of War during the First Restoration.

"Forward!" lack guts, who huddle like sheep behind one another? What are we to believe?

So, let us get at the truth of the story!

Frederick's old soldiers, in spite of their discipline and training, cannot follow the methods taught and ordered. They can no more execute fire at command than they can execute the advance on the drill ground at Potsdam. They use fire at will. They fire rapidly, instinctively—with an instinct more powerful than discipline—two shots for one. This fire becomes a thunderous roll, not of salvos, but of rapid fire at will. Whoever fires most, hits most, so the soldier figures, and so indeed does Frederick, who encouraged fire in this same battle of Mollwitz. Thereafter, he ordered doubling the number of cartridges issued to the soldier, giving them sixty instead of thirty.

Moreover, if fire at command has been possible, who knows what they could have done? If Frederick's soldiers had been capable, they would have cut down battalions like so much wheat. If he had allowed them to aim calmly, no man interfering with another, each seeing clearly, then at the signal all firing together, could anyone stand against them? At the first volley the enemy would have broken and run, or risk annihilation. But if we look at the final results at Mollwitz, we see that the same number was killed on the side that used fire at command as on the side that did not. The Prussians lost 960 dead, the Austrians 966.

But it is said that if fire was not more deadly, it was because setting sights was then unknown. What if it was? There was no adjustment of fire perhaps, but there were well-known regulations. We do not say it was practiced, but it was very well known. Cromwell often said, "Put your confidence in God, my children, and fire at their shoelaces."

Do we set our sights better today? It is doubtful. If the able soldiers of Cromwell, of Frederick, of the Republic, and of Napoleon could not set their sights, can we?

Thus, this fire at command, which was possible in rare circumstances, and then only at the commencement of action, was entirely ineffective.

Hardy spirits, seeing such little effect from long-range firing in battle, counseled holding fire until the enemy was close, at twenty paces, before firing a single volley and driving him back. You do not have to set sights at twenty paces. To what end?

Marshal Saxe says,

At the battle of Castiglione, the Imperial troops let the French approach to twenty paces, hoping to destroy them with a volley. At that distance they fired very coolly and with all precautions, but they were broken before the smoke cleared. At the battle of Belgrade (1717), I saw two battalions who, at thirty paces, aimed and fired at a group of Turks. The Turks cut them up, with only two or three escaping. The Turkish loss was only thirty-two dead.

No matter what the Marshal says, we doubt that these men were composed; because men who could hold their fire up to such a near approach of the enemy, with the best weapon in the world, and fire into these masses, would have killed the first rank, thrown the others into confusion, and would never have been cut up as we have seen. To make these men attentively await the enemy until twenty or thirty paces to open fire certainly subjects them to very great moral pressure. Held by discipline, they waited, but as one might wait for a roof to fall, for a bomb to explode, full of violent emotion yet contained, and when the order is given to raise the arms and fire, the crisis is upon them. The roof collapses, the bomb explodes, you flinch and fire in the air, and if you kill anyone it is by accident.

This is what happened before the advent of skirmishers. Salvos were tried; in action, they immediately became fire at will. Executed against troops advancing without firing they were ineffective. They did not arrest the assault by the enemy, and the troops who had depended on the salvos with such confidence were demoralized and ran. But when skirmishers were employed, salvos became impossible, and the armies who remained confident in this ancient tactic learned this at their expense.

In the first days of the Revolution our troops, without drills or training, could not fight in line. To advance on the enemy, part of the battalion was detached as skirmishers. The rest marched into battle and engaged without keeping ranks. The combat was conducted by groups without formal order. The art was to support the skirmishers with reserves. The skirmishers always commenced the action, if they indeed did not finish it as well.

To oppose skirmishers with fire by rank was the height of folly.

Skirmishers fought skirmishers. Once this tactic was adopted, they were supported and reinforced by troops in formation. In the thick of general firing, fire at command became impossible and was replaced by firing at will.

Demouriez,[16] at the battle of Jammapes, threw out whole battalions of skirmishers and supported them with light cavalry and did wonders with

---

16. Jean Francoise du Perier Dumouriez (1739–1823), French general and Revolutionary politician, veteran of the Seven Years War. Minister of war for the Girondins when the Prussians invaded in 1792, he took command of the Army of the North and defeated the Prussians at the battle of Valmy (September 20) and the Austrians at the battle of Jammapes

them. They surrounded the Austrian redoubts and rained a hail of bullets so violent on the cannoneers they abandoned their pieces.

The Austrians, dazzled by this mode of combat, vainly reinforced their light troops with detachments of heavy infantry. Their skirmishers could not withstand our numbers and impetuosity, and presently their line was forced back, beaten by a storm of bullets. The noise of battle, the firing, increased; the defeated troops, no long able to hear commands, threw down their arms and ran in disorder.

So, firing in line, heavy as it might be, is not effective in counterbalancing numerous detachments of skirmishers. A mass of bullets fired aimlessly is impotent against isolated individuals, protected by the slightest folds of ground against the enemy's fire, while the massed battalions offer a large and relatively harmless target. The dense line, appearing so powerful, withers under the fire of small groups, so feeble in appearance (General Renard).

The Prussians suffered likewise at Jena. In the same way, their lines tried to employ fire at command against our skirmishers. You may as well fire on a handful of fleas.

We are told of the English salvos at the battle of Sainte-Euphémie, in Calabria, and later in Spain. But it was only possible for the English in these particular cases precisely for the reason that their troops charged at the outset, without sending out skirmishers.

The battle of Saint-Euphémie lasted only half an hour; it was badly conceived and badly executed. "And if," General Duhesme[17] says, "the battalions charging had been preceded by detachments of skirmishers who had already begun to thin the enemy's ranks, and, closing in, the head of columns had charged, the English line would not have maintained that coolness which made their fire so effective and accurate. And certainly, it would not have waited so long to commence firing, had it been vigorously harassed by skirmishers."

An English author, writing on the history of weapons, uses the term *rolling fire*, well directed, of British troops. He says *rolling fire* and does not men-

---

(November 6). After defeats at Neerwinden and Leuven, Dumouriez defected to the Austrians. He died in exile in England.

17. Guillaume Philibert Duhesme (1766–1815), French general who began his career as colonel of a free corps in 1792, corps commander in the Army of the Reserve at Marengo, veteran of the Peninsular campaign, commander of the Young Guard Division of the Imperial Guard at Ligny during the Waterloo campaign, mortally wounded in action at Plancenoit. Author of *Essai historique de l'infanterie légère* (1806).

tion salvos. Perhaps we are mistaken in our accounts, taking battalion fire for the formal fire at command in our regulations.

The same assumption appears in the work on the infantry by the Marquis de Chambray,[18] who knew the English army well. He says that the English, in Spain, almost always fired in two ranks. They employed battalion fire only when attacked by our troops without skirmishers, firing on the flanks of our columns. And he says, "Fire by battalion, by half-battalion, and by platoon is only for the target range. The fire actually used most often in war is that in two ranks, the only one used by the French." Later, he says, "Experience proves fire in two ranks the only one to be used against the enemy." And before him, Marshal de Saxe wrote, "Avoid dangerous maneuvers such as fire by platoon, which have often caused shameful defeats." This is as true now as when it was written.

Fire at command, by platoon, by battalion, etc., is used when the enemy, having repulsed skirmishers and reached the proper range, either charges or opens fire. If the latter, there is an exchange that lasts until one or the other gives way or charges. If the enemy charges, what happens? He advances, preceded by skirmishers who deliver a hail of bullets, absorbing all the soldiers' attention. You want the line to open fire, but the voices of your officers cannot be heard. The soldiers fire at will, while there is a cartridge left. The enemy may find a fold in the terrain for cover. He may change his formation from deployed order to columns with wide intervals, or somehow change his dispositions. The soldiers continue to fire, and the officers, who are behind their troops, lost in the smoke, can do nothing about it.

All this has been said before, and fire at command has been abandoned. So why take it up again? It probably comes to us from the Prussians. In effect, the reports of their last campaign (1866), made by the general staff, state that it was very effectively employed, and cite numerous examples.

But a Prussian officer who took part in the campaign in the ranks, and who saw the affair up close, says,

In examining the battles of 1866 for common characteristics of firing, one is struck by one representative feature: it is the extraordinary extension of the front line at the expense of depth. Either the front is stretched out into a single, long, thin line, or it is broken into isolated

---

18. Georges de Chambray (1783–1848), French field marshal (1830), general of artillery, historian, veteran of numerous campaigns from Ulm-Austerlitz to the Russian campaign, in which he was taken prisoner. Author of *Histoire de l'expédition de Russie* (1823).

pieces that fight on their own. Above all, there is manifested a tendency to envelop the enemy by extending the wings. There is no longer a question of preserving the original order of battle; the different groups are confused by the action, even before the action. Detachments and large elements of any corps are made up of diverse and heterogeneous parts. The fighting is almost exclusively conducted by columns of companies, rarely of half-battalions. The tactics of these columns consist of throwing out strong detachments of skirmishers; bit by bit, their supports are engaged and deployed; thus the whole first line is broken, scattered, like a horde of irregular cavalry. The second line, which has kept close order, tries to quickly join the first, mainly to join the fight but also because they have been hit by high shots aimed at the first line. It suffers heavy losses because it is still compact and supports them impatiently because it does not yet feel the fever of the fighting. Most of the second line forces itself into the first, and because there is more room on the wings, it gravitates toward them. Very often, even the reserve is so involved it cannot fulfill its mission. In reality, all the fighting of the first two lines is nothing more than a series of engagements between company commands and the enemy each one faces. Superior officers cannot follow all the units on horseback as they push ahead over all sorts of terrain. They must dismount and attach themselves to the first part of their command they meet. Unable to manage their whole command, compelled to do something, they command the smaller unit. It is not always better commanded for all that. Even generals find themselves in this situation!

That, of course, is something we well understand; it is certainly what happens.

As for the examples cited in the general staff reports, they regard companies or half-battalions at most, and regardless of the complacency with which they are cited, they must have been rare and should not be taken as a rule.

6. Fire at Will–Its Efficacy

Thus, fire at command, formerly as now, is impractical, and as a consequence is not practiced in battle. The only means employed are fire at will and the fire of skirmishers. Let us consider their efficacy.

Very competent men have compiled statistics on this point.

Guilbert thinks that for each million cartridges fired, no more than 2,000 men are killed.

Gassendi[19] assures us that, of 3,000 rounds fired, only one finds a target.

Piobert[20] says that the estimate, based on the result of long wars, is that 3,000 to 10,000 cartridges are expended for each man struck.

Today, with accurate and long-range weapons, have things changed much? We do not think so. Compare the number of bullets fired with the number of men felled, with a deduction for the effect of artillery fire, which must be considered.

A German author believes that with the Prussian Needle gun, strikes are 60 percent of the shots fired. How then to explain the disappointment of M. Dreyse,[21] the happy inventor of the Needle gun, when he compared Prussian and Austrian losses? This good old gentleman was astonished to see that the results of his rifle had not met his expectations.

Fire at will, as we shall show, is a fire to occupy the men in the ranks, but it is not very effective. We could offer several examples, but we only cite one, and it is conclusive.

General Duhesme says,

Has it not been remarked that, before a firing line there rises a veil of smoke which on one side or another hides troops from view and makes the fire of the best placed troops uncertain and practically without effect? I proved it conclusively at the battle of Caldiero, in one of the successive advances that occurred on my left wing. I saw some battalions that I had rallied stop and use individual fire that they could not sustain for long. I went there, and I saw through the cloud of smoke nothing but gun flashes, the glint of bayonets, and the tops of the grenadiers' hats. We were not far from the enemy, perhaps sixty paces. I went into the ranks, which had neither closed nor aligned, and with my hand raised the soldiers' rifles to get them to stop firing and to advance. I was on horseback, followed by a dozen orderlies. None of

19. Jean Jacques Basilien, Comte de Gassendi (1748–1828), French army officer, general of artillery under Napoleon, parliamentarian. Author of a manual of instruction on the tactical use of artillery.

20. Guillaume Piobert (1793–1871), French army officer, scientist, expert in ballistics. Now chiefly remembered as the author of "Piobert's Law," which he conceived to explain the behavior of gunpowder.

21. Johann Nicolaus von Dreyse (1787–1867), German inventor of the so-called Needle gun, perhaps the earliest of the bolt-action rifles. Dreyse's gun was adopted by the Prussian army in 1840, first employed against the Austrian army in the battle of Königgrätz, and not replaced until the Franco-Prussian War.

us was wounded, nor did I see an infantryman fall. Well then! Hardly had our line started when the Austrians, without paying any attention to the obstacle that separated us, made their retreat.

It is probable that had the Austrians begun moving first, the French would have retreated. They were veterans of the Empire, certainly as reliable as our own men, who gave this example of a lack of coolness.

In ranks, fire at will is the only possible method for our officers and men, but with the excitement, the smoke, the confusion, one is happy to obtain even horizontal fire, much less aimed fire.

In fire at will, even without trembling, men bump into each other. Whoever advances, or reacts to the recoil of his weapon, interrupts the shot of his comrade. With full packs, the second rank does not have a clear shot; they fire into the air. On the firing range, spacing men in formation to extreme limits, firing very slowly, men can be found who are composed and not much disturbed by the crack of the rifle in their ears, who let the smoke disperse and see a clear shot. And the percentages of results show much more regularity than with fire at command.

But, in front of the enemy, fire at will becomes an instantly hazardous fire. Everyone fires as much as possible; that is to say, as badly as possible. There are physical and mental reasons:

Even at close range in battle, the artillery can fire well. The gunner, protected somewhat by his piece, only needs a moment of coolness in which to lay his gun properly. That his pulse is racing does not affect his line of sight if he is deliberate, and his eye remains steady until he fires.

The rifleman, like the gunner, exerts his willpower to hold his fire and aim his weapon; only a moment is needed to fire; but his blood pulses, his nervous system is excited, opposing the immobility of the weapon in his hands. He instinctively wants to shoot, so as to *prevent the departure of the bullet meant for him.* However heavy the fire, this vague reasoning, unformed in his mind, controls with all its force the instinct of self-preservation. Even the bravest and most reliable soldiers then fire madly. *The greater number fire from the hip.*

The theory of the firing range is that with continual pressure on the trigger, the shot surprises the rifleman. But who practices it under fire?

However, the tendency in France is to strive only for accuracy. What good will it do when smoke, fog, darkness, long range, excitement, the lack of composure, forbid a clear shot?

It is a hard thing to say, after the feats of fire at Sebastopol, and in Italy, that accurate weapons have given us no more valuable service than a simple rifle. All the same, to one who has seen it, facts are facts. But see how history is written: it is alleged that the Russians were beaten at Inkerman by the range and accuracy of the weapons of the French troops. But the battle was fought in thickets and wooded country, and in a dense fog. And when the weather cleared, our soldiers and our chasseurs were out of ammunition and drew from the Russian's pouches, amply provided with round balls and small-caliber bullets. The facts are that the Russians were defeated by superior morale; that firing at random, without aiming, had only material effect.

When one fires only at random, who fires most hits most. Or perhaps it is better said that [he] who fires least expects to be hit most.

Frederick was impressed with this, because he did not believe in the Potsdam maneuvers. The wily Frederick regarded fire as a way to calm and occupy unreliable soldiers; and it proved his talent that he could practice that which in the hands of any other general might have been a mistake. He knew very well how to count on the effect of his fire, how many thousand cartridges were required to kill or wound an enemy. Also, at first, his soldiers were issued thirty cartridges; finding this number insufficient, after Mollwitz, he issued sixty.

Today, as in Frederick's, rapid, random fire, the only mode practicable, has contributed to the prestige of the Prussians. This tradition of rapid fire was lost after Frederick, but the Prussians have revived it by practicing common sense. Our own veterans of the Empire have preserved this idea, which derives from instinct. They enlarged their vents, indifferent to blowbacks, to avoid having to open the chamber and prime. Because the bullet has a good deal of clearance when the cartridge is torn and loaded, a blow of the butt on the ground charges and primes the weapon.

But today, as then, despite the skill acquired in individual fire, men do not aim and fire as badly as soon as they are formed into platoons to fire.

Prussian officers, who are practical men, know that adjusting sights in the heat of action is impracticable, and that in fire by volleys the troops tend to use the full sight. So in the war of 1866, they ordered their men to fire very low, almost without sighting, in order to benefit from ricochets.

7. Fire by Rank Is a Fire to Occupy Men in the Ranks

But if fire at will is not effective, what is its use? As we have already said, it is to occupy the men in the ranks.

In ordinary fire, the very act of breathing communicates itself and interferes with firing. How then can it be claimed that on the field of battle, in rank, men can fire even moderately well when they fire only to calm themselves and forget danger?

Napoleon said, "The instinct of man is to not let himself be killed without defending himself." And, in effect, man in combat is a creature in whom the instinct of self-preservation dominates all others at times. Discipline is meant to dominate this instinct by a greater terror of shame or of punishment. But it is never entirely able to achieve this purpose; there is a point beyond which it is ineffective. Once this point is reached, the soldier must fire or he will either advance or go back. Let us say, then, that fire is a safety vent for excitement.

In serious affairs, it is thus difficult, if not impossible, to control fire. Here is an example from Marshal de Saxe:

> Charles XII, King of Sweden, wanted to introduce into his infantry the method of charging with the bayonet. He spoke of it often, and it was known in the army that this was his idea. Finally at the battle of _____ [left blank by the author] against the Russians, he went to his regiment of infantry when the fighting started, made a fine speech, dismounted before the colors, and himself led the regiment in the charge. When he was thirty paces from the enemy the whole regiment fired, in spite of his orders and his presence. Otherwise, it did very well and broke the enemy. The king was so annoyed, he passed through the ranks without a word, mounted his horse, and rode away without saying a word.

So, if the soldier is not ordered to fire, he will fire anyway to distract himself and forget danger. The fire of Frederick's Prussians had no other purpose. Marshal de Saxe saw this. "The speed with which the Prussians load their rifles," he says, "is advantageous in that it occupies the soldiers and forbids reflection while he is in the presence of the enemy. It is an error to believe that the five last victories won by the nation in its last war were due to fire. It has been noted that in most of these actions, more Prussians were killed by rifle fire than there were of their enemies."

It is sad to think that the soldier in line is only a firing machine. Firing has been and always will be his principal object, to fire as many shots in as short a time as possible. But the victor may not always be the one who kills the most: he is fortunate who best knows how to overthrow the morale of his enemy.

One cannot count on the composure of men. And as it is necessary above all to keep up their morale, one ought to try above all to occupy and calm them. This can best be done by frequent shooting. There will be little effect, and it would be absurd to expect them to be calm enough to fire slowly, adjust their ranges, and above all aim carefully.

8. *The Deadly Fire Is the Fire by Skirmishers*

In firing together, when the men are formed into platoons or battalions, all weapons have the same value, and if it is assumed today that fire must decide engagements, the method of fighting that must be adopted is that which gives the most effect to the weapon: the fighting of the skirmishers.

Theirs is the kind of fire that is the most lethal. We could provide many examples, but the two following instances from General Duhesme will suffice:

"A French officer who served with the Austrians in one of the recent wars," says General Duhesme, "told me that from the fire of a French battalion 100 paces from them, his company lost only three or four men, while at the same time they had had more than thirty killed or wounded by the fire of a group of skirmishers in a little wood on their flank 300 paces away."

"At the passage of the Minico, in 1801, the 2nd Battalion of the 91st took fire from a battalion of Bussi's regiment without losing a man: the skirmishers of that same formation killed more than thirty men in a few minutes while protecting the retreat of their formation."

Skirmishers' fire is, then, the most lethal in war, because the few men who remain cool enough to aim are not otherwise bothered while employed as skirmishers. They will perform better as they are better hidden and better trained in shooting.

As accurate firing is better only in isolated firing, we may expect that accurate weapons will tend to make skirmishing more frequent and more decisive.

As for the rest, experience says that the use of skirmishers is compulsory in war. Today all troops seriously engaged instantly become groups of skirmishers, and the only precise fire possible is from hidden snipers.

However, the military education we have received, in the spirit of the times, clouds our mind with doubt regarding skirmishing. We accept it with regret. Our own experience being incomplete, insufficient, we content ourselves with the supposition that gives us satisfaction. The war of skirmishers, no matter how thoroughly its usefulness has been proven, is accepted with reservation, because we are forced by circumstance to engage our troops by degrees, in spite of ourselves, often inconsistently. But, we are convinced that today successive engagement is essential in war.

But let us have no illusions about the efficacy of the fire of skirmishers. Regardless of accurate, long-range weapons, regardless of all the training that can be given the soldier, their fire can never have more than a relative effect, which should not be exaggerated.

The fire of skirmishers is generally aimed at other skirmishers. A body of troops indeed does not permit itself to be fired on by skirmishers without returning fire. And it is absurd to expect skirmishers to fire on a formation protected by its own skirmishers. To demand of troops firing individually, almost alone, that they not reply to fire by enemy skirmishers nearby, but to aim instead at a distant formation that is not harming them, is to ask an impossible unselfishness.

As skirmishers, the men are very dispersed. To watch the adjustments of range is difficult. The men are practically alone. Those who remain cool may try to adjust their range, but first one must see where one's shots fall, then if the terrain permits (and it seldom does) to distinguish them from shots fired at the same time by your comrades. All these men will be more unnerved, will fire faster and less accurately as the fight intensifies and the enemy grows more determined. And discouragement is more contagious than composure.

The target is a line of skirmishers, a target offering so little breadth and above all depth, that beyond point-blank range, a precise calculation of range is necessary to have an effect. This is impossible, because the range varies at each instant with the movement of the skirmishers.[22]*

Thus, with skirmishers against skirmishers, there are only scattered shots against scattered shots. The fire of skirmishers, marching, on the training range, proves this, even though each man knows exactly the range and has the time and calmness to set his sights. It is impossible for skirmishers in motion to set sights beyond 400 meters, and even this is pretty extreme even though the weapon itself is accurate well beyond this.

---

22. *Nothing is more difficult than estimating range; nothing more easily deceives the eye. Practice and the use of instruments cannot make a man infallible. At Sebastopol, for two months, a distance of 1,000 to 1,200 meters could not be determined by the rifle, because of an inability to see where shots fell. For three months it was impossible to calculate with ranging shots, although all ranges were attempted; the distance to a certain battery was only 500 meters away, but higher and separated from us by a ravine. One day, after three months, two shots at 500 meters registered on target. Everybody estimated this distance as over 1,000 meters. Once the village was taken and the point of observation changed, the truth became clear.

Also, a good shot is born. There are men, especially those instructing officers at the firing range, who become excellent shots after years of practice. But it is impossible to train all soldiers this way without an enormous expenditure of ammunition and without abandoning all other training. And then there would be no results with half of them.

In sum, we find that fire is effective only at point-blank range. Even in our most recent wars there have been very few cases in which men who were blessed with coolness and able leaders have proved an exception. With those exceptions noted, we can say that accurate, long-range weapons have not had any real effect at a range greater than point-blank.

It has been offered, as evidence of the usefulness of accurate weapons, the terrible, decisive results obtained by the British in India with the Enfield rifle. But these results have been achieved against poorly armed enemies. The British therefore had the security, the confidence, and, as a consequence, the coolness necessary for the use of accurate weapons. These are completely different when one faces an enemy equally well armed and who, as a consequence, gives as good as he gets.

9. The Absolute Impossibility of Fire at Command

Returning to the technique of fire at command, which tends to be demanded of troops in line: can regular and efficient fire be hoped for from troops in line? Should it be?

No, because man cannot be made other than what he is, and neither can the line. Even on the firing range or on the maneuver field, what does fire at command accomplish?

On the firing range, all the men in two ranks take up the firing position in unison; all are perfectly quiet. Men in the first rank are not interrupted by their neighbors. The men in the second rank are likewise undisturbed, and because the men in the rank in front are settled, they can aim through the intervals with as much ease as those in the first rank enjoy.

Firing is executed at command, simultaneously, so no man's weapon is jostled at the moment of the shot by the movement of others. All conditions are entirely favorable for this mode of fire. Moreover, the command is given with skill and composure by an officer who has perfectly aligned his men (a rare thing even on the drill ground). The results are considerably greater than those of fire at will when executed with exacting attention, results that are sometime astonishing.

But fire at command, demanding as it does utmost composure of the officer, even more than that of the men, is not practicable in the presence of the enemy except in the very special case of picked officers, picked men, picked ground, range, cover, etc. Even in maneuvers, its execution is farcical. There is no formation in which the soldiers do not anticipate the command to fire, so commanders order it as quickly as they can, often while the march is still in motion.

It is useless to speak of the sight-leaf[23] in the presence of the enemy, in officers and men attempting to execute in the presence of the enemy that of which they are utterly incapable even on the training field. We have seen a firing instructor, an officer of coolness and assurance, who, on the range fired practice rounds every day for a month, land four shots at a range of 600 meters with the sight-leaf set at point-blank.

We should not credit too much those who, in matters of war, take the weapon as a starting point and unhesitatingly assume the man serving it will always follow prescribed rules and precepts. The fighting man is flesh and blood. He is both body and soul and, strong as the soul might be, it cannot so dominate the body that there is no revolt of the flesh, no vexation of the spirit when faced with destruction. We should learn to distrust mathematics and material dynamics when they are applied to matters of combat. We should beware of lessons drawn from the firing range and the training grounds. There, our experience is with the calm, settled, rested, attentive, obedient soldier; in short, with an intelligent and tractable man, and not with the nervous, easily swayed, moved, troubled, distraught, excited, restless being who does not even control himself—who is the fighting man from general to private. There are strong men, exceptions, but they are rare.

These illusions, persistent and tenacious, always repair the next day the most damaging injuries inflicted upon them by reality. Their least damaging effect is to encourage prescribing the impracticable, as if ordering it were not really an attack on discipline and did not result in confusing officers and men by the unexpected and by surprise at the contrast between battle and the theories of peacetime training.

Certainly, battle is always surprising, but it surprises less if good sense and recognition of the truth have influenced the fighting man's training.

Man formed in a disciplined, organized body for combat is invincible before an unorganized mass. But against a similar formation he reverts to the primitive man who flees a force that proves itself stronger, or that he feels

---

23. That is, the adjustable rear sight on a weapon that sets the elevation of one's shot.

is stronger. The heart of the soldier is always the human heart. Discipline holds enemies face to face a little longer, but the instinct of self-preservation preserves its empire and with it the sense of fear.

Fear. . . !

There are commanders, there are soldiers, who know no fear, but they are of a rare mold. The mass trembles, because it cannot suppress the flesh. And this trembling must be reckoned with in all organization, discipline, formation, maneuver, movement, and modes of action. For in all these matters, the soldier tends to be disturbed, to be misled, to underestimate himself and to exaggerate the offensive spirit of the enemy.

On the battlefield, death is in the air, blind, invisible, making his presence known by fearful whistling that makes men duck their heads. The recruit crouches, bunches up, trying to protect himself by an instinctive, unformulated reasoning. He guesses that the greater number facing danger the better the chance of escaping. But he soon sees that flesh attracts lead. Then, overcome by terror, he inevitably retreats from the fire, or he "escapes by advancing," in the picturesque and profound words of General Burbaki.[24]

The soldier escapes his commander, we say. Yes, he escapes! But is it not clear that he escapes because until now no one has bothered about his character, his temperament, and the impressionable and excitable nature of man? He has always been held to impossibilities when methods of fighting were prescribed. The same thing is done today. Tomorrow, as yesterday, he will escape.

There is of course a moment when all soldiers escape, either forward or to the rear. But the organization, the methods of combat should have no other objective than to delay this crisis as long as possible. Yet, they hasten it.

All our commanders quite justifiably dread, because of their experience, that the soldier will expend his ammunition too quickly in the face of the enemy. This preoccupation is a serious matter certainly worthy of attention. How to prevent this useless and dangerous waste of ammunition is the question. Our soldiers display little coolness; once in danger they fire, to calm themselves, to occupy the time; they cannot be stopped.

Some people cannot be embarrassed, and with the best faith in the world, say, "What is this? You are concerned about stopping the fire of your

---

24. Charles-Denis-Sauter Bourbaki (1816–1897), French general, veteran of the Algerian wars, the Crimean War, the Italian War, and the Franco-Prussian War. A much-decorated and well-known officer of Zouaves, by 1869 he was aide-de-camp to Napoleon III.

soldiers? That is not difficult. You see that they show little composure, and shoot despite their officers, even in spite of themselves? All right, demand of them and their officers methods of fire that require extremes of coolness, calm, and assurance, even in training. They are incapable of giving a little? Ask more and you will get it. There, you have found a mode of combat, a simple method, good and terrible, that no one has ever heard of." This is indeed a fine theory. It would make the wily Frederick, who surely did not believe in such maneuvers, laugh until he cried.[25]*

This is to solve a problem by a means always recognized as impossible, and more impossible today.

Fearing that the soldier will escape from command, cannot better means be found to hold him rather than demand impracticable fire of him and his officer? This, ordered yet not executed by the soldiers, or even by the officers, is an attack on the discipline of the unit. "Never order the impossible," says discipline, "for the impossible then becomes disobedience."

How many conditions are required to make fire at command possible, conditions among the soldiers, among their officers. Perfect these conditions, they say. All right, perfect their training, their discipline, etc.; but to obtain fire at command it is necessary to perfect their nerves, their physical power, their moral force, to make bronze images of them, to abolish excitement, the trembling of the flesh. Can anyone do this?

Frederick's soldiers submitted by blows of the baton to a terrible state of obedience. Yet their fire was fire at will. Discipline had reached its limits.

Man in battle, let us repeat, is a being to whom the instinct of self-preservation at times dominates all else. Discipline, whose purpose is to dominate this instinct by dread of a greater terror, cannot completely abolish it. Discipline goes only so far and no farther.

Certainly, we cannot deny extraordinary examples when discipline and devotion have raised man above himself, but these are extraordinary, very rare. They are admired as exceptions, and exceptions prove the rule.

As to perfection, consider the Spartans. If man was ever perfected for war, it was he, and yet he has been beaten, and run. In spite of training, moral and physical force has limits. Spartans, who should have stood to the last man on the battlefield, ran.

---

25. *His war instructions prove this. His best generals, Zeiten, Warnery, knew of such methods, saw nothing practicable in them and guarded against them in war as indeed he himself did. But Europe believed him, tried to imitate him on the field of battle, and aligned her troops to be defeated by him. This is what he wanted. He even deceived the Prussians. But they came back to sound methods after 1808, in 1813, and after.

The British with their phlegmatic coolness and their terrible rolling fire, the Russians, with that inertia that is seen as tenacity, have given way before an attack. The German has given way, he who because of his subordination and stability has been called excellent war material.

Again, an objection is raised: perhaps with recruits the method may be unworkable, but with veterans? But with whom does one begin a war? Methods are designed precisely for young and inexperienced troops.

Then they ask, if the Prussians used this method of fire successfully in the last war, why should we not do the same? Supposing that the Prussians actually did use it—and this is far from being proved—it does not follow that it will work for us. This mania for borrowing German tactics is not new, although it has always been protested. Marshal Luchner[26] said, "No matter how much they torment their men, fortunately they will never make them Prussians." Later, Gouvion Saint-Cyr said, "The men are drilled in various exercises thought necessary to fit them for war, but there is no question of adopting exercises to suit the French military genius, the French character and temperament. It has not been thought necessary to take this into account; it has been easier to borrow from the Germans."

To employ preconceived tactics is more suitable to the phlegmatic Germans than it is to our soldiers. The Germans obey well enough, but they try to follow tactics that are contrary to nature. The Frenchman, no, he cannot. He is more spontaneous, more excitable and impressionable, less calm, less obedient, and in our last wars he has promptly and completely violated both the letter and the spirit of our regulations. "The German," says a Prussian officer,

has sentiments of duty and obedience. He submits to a severe discipline. He is devoted, although not animated by a *lively spirit*. Easygoing, rather plodding than active, intellectually tranquil, reflective, without dash or divine fire, wishing but not mad to conquer, obeying calmly and conscientiously, but mechanically and without enthusiasm, fighting with a resigned valor, with heroism, he may allow himself to be sacrificed uselessly, but he sells his life dearly. Without warlike tendencies, not bellicose, unambitious, he is nevertheless excellent war material

---

26. Nicolas Luckner (1722–1794), French field marshal of Bavarian descent, veteran, as a commander of hussars at the battle of Rossbach during the Seven Years War, entered service of the French army in 1763, commander of the Army of the Rhine during the early days of the Revolution, denounced and sentenced to death by the Revolutionary Court in 1794.

because of his subordination and stability. What must be inculcated in him is a will of his own, a personal impulse to send him forward.

Given this unflattering portrait, which we believe is a little extreme, even if by a compatriot, it is possible that the Germans can be handled in tactics that are impossible with the French. But, did the Prussians actually use these tactics? Remember Blücher's urgent warning to his brigade commanders, not to allow their bayonet attacks to degenerate into fusillades. Note the article in the current Prussian firing regulations, which prescribes test shots before delivering fire, *so as to dissipate the kind of excitement that possesses the soldier when his drill has been interrupted for some time.*

In conclusion, if fire at command was impossible with the ancient rifle, it is more to our disadvantage today, for the simple reason that trembling increases as destructive power increases. Under Turenne, lines stood longer than today because the musket was used and the battle developed more slowly. Today, when everyone has rapid-fire rifles, are things easier? Alas, no! The relationship between weapons and the man remain the same. Give me a musket, I fire at sixty paces; a rifle, at 200, a Chassepot,[27] at 400. But perhaps I am less composed and steady than at the old sixty paces, because with rapid fire the new weapon is more terrible at 400 paces, both for the enemy and me, than the musket was at sixty paces. And is there ever more accuracy? No. Rifles were used before the Revolution, and yet this very well known weapon was seldom seen in war, and its efficacy, as shown in rare cases, was unsatisfactory. Accurate fire with it at combat distances from 200 to 400 meters was illusory, and it was abandoned in favor of the old rifle. Did the foot chasseurs know fire at command? Elite troops, dependable, did they use it? No, yet it would have been a fine way of using their weapons. Today we have weapons that are accurate at 600 to 700 meters. Does that mean that accurate fire is possible at that range? No. If your enemy is armed as we are, fire at that range will show the same results that have been shown for 400 meters. The same losses will be taken, and the composure shown will be the same—that is, it will be absent. If one fires three times as fast, three times as many men will fall, and it will be three times as difficult to remain calm.

---

27. The *Fusil modèle 1866* (Chassepot) was the standard small arm of the French army at the time Ardant du Picq wrote. Replacing the Minié muzzle-loading rifle, the Chassepot was the first bolt-action, breech-loading military rifle. Its range was 1,200 yards, twice that of the Prussians' Dreyse Needle gun.

Just as it was impossible to execute fire at command before, so it is today. Before, no sight-setting was possible; it is no better today.

But if this fire is impossible, why advocate it? Let us keep to the realm of the possible or we will make grave miscalculations. "In our art," said General Daine,[28] "theorists abound, practical men are extremely rare. And when the moment of action arrives, principles are often found to be confused, application impossible, and the most erudite officers remain inactive, unable to use the scientific treasures that they have amassed."

Let us then search, with practical men, for that which is possible, and carefully collect the lessons of their experience, remembering Bacon's maxim, "Experience surpasses science."

---

28. Nicolas Joseph Daine (1782–1843), Belgian army officer who campaigned with the French army from 1795 to 1813. Appointed brigadier in United Kingdom of the Netherlands in 1816, he was commander of provisional armed forces of Limburg during the Belgian revolution of 1830.

Appendix II
Historical Documents

1. Cavalry (Extract from Xenophon)

The unexpectedness of an event accentuates it, be it pleasant or terrible. This is nowhere better seen than in war, where surprise terrorizes even the strongest.

When two armies are in touch or merely separated by the field of battle, there are first, on the part of the cavalry, skirmishes, thrusts, wheels to stop or pursue the enemy, after which usually each goes cautiously and does not put forth its greatest effort until the critical part of the conflict. Or, having commenced as usual, the opposite is done and one moves swiftly, after the wheel, either to flee or to pursue. This is the method by which one can, with the least possible risk, most harm the enemy, charging at top speed when supported, or fleeing at the same speed to escape the enemy. If it is possible in these skirmishes to leave behind, formed in column and unobserved, four or five of the bravest and best mounted men in each troop, they may be very well employed to fall on the enemy at the moment of the wheel.

(Xenophon did not mention a shield, only a band on his left arm.)

2. Marius against the Cimbrians (Extract from Plutarch's "Life of Marius")

Boiroix, king of the Cimbrians, at the head of a small troop of cavalry, approached Marius' camp and challenged him to fix a day and place to decide who would rule the country. Marius answered that Romans did not ask their enemies when to fight, but that he was willing to satisfy the Cimbrians. They agreed then to give battle in three days on the plain of Verceil, a convenient place for the Romans to deploy their cavalry and for the barbarians to extend their large army. On the day set, the two opponents were in battle formation. Catulus had 20,300 men. Marius had 32,000, placed on the wings and consequently on either side of those of Catulus, in the center. So writes Sylla, who was there. They say that Marius gave this disposition to the two parts of his army because he hoped to fall with his two wings on the barbarian phalanxes and wished the victory to come only to his command, without Catulus taking any part or even meeting with the enemy. Indeed, as the front of battle was very broad, the wings were separated from the center, which was broken through. They add that Catulus reported this disposition in the explanation that he had to make and complained bitterly of Marius' bad faith. The Cimbrian infantry came out of its positions in good order and in battle array formed a solid phalanx as broad as it was wide, thirty stades or about 18,000 feet. Their 15,000 horsemen were magnificently equipped. Their helmets were crowned by the gaping mouths of savage beasts, above which were high plumes which looked like wings. This accentuated their height. They were protected by iron cuirasses and had shields of an astonishing whiteness. Each had two javelins to throw from a distance, and in close fighting they used a long heavy sword.

In the battle the cavalry did not attack the Romans in front, but turning to the right they gradually extended with the idea of enclosing the Romans before their infantry and themselves. The Roman generals instantly perceived the ruse. But they were not able to restrain their men, one of whom, shouting that the enemy was flying, led all the others to pursue. Meanwhile the barbarian infantry advanced like the waves of a great sea.

Marius washed his hands, raised them to heaven, and vowed to offer a hecatomb to the gods. Catulus for his part also raised his hands to heaven and promised to consecrate the fortune of the day. Marius also made a sacrifice, and when the priest showed him the victim's entrails, cried, "Victory is mine!" But, as the two armies were set in motion, something happened, which, according to Sylla, seemed divine vengeance on Marius. The movements of such a prodigious multitude raised such a cloud of dust that the two armies could not see each other. Marius, who had advanced first with his troops to fall on the enemy's formation, missed it in the dust, and having passed beyond it, wandered for a long time in the plain. Meanwhile fortune turned the barbarians toward Catulus, who had to meet their whole attack with his soldiers, among whom was Sylla. The heat of the day and the burning rays of the sun, which was in the eyes of the Cimbrians, helped the Romans. The barbarians, reared in cold wooded places, hardened to extreme cold, could not stand the heat. Sweating, panting, they shaded their faces from the sun with their shields. The battle occurred after the summer solstice, three days before the new moon of the month of August, then called Sextilis. The cloud of dust sustained the Romans' courage by concealing the number of the enemy. Each battalion advancing against the enemy in front of them was engaged, before the sight of such a great horde of barbarians could shake them. Furthermore, hardship and hard work had so toughened them that in spite of the heat and impetuousness with which they attacked, no Roman was seen to sweat or pant. This, it is said, is testified to by Catulus himself in eulogizing the conduct of his troops.

Most of the enemy, above all the bravest, were cut to pieces, for, to keep the front ranks from breaking, they were tied together by long chains attached to their belts. The victors pursued the fugitives to their entrenched camp.

The Romans took more than 60,000 Cimbrians prisoners and killed twice as many.

3. The Battle of the Alma (Extract from the correspondence of Colonel Ardant du Picq. A letter sent from Huy, February 9, 1869, by Captain de V___, a company officer in the attack battalion)

My company, with the 3rd, commanded by Captain D___, was designed to cover the battalion.

At 800 or 900 meters from the Alma, we saw a sort of wall, crowned with white, whose use we could not understand. Then, at not more than 300 meters, this wall delivered against us a lively battalion fire and deployed at the run. It was a Russian battalion whose uniform, partridge-gray or chestnut-gray color, with white helmet, had, with the help of the bright sun, produced the illusion. This, parenthetically, showed me that this color is certainly the most sensible, as it can cause such errors.[29]* We replied actively, but there was effect on neither side

---

29. *It should be noted here that French uniforms are of an absurd color, serving only to take the eye at a review. So the chasseurs, in black, are seen much farther than a rifleman of

because the men fired too fast and too high. . . . The advance was then taken up, and I don't know from whom the order can have come. . . . We went on the run, crossing the river easily enough, and while we were assembling to scramble up the hill we saw the rest of the battalion attacking, without order, companies mixed up, crying "Forward!" and singing, etc. We did the same, again took up the attack, and were lucky enough to reach the summit of the plateau first. The Russians, astounded, massed in a square. Why? I suppose that, turned on the left, attacked in the center, they thought themselves surrounded, and took this strange formation. At this moment a most inopportune bugle call was sounded by order of Major De M____ temporarily commanding a battalion of foot chasseurs. This officer had perceived the Russian cavalry in motion and believed that its object was to charge us, while, on the contrary, it was maneuvering to escape the shells fired into it while in squadron formation by the Megere, a vessel of the fleet. This order given by bugle signal was executed as rapidly as had been the attack, such is the instinct of self-preservation that urges man to flee danger above all when ordered to flee. Happily a levelheaded officer, Captain Daguerre, seeing the gross mistake, commanded "Forward!" in a stentorian tone. This halted the retreat and caused us again to take up the attack. The attack made us masters of the telegraph-line, and the battle was won. At this second charge the Russians gave, turned, and hardly any of them were wounded with the bayonet. So then a major commanding a battalion, without orders, sounds a bugle call and endangers success. A simple captain commands "Forward!" and decides the victory. This is the history of yesterday, which may be useful tomorrow.

It appears from this that, apart from the able conception of the commander-in-chief, the detail of execution was abominable, and that to base on successes new rules of battle would lead to lamentable errors. Let us sum up:

First: A private chasseur d'Afrique gave the order to attack;

Second: The troops went to the attack mixed up with each other. We needed nearly an hour merely to reform the brigade. This one called, that one congratulated himself, the superior officers cried out, etc., etc. There was confusion that would have meant disaster if the cavalry

---

the line is in his gray coat. The red trousers are seen farther than the gray—thus gray ought to be the basic color of the infantry uniform, above all that of the skirmishers. At nightfall the Russians came up to our trenches without being seen by anyone, thanks to their partridge-gray coats.

charge, which was believed to threaten us, had been executed. Disorder broke out in the companies at the first shot. Once engaged, commanders of formations no longer had them in hand, and they intermingled, so that it was not easy to locate oneself;

Third: There was no silence in ranks. Officers, noncommissioned officers and soldiers commanded, shouted, etc.; the bugle sounded the commands they heard coming from nobody knew where;

Fourth: There was no maneuvering from the first shot to the last. I do not remember being among my own men; it was only at the end that we found each other. Zouaves, chasseurs, soldiers of the 20th Line formed an attack group—that was all. About four o'clock there was a first roll call. About a third of the battalion was missing; at nine at night there was a second roll call. Only about fifty men were missing, thirty of whom were wounded. Where the rest were I do not know.

Fifth: To lighten the men, packs had been left on the plain at the moment fire opened, and as the operation had not been worked out in advance, no measures were taken to guard them. In the evening most of the men found their packs incomplete, lacking all the little indispensables that one cannot get in the position in which we were.

It is evidently a vital necessity to restrain the individual initiative of subordinates and leave command to the chiefs, and above all to watch the training for the soldiers who are always ready, as they approach, to run on the enemy with the bayonet. I have always noted that if a body which is charged does not hold firm, it breaks and takes flight, but that if it holds well, the charging body halts some paces away before it strikes. I shall tell you something notable that I saw at Castel-Fidardo. They talk a lot of the bayonet. For my part I saw it used once, in the night, in a trench. Also, it is noted that in the hospital, practically all the wounded treated were from fire, rarely from the bayonet.

4. *The Battle of the Alma (Extract from the correspondence of Colonel A. du Picq. Letters dated in November 1868 and February 1869 sent from Renne by Captain P____ of the 17th Battalion of the foot chasseurs, with remarks by the colonel and responses of Captain P_____)*

Letter from Captain P____:

. . . It is there that I had time to admire the coolness of my brave Captain Daguerre, advancing on a mare under the enemy's eyes, and observing imperturbably, like a tourist, all the movements of our opponents.

I will always pay homage to his calm and collected bravery. . . . Remarks by the Colonel:

Did not Captain Daguerre change the bugle call "Retreat," ordered by ____ to the bugle call "Forward"?

Answer of Captain P_____:

In fact, when protected in the wood by pieces of wall, we were firing on the Russians. We heard behind us the bugle sounding "Retreat" at the order of ____. At this moment my captain, indignant, ordered "Forward" sounded to reestablish confidence, which had been shaken by the distraction or by the inadvertence of ____.

5. The Battle of Inkerman (Extracts from the correspondence of Colonel Ardant du Picq)

Letter from Lyon, March 21, 1869, by Major de G_____, 17th Regiment of the Line:

. . . The 1st Battalion of the 7th Light Regiment had hardly arrived close to the telegraph when it received a new order to rush to the help of the English army, which, too weak to hold such a large army, had been broken in the center of its line and driven back on its camps.

The 1st Battalion of the 7th Light Regiment, Major Vaissier, had the honor to arrive first in the presence of the Russians after moving three kilometers on the run. Received by the enthusiastic cheers of the English, it formed for battle, then carried away by burning cries of "Forward, with the bayonet!" from its brave major it threw itself headlong on the Russian columns, which broke.

For two hours the 1st Battalion of the 7th Light Regiment, a battalion of the 6th Line Regiment, four companies of the 3rd Battalion of foot chasseurs, and five companies of Algerian chasseurs held the head of the Russian army, which continued to debouch in massed columns from the ravine and plateau of Inkerman.

Three times the battalion was obliged to fall back some paces to rally. Three times it charged with the bayonet, with the same ardor and success.

At four in the afternoon the Russians were in rout, and were pursued into the valley of Inkerman.

On this memorable day all the officers, noncommissioned officers and soldiers of the 7th Light Regiment performed their duty nobly, rivaling each other in bravery and self-sacrifice.

Notes on Inkerman by Colonel du Picq from the letters of Captain B_____:

In what formation were the Russians? In column, of which the head fired, and whose platoons tried to get from behind to enter the action?

When Major Vaissier advanced was he followed by everyone? At what distance? In what formation were the attackers? In disordered masses? In one rank? In two? In mass? Did the Russians immediately turn tail, receiving shots and the bayonet in the back? Did they fall back on the mass which itself was coming up? What was the duration of this attack against a mass, whose depth prevented its falling back?

Did we receive bayonet wounds?

Did we fall back before the active reaction of the mass or merely because, after the first shot, the isolated soldiers fell back to find companions and with them a new confidence?

Was the second charge made like the first one? Was the 6th Line Regiment engaged as the first support of the 7th Light Regiment? How were the Zouaves engaged?

6. *The Battle of Magenta (Extract from the correspondence of Colonel Ardant du Picq. Letters from Captain C____, dated August 23, 1868)*

At Magenta I was in Espinasse's division, of Marshal MacMahon's corps. This division was on the extreme left of the troops that had passed the Ticino at Turbigo and was moving on Magenta by the left bank. Close to the village a fusillade at close range apprised us that the enemy was before us. The country, covered with trees, hedges, and vines, had hidden them.

Our 1st Battalion and the 2nd Foreign Regiment drove the Austrians into Magenta.

Meanwhile, the 2nd and 3rd Battalions of Zouaves, with which I was, remained in reserve, arms stacked, under control of the division commander. Apparently quite an interval had been left between Espinasse's

division and la Moterouge's, the 1st of the corps, and, at the moment
of engagement, at least an Austrian brigade had entered the gap, and
had taken in flank and rear the elements of our division engaged before Magenta. Happily the wooded country concealed the situation or
I doubt whether our troops engaged would have held on as they did.
At any rate the two reserve battalions had not moved. The fusillade
extended to our right and left as if to surround us; bullets already came
from our right flank. The general had put five guns in front of us, to
fire on the village, and at the same time I received the order to move
my section to the right, to drive off the invisible enemy who was firing
on us. I remember that I had quit the column with my section when I
saw a frightened artillery captain run toward us, crying, "General, General, we are losing a piece!" The general answered, "Come! Zouaves,
packs off." At the words, the two battalions leaped forward like a flock
of sheep, dropping packs everywhere. The Austrians were not seen at
first. It was only after advancing for an instant that they were seen.
They were already dragging off the piece that they had taken. Surprise
and terror so possessed the Austrians, who did not know we were so
near, that they ran without using their arms. The piece was retaken;
the regimental standard was captured by a man in my company. About
200 prisoners were taken, and the Austrian regiment—Hartmann's 9th
Infantry—was dispersed like sheep in flight, five battalions of them. I
believe that had the country not been thick the result might have been
different. The incident lasted perhaps ten minutes.

The two battalions took up their first position. They had no losses,
and their morale was in the clouds. After about an hour General Espinasse put himself at the head of the two battalions and marched us on
the village. We were in column of platoons with section intervals. The
advance was made by echelon, the 2nd Battalion in front, the 3rd a
little to the rear, and a company in front deployed as skirmishers.

At 150 paces from the Austrians, wavering was evident in their lines;
the first ranks threw themselves back on those in the rear. At that instant the general ordered again, 'Come! Packs off. At the double!' Everybody ran forward, shedding his pack where he was.

The Austrians did not wait for us. We entered the village mixed up
with them. The fighting in houses lasted quite a while. Most of the
Austrians retired. Those who remained in the houses had to surrender.
I found myself, with some fifty officers and men, in a big house from
which we took 400 men and five officers, Colonel Hauser among them.

My opinion is that we were very lucky at Magenta. The thick country in which we fought favored us in hiding our inferior number from the Austrians. I do not believe we would have succeeded so well in open country. In the gun episode the Austrians were surprised, stunned. Those whom we took still held their arms, without either abandoning them or using them. It was a typical Zouave attack, which, when it succeeds, has astonishing results; but if one is not lucky it sometimes costs dearly. Note the 3rd Zouaves at Palestro, the 1st Zouaves at Marignano. General Espinasse's advance on the village, at the head of two battalions, was the finest and most imposing sight I have ever seen. Apart from that advance, the fighting was always by skirmishers and in large groups.

7. The Battle of Solferino (Extract from the correspondence of Colonel Ardant du Picq. Letters from Captain C___)

The 55th Infantry was part of the 3rd Division of the IV Corps.

Coming out of Medole, the regiment was halted on the right of the road and formed, as each company arrived, in close column. Fascines were made.

An aide-de-camp came up and gave an order to the colonel.

The regiment was then put on the road, marched some yards and formed in battalion masses on the right of the line of battle. This movement was executed very regularly although bullets commenced to find us. Arms were rested, and we stayed there, exposed to fire, without doing anything, not even sending out a skirmisher. For that matter, during the whole campaign, it seemed to me that the skirmisher school might never have existed.

Then up came a Major of Engineers, from General Niel, to get a battalion from the regiment. The 3rd Battalion being on the left received the order to march. The major commanding ordered "by the left flank," and we marched by the flank, in close column, in the face of the enemy, up to Casa-Nova farm, I believe, where General Niel was.

The battalion halted a moment, faced to the front, and closed a little.

"Stay here," said General Niel, "you are my only reserve!"

Then the general, glancing in front of the farm, said to the major, after one or two minutes, "Major, fix bayonets, sound the charge, and forward!"

This last movement was still properly executed at the start, and for about 100 yards of advance.

Shrapnel annoyed the battalion, and the men shouldered arms to march better.

At about 100 yards from the farm, the cry "Packs down!" came from I do not know where. The cry was instantly repeated in the battalion. Packs were thrown down, anywhere, and with wild yells the advance was renewed, in the wildest disorder.

From that moment, and for the rest of the day, the 3rd Battalion as a unit disappeared.

Toward the end of the day, after an attempt had been made to get the regiment together, and at the end of half an hour of backing and filling, there was a roll call.

The third company of grenadiers had on starting off in the morning 132 to 135 present. At this first roll call, forty-seven answered, a number I can swear to, but many of the men were still hunting packs and rations. The next day at reveille roll call, ninety-three or -four answered. Many came back in the night.

This was the strength for many days I still remember, for I was charged with company supply from June 25.

An additional bit of information—it was generally known a few days later that at least twenty men of the 4th company of grenadiers were never on the field of battle. Wounded of the company, returned for transport to Medole, said later that they had seen some twenty of the company close to Medole, lying in the grass while their comrades fought. They even gave some names, but could not name them all. The company had only been formed for war on April 19, and had received that same day forty-nine new grenadiers and twenty-nine at Milan, which made seventy-eight recruits in two months. None of these men were tried or punished. Their comrades rode them hard, that was all.

8. Mentana (Extract from the correspondence of Colonel Ardant du Picq. Letters from Captain C_____, dated August 23, 1868)

November 3, at two in the morning, we took up arms to go to Monte-Rotondo. We did not yet know that we would beat the Garibaldians at Mentana.

The Papal army had about 3,000 men, we about 2,500. At one o'clock the Papal forces met their enemies. The Zouaves attacked vigorously, but the first engagements were without great losses on either side. There is nothing particular in this first episode. The usual thing happened, a force advances and is not halted by the fire of its adversary who ends by showing his heels. The Papal Zouaves are marked by no ordinary spirit. In comparing them with soldiers of the Antibes legion, one is forced to the conclusion that the man who fights for an idea fights better than one who fights for money. At each advance of the Papal forces, we advanced also. We were not greatly concerned about the fight, as we hardly thought that we would have to participate, not dreaming that we could be held by the volunteers. However, that did not happen.

It was about three o'clock. At that time three companies of the battalion were employed in protecting the artillery—three or four pieces placed about the battlefield. The head of the French column was then formed by the last three companies of the battalion, one of the 1st Line Regiment; the other regiments were immediately behind. Colonel Fremont of the 1st Line Regiment, after having studied the battlefield, took two chasseur companies, followed by a battalion of his regiment and bore to the right to turn the village.

Meanwhile, the 1st Line Regiment moved farther to the right in the direction of Monte-Rotondo, against which at two different times it opened up to fire at will, which seemed a veritable hurricane. Due to the distance or to the terrain the material result of the fire seemed to be negligible. The moral result must have been considerable; it precipitated a flood of fugitives on the road from Mentana to Monte-Rotondo, dominated by our sharpshooters, who opened on the fugitives a fire more deadly than that of the chassepots. We stayed in the same position until night, when we retired to a position near Mentana, where we bivouacked.

My company was one of the two chasseur companies that attacked on the right with the 1st Line Regiment. My company had ninety-eight rifles (we had not yet received the chassepots). It forced the volunteers from solidly held positions where they left a gun and a considerable number of rifles. In addition, it put nearly seventy men out of action, judging by those who remained on the field. It had one man slightly wounded, a belt and a carbine broken by bullets.

There remained with the general, after our movement to the right, three companies of chasseurs, a battalion of the 29th, and three of the 59th. I do not include many elements of the Papal army that had not been engaged. Some of my comrades told me of having been engaged with a chasseur company of the 59th in a sunken road, whose sides had not been occupied. The general was with this column. Having arrived close to the village, some shots either from the houses or from enemy sharpshooters, who might easily have gotten on the undefended flanks, provoked a terrible fusillade in the column. In spite of the orders and efforts of the officers, everybody fired, at the risk of killing each other, and this probably happened. It was only when some men, led by officers, were able to climb the sides of the road that this firing ceased. I do not think that this was a well understood use of new arms.

The fusillade of the 1st Line Regiment against Monte-Rotondo was not very effective, I believe negligible. I do not refer to the moral result, which was great.

The Garibaldians were numerous about Monte-Rotondo. But the terrain like all that around Italian villages was covered with trees, hedges, etc. Under these conditions, I believe that the fire of sharpshooters would have been more effective than volleys, where the men estimate distances badly and do not aim.

Appendix III
Record of Military Service
of Colonel Ardant du Picq

Ardant du Picq (Charles-Jean-Jacques-Joseph), born October 19, 1821, at Perigeux (Dordogne).

Entered military service as a student of *l'Ecole speciale militaire* [de Saint-Cyr], November 15, 1842.

Sub-Lieutenant, 67th Regiment of the Line, October 1, 1844.

Lieutenant, May 15, 1848.

Captain, August 15, 1852.

Transferred to 9th Battalion, Foot Chasseurs, December 25, 1853.

Major, 100th Regiment of the Line, February 15, 1856.

Transferred to the 16th Battalion of Chasseurs, March 17, 1856.

Transferred to the 37th Regiment of the Line, January 23, 1863.

Lieutenant Colonel of 55th Regiment of the Line, January 16, 1864.

Colonel of the 10th Regiment of Infantry of the Line, February 27, 1869.

Died of wounds at the military hospital in Metz, August 18, 1870.

Campaigns and Wounds

Orient, March 29, 1854, to May 27, 1856. Taken prisoner of war at the storming of the central bastion (Sebastopol), September 8, 1855; returned from enemy's prisons, December 13, 1855.

Syrian Campaign, August 6, 1860, to June 18, 1861. Served in Africa from February 24, 1864, to April 14, 1866. Franco-Prussian War, July 15, 1870, to August 18, 1870.

Mortally wounded, August 15, 1870. Comminute fracture of the right thigh, torn gash in right thigh, contusion of the abdomen—by shell burst, Longeville-lés-Metz (Moselle).

Decorations

Chevalier of the Imperial Order of the Legion of Honor, December 29, 1860.

Officer of the Imperial Order of the Legion of Honor, September 10, 1868.

Received medal of H. M. the Queen of England.

Received medal for bravery in Sardinia.

Authorized the decoration of the fourth class of the Ottoman Medjidie order.

Appendix IV

"Extract from the History of the 10th Infantry Regiment"[30]

On July 22, three active battalions of the 10th Regiment of the Infantry of the Line left Limoges and Angouleme by rail, arriving on July 23 at the camp at Châlons, where the VI Corps of the Rhine was concentrating and organizing under the command of Marshal Canrobert. The regiment, within this army corps, belonged to the 1st Brigade (Pechot) of the 1st Division (Trixier).

The mobilization for war, begun at Limoges, was completed at Châlons.

The battalions were brought to a strength of 720 men, and the regiment counted 2,200 and 10 present, not including the band, the sappers, and the headquarters section, which raised the total effectives to 2,300 men.

The troops of the VI Corps were soon organized and were reviewed by Marshal Canrobert on July 31.

On August 5, the division was ordered to move to Nancy. It embarked on nine trains, most of them departing by 6 A.M. Arriving at its destination in the evening, the 1st Brigade camped on the Leopold Racetrack, and the 10th Regiment established itself on the Place de la Grève.

The details of Forbach and Reichshofen soon caused these plans to be modified. The VI Corps was ordered to return to Châlons. The last troops of the 2nd Brigade, delayed at Toul and Commercy, were returned on the same trains.

The 1st Brigade entrained at Nancy, on the night of August 8, arriving at the Châlons camp on the afternoon of August 9.

---

30. "Extrait de l'historique du 10e régiment d'infanterie," in Ardant du Picq, *Études sur le combat*, ed. Ernest Judet (Paris: Librairie Chapelot, 1903), xliii–xlvii.

The VI Corps, however, was to remain but a few days in camp. On the 10th it received orders to go to Metz. On the morning of the 11th, the regiment was again placed on three trains. The first train, carrying the staff and the 1st Battalion, arrived at Metz without incident. The second train, transporting the 2nd Battalion and four companies of the 3rd, was stopped at about 11 P.M. near the Frouard branch.

The telegraph line was cut by a Prussian party near Dieulouard, for a length of two kilometers, and it was feared the [railroad] was damaged.

In order not to delay his arrival at Metz, nor the progress of the trains following, Major Morin at the head of the column directed his command to detrain and continue to Metz.

He caused the company at the head of the train to alight (6th Company, 2nd Battalion, commanded by Captain Valpajola) and sent it reconnoitering on the [railroad], about 300 meters in advance of the train. All precautions were taken to assure the security of the train, which regulated its progress on that of the scouts.

After a run of about eight kilometers in this way, at Marbache station, all danger having disappeared and communication with Metz having been established, the train resumed its regulation speed. In consequence of the slowing up of the second column, the third followed at a short distance until it also arrived. On the afternoon of the 12th, the regiment was entirely united.

The division of which it was a part was sent beyond Montigny and it camped there as follows:

The 9th Chasseurs and the 4th Regiment of the Line, ahead of the Thionville railroad, the right on the Moselle, the left on the Pont-à-Mousson highway; the 10th Regiment of the Line, the right supported at the branch of the Thionville and Nancy lines, the left in the direction of Saint-Privat, in front of the Montigny repair shops of the Eastern Railroad lines.

The regiment was thus placed in the rear of a redoubt under construction. The company of engineers was placed at the left of the 10th near the earthworks on which it was to work.

Along the ridge of the plateau, toward the Seille, was the 2nd Brigade, which rested its left on the river and its right perpendicular to the Saint-Privat road, behind the field-work of this name. The divisional batteries were farther behind it.

The division kept this position August 13th and during the morning of the 14th. In the afternoon, an alarm made the division take arms, during the engagement that took place on the side of Vallieres and Saint-Julien (the battle of Borny). The regiment immediate occupied positions on the left of the village of Montigny.

At nightfall, the division retired to the rear of the railroad cut and received orders to hold itself in readiness to leave during the night.

The regiment remained thus under arms, the 3rd Battalion (Major Deschesnes) passing the night on grand guard in front of the Montigny redoubt.

Before daybreak, the division marched over the bank of the Thionville railroad, crossed the Moselle, and, marching toward Gravelotte, descended into the plain south of Longeville-lés-Metz, where the principal halt was made and coffee prepared.

Scarcely had stacks been made, and the men set to making fires, about 7 A.M., when shells exploded in the midst of the troops. The shots came from the Bradin farm, situated on the heights of Montigny, which the division had just left the same morning, and which a German cavalry reconnaissance patrol, supported by two pieces, had suddenly occupied.

The Colonel had arms taken at once and disposed the regiment north of the road, which, being elevated, provided sufficient cover for defilading the men.

He himself stood in the road to put heart into his troops by his attitude, they having been a little startled by this surprise and the baptism of fire that they received under such disadvantageous circumstances.

Suddenly, a shell burst over the road, a few feet from the Colonel, and mutilated his legs in a frightful manner.

The same shell caused other ravages in the ranks of the 10th. The commander of the 3rd Battalion, Major Deschesnes, was mortally wounded, Captain Reboulet was killed, Lieutenant Pone (3rd Battalion, 1st Company), and eight men of the regiment were wounded. The Colonel was immediately taken to the other side of the highway into the midst of his soldiers and a surgeon was called, those of the regiment already engaged in caring for other victims of the terrible shot.

In the meantime, Colonel Ardant du Picq asked for Lieutenant Colonel Doleac, delivered to him his saddlebags containing important papers concerning the regiment, and gave him his field glasses. Then, without uttering the least sound of pain, notwithstanding the frightful injury from which he must have suffered horribly, he said with calmness: "My regret is to be struck in this way, without having been able to lead my regiment on the enemy."

They wanted him to take a little brandy, but he refused and accepted some water that a soldier offered him.

A surgeon arrived finally. The Colonel, showing him his right leg open in two places, made with his hand the sign of amputating at the thigh, saying: "Doctor, it is necessary to amputate my leg here."

At this moment a soldier wounded in the shoulder, and placed near the Colonel, groaned aloud. Forgetting his own condition, the Colonel said immediately to the surgeon: "See first, Doctor, what is the matter with this brave man. I can wait."

Because of the lack of instruments it was not possible to perform the amputation on the ground, as the Colonel desired, so he was transported to the Metz hospital.

Four days later (August 19),[31] Colonel Ardant du Picq died like a hero of old, without uttering the least complaint. Far from his regiment, far from his family, he uttered several times the words that summed up his affections: "My wife, my children, my regiment, adieu!"

---

31. The date given here does not agree with that given in the extract from du Picq's service dossier.

Appendix V
A Brother's Reminiscence[32]

Paris, 12 October 1903

Sir,

Here are some random biographical notes on the author of *Études sur le combat* that you asked of me.

My brother entered Saint-Cyr quite late, at twenty-one years of age, which I believe was the age limit at the time. That was not his preference, which was for a naval career, in which adventure offered him an opportunity for his energy, and which he would have entered if circumstances permitted. His childhood was turbulent and somewhat intractable; but in adolescence he retained a very pronounced taste for physical exercise, especially for gymnastics, little practiced then, to which he was naturally inclined because of his agility and muscular strength.

He was successful in his classes, especially in those to his taste, mainly French composition. In this he rose above the usual level of schoolboy exercises when the subject interested him. Certain other branches that were uninteresting or antipathetic to him—for instance, Latin grammar—he neglected. I do not remember ever having seen him attend a distribution of prizes, although he was highly interested, or perhaps too much so. On these occasions, he would disappear generally after breakfast and not be seen until evening. His bent was toward mechanical notions and handiwork. He was not uninterested in mathematics, but his interest in this was ordinary. He was nearly refused entrance to Saint-Cyr. He was confused before the examiners and the results of the first part of the tests were almost negligible. He consoled himself with his favorite maxim as a young man, "Onward philosophy." Considering the first test as over and done with, he faced the second test with

---

32. Written at the request of Ernest Judet, for inclusion with his 1903 edition. See Ardant du Picq, *Études sur le combat*, xxxv–xxxix.

177

perfect indifference. This gave him another opportunity and he came out with honors. As he had done well with the written test on "Hannibal's campaigns," he was given a passing grade.

At school he was liked by all his comrades for his good humor and frank and sympathetic character. Later, in the regiment, he gained naturally and without effort the affection of his equals and the respect of his subordinates. The latter were grateful to him for the real, cordial, and inspiring interest he showed in their welfare, for he was familiar with the details of the service and with the soldier's equipment. He would not compromise on such matters, and prevaricators who had to do with him did not emerge creditably.

It can be said that after reaching manhood he never lied. The absolute frankness from which he never departed under any circumstances gave him prestige superior to his rank. A mere lieutenant, he voted "No" to the coup d'état of December 2 and was admonished by his colonel, who was sorry to see him compromise his future so. He replied with his usual rectitude: "Colonel, since my opinion was asked for, I must suppose that it was wanted."

On the eve of the Crimean War, his regiment (the 67th) not seeming destined to take the field, he asked for and obtained a transfer to the light infantry (9th Battalion). It was with this battalion that he served in the campaign. When it commenced, he made his first appearance in the fatal Dobrutscha expedition. This was undertaken in a most unhealthy region, on the chance of finding Cossacks who would have furnished matter for a communiqué. No Cossacks were found, but cholera was. It cut down in a few hours a large portion of the total strength. My brother, left with the rear guard to bury the dead, burn their effects, and retrieve the sick, was in his turn infected. The attack was very violent and he recovered only because he would not give in to the illness. Evacuated to the Varna hospital, he was driven out the first night by the burning of the town and was obliged to take refuge in the surrounding fields where the healthfulness of the air gave him unexpected relief. Returned to France as a convalescent, he remained there until the month of December (1854). He then rejoined his regiment and withstood to the end the rigors of the winter and the slowness of the siege.

Salle's division, to which the Trochu brigade belonged, and in which my brother served, was charged with the attack on the central bastion. This operation was considered a simple diversion without a chance of success. My brother, commanding the storming column of his battalion, had the good fortune to come out safe and sound from the deadly fire to which he was exposed and that deprived the battalion of several good officers. He entered the bastion with a dozen men. All were naturally made prisoners after a resistance that would have cost my brother his life if the bugler at his side had not warded off a saber blow at his head. Upon his return from captivity, in the first months of 1856, he was immediately made major in the 100th Regiment of the Line, at the insistence of General Trochu, who regarded him highly. He was called the following year to command the 16th Battalion of Foot Chasseurs. He served with this battalion during the Syrian campaign where there was but little serious action.

Back again in France, his promotion to the grade of lieutenant colonel, notwithstanding his excellent ratings and his place on the promotion list, was long retarded by the ill will of Marshal Randon, the minister of war. Marshal Randon complained of his independent character and bore him malice from an incident relative to the furnishing of shoes intended for his battalion. My brother, questioned by Marshal Niel about the quality of the lot of shoes, had frankly declared it bad.

Promoted finally to lieutenant colonel in the 55th in Algeria, he took the field there in two campaigns, I believe. Appointed colonel of the 10th of the Line in February 1869, he was stationed at Lorient and at Limoges during the eighteen months before the war with Germany. He busied himself during this period with the preparation of his work, soliciting from all sides firsthand information. It was slow in coming in, due certainly to indifference rather than ill will. He made several trips to Paris for the purpose of opening the eyes of those in authority to the defective state of the army and the perils of the situation. Vain attempts! "They take all that philosophically," he used to say.

Please accept, Sir, with renewed acknowledgements of gratitude, the expression of my most distinguished sentiments.

C. Ardant du Picq

P.S. Regarding the question of atavism in which you showed some interest in our first conversation, I may say that our paternal line does not in my knowledge include any military man. The oldest ancestor I know of, according to an album of engravings by Albert Dürer, recovered in a garret, was a gold and silversmith at Limoges toward the end of the sixteenth century. His descendents have always been traders down to my grandfather who, from what I have heard said, did not in the least attend to his trade. The case is different with my mother's family, which came from Lorraine. Our great-grandfather was a soldier, our grandfather also, and two, at least, of my mother's brothers gave their lives on the battlefields of the First Empire. At present, the family has two representatives in the army, the one a son of my brother's, the other a first cousin, once removed, both bearing our name.

Appendix VI
The Circular Letter

General,

In the last century, after the advancements of the rifle and the field artillery by Frederick, and the Prussian successes in war—today, after the improvement of the new rifle and cannon to which, in part, those recent victories are due—we see all thinking men in the army asking: how shall we fight tomorrow? We have no credo on the subject of combat. And the most contradictory methods confuse the intelligence of military men.

Why? A common mistake at the starting point. One might say that no one is willing to acknowledge that one must understand yesterday in order to know tomorrow, for the affairs of yesterday are nowhere plainly written. The lessons of yesterday exist only in the memory of those who know how to see, and they have never spoken. I appeal to one of those.

The smallest detail, taken from an action of war, is more instructive to me, a soldier, than all the Thiers and Jominis in the world who no doubt speak for heads of state and armies; but they never show me what I wish to know—a battalion, a company, a squad, in action.

So, concerning a regiment, a battalion, a company, a squad, it would be interesting to know the disposition taken to meet the enemy, or the order of march toward them. What becomes of this disposition or this march order under the isolated or combined influences of the accidents of terrain and the approach of danger?

Is this order changed or does it remain in force when approaching the enemy?

What happens to it when it comes within range of the guns, within range of the bullets?

At what distance is a voluntary or an ordered disposition taken before beginning operations or opening fire, for charging, or both?

How did the fight begin? What about the firing? How did the men adapt themselves? (This can be seen from results—how many bullets fired, how many casualties—when the data are available.) How was the charge made? At what distance did the enemy run from it? At what distance did the charge fall back because of the enemy's good order and dispositions, or before one or another movement of the enemy? What did it cost? What can be said about all these with reference to the enemy?

What of the behavior—that is, the order, the disorder, the shouts, the silence, the confusion, the composure of the officers and men—whether ours or the enemy's, before, during, and after combat?

How was the soldier controlled and directed during the action? At what instant has he a tendency to quit the line to remain behind or to rush ahead?

At what moment, if the control were escaping the commander's hands, is it no longer possible to exercise it?

At what instant has this control escaped the battalion commander? When from the captain, the section leader, the squad leader? At what time, in brief, if such a thing did happen, was there only disorganization, whether at the front or to the rear, carrying along pell-mell with it both the commanders and the men?

Where and when did this happen?

Where and when were the leaders able to resume control of the men?

When, before, during, or after the day, was the battalion roll call, the company roll call, made? The results of these?

How many dead, wounded, on both sides? What kind of wounds suffered by the officers, the noncommissioned officers, corporals, privates, etc., etc.?

All these details, in a word, illuminate the material or the moral side of the action, or make it easier to visualize. Possibly, the closer the examination of these things, the more instructive for us, the soldiers, than all the imaginable discussions on the plans and general conduct of the campaigns of the greatest captain's grand maneuvers.

From colonel to private we are soldiers, not generals, and it is therefore our trade that we desire to know.

Certainly, one cannot obtain all the possible details from one affair. But certainly, a series of true accounts should reveal characteristic details that in themselves are likely to show in a striking, irrefutable way what was necessary and forcibly occurring at such and such a moment

of action. Take the estimate of the solider obtained in this way as a
base for what might possibly be a rational method of fighting. That will
guard us against *a priori* and pedantic school methods.

Whoever has seen combat relies on a method based on his experience. But experience is long and life is short. The experiences of each,
therefore, cannot be completed except by those of others.

And that is why, General, I venture to address myself to you for your
experiences.

Proofs have weight.

As for the rest, whether you agree to assist or not, kindly accept the
assurance of most respectful devotion from your obedient servant.